OFF BASE

OFF BASE

CONFESSIONS OF A THIEF

RICKEY HENDERSON

WITH JOHN SHEA

HarperCollins*Publishers*

HarperCollins books may be purchased for educational, business, or sales promotional use. For information, please call or write: Special Markets Department, HarperCollins Publishers, Inc., 10 East 53rd Street, New York, NY 10022. Telephone: (212) 207-7528; Fax: (212) 207-7222.

FIRST EDITION

Designed by George J. McKeon

LIBRARY OF CONGRESS CATALOG CARD NUMBER 91-58365
ISBN 0-06-017975-9

92 93 94 95 96 CC/HC 10 9 8 7 6 5 4 3 2 1

To my wonderful daughters, Angela and Alexis.
In memory of my grandmother.

—R.H.

To Mom and Zdena and Jan, my brothers, Terry, Mike,
Dan, and Frank, and Dad.

—J.S.

CONTENTS

ACKNOWLEDGMENTS

We would like to gratefully acknowledge the contributions of several people whose cooperation, inspiration, hard work, tolerance, understanding, memories, and blessings contributed to this project.

Thanks for helping to reconstruct the early years: family members Bobbie Henderson, Tyrone Henderson, and Pamela Palmer; godmother Mrs. Tommie Wilkerson; friends Fred Atkins, Aaron Turner, and Dave Stewart; coaches Bob Cryer, Wayne Brooks, Jim Brown, Hank Thomasson, and Clinton White; Bushrod Park's Michael Hammock and Leslie Colbert; Oakland Tech High School librarian Betty Jones; and Pine Bluff historian James Leslie.

Thanks for helping to bring the professional years into perspective: Lou Brock, Charlie Finley, George Steinbrenner, Syd Thrift, Tom Trebelhorn, Steve Boros, Dave Righetti, Dr. Bill Harrison, Jim Guinn, Mickey Morabito, Steve Vucinich, Jose Cangiano, Terry Garcia, Victor Cuevas, A's media relations officials Jay Alves, Mike Selleck, and Kathy Jacobson, and Yankees media relations officials Jeff Idelson and Brian Walker.

Thanks for helping to provide a delicate professional, personal, and legal balance: Shari Wenk of Burns Sports Celebrity Service, Dr. Miles McAfee and Aaron Turner of Golden Gate Sports Management Firm, and editors Tom Miller, Jim Hornfishcher, and Cynthia Barrett of HarperCollins Publishers.

Thanks to editors Jay Silverberg and Mark Whittington of the *Marin Independent Journal* and Jerry Langdon of Gannett News Service and freelance editors Terry Shea of Bolinas School, Jon Stein of Union School, and Rob Krier of the *San Diego Union-Tribune*.

Thanks also to our other friends in the media who provided their expertise: Bill Plaschke, *Los Angeles Times*; Tom Pedulla, Westchester Rockland Newspapers; Moss Klein, *Newark Star-Ledger*; Bill Weiss, Howe Sportsdata; Wayne Graczyk, *Tokyo Weekender*; John Hickey, *The (Hayward) Daily Review*; Larry Stone, *San Francisco Examiner*; Henry Schulman, *Oakland Tribune*; Richard Grossinger, North Atlantic Books; Thom Ross, sports artist.

A special thanks to Kjersti Harter and the Foster City Holiday Inn staff, and the St. Isabella CYO fourth-grade basketball team.

OFF BASE

THE EVOLUTION OF A HOT DOG

Yes, I am a hot dog.

Look up all the baseball players who were ever called hot dogs. Every last one of those guys could play. You're not called a hot dog unless you *can* play. Unless you have style. Ever hear of a hot dog who couldn't play?

A guy in the stands was all over me one day during a spring training game. He kept hollering that I was a hot dog. He wore a T-shirt that read, "Rickey Henderson is living proof that the cost of hot dogs rises every year." After the game, I asked the guy why he thought I was a hot dog. He kept saying, "You're a million-dollar hot dog, you're a million-dollar hot dog." I asked him again. He couldn't answer. He turned and walked away. He couldn't give me the definition of a hot dog. You see, if he had, he would have complimented me.

Another word for hot dog is showman. Yes, I'm a hot dog. Yes, I'm a showman. But remember, this is baseball. This is entertainment. I'm an entertainer. All baseball players are entertainers, although I must say that some players might look like they have no fun whatsoever. Baseball was made to be fun. As an athlete, that's how I approach the game, and that's how fans approach the game. They come out to the ball park and spend money—in some parks, a lot of money—to have a good time, not to sit through three hours of boredom. If I brought my kids to a baseball game, I know they'd want to be entertained. I'd want for them to have something extra to think about besides the situation in the game. I feel it's my job to entertain the fans, not only by playing to win but by adding a bit of spice to their day. I want the fans to walk away saying to themselves, "Hey, I enjoyed that game." Or, "Hey, I enjoyed what Rickey did. He really caught my eye." That's doing your job as an entertainer.

I do a lot of things out of the ordinary. I might jog slowly around the bases after hitting a home run. I might take my time in the batter's box or getting to first base after a walk. I might snatch-catch a fly ball out of the air. I might walk over to the crowd and chat with a fan in the front row. I might wear fluorescent wristbands. I might arrive at spring training a day or two after my teammates. I might show a lot of emotion between the chalk lines. But that's all me. I'm just trying to have fun and approach the game the same way I've always approached it. That's the way I've been successful, and that's the way I've been able to show the fans a good time.

Call it Rickey Time.

An old teammate of mine once said in my defense, "It's hard to make a Jaguar look like a Volkswagen." I like that. A Jaguar has too much style to be covered by the body of a Volkswagen. In other words, I'm not going to hide what I am. Maybe that's bad. I don't know. If my actions offend anybody, I'm sorry. I mean no harm to anybody. But I'm not a conformist. I never have been, and I don't think I ever will be. Call me a hot dog, but don't call me a conformist.

People labeled me a hot dog long before I became known as the game's greatest base stealer in 1991, long before I won the American League MVP award in 1990, long before I brought the Oakland A's a world championship in 1989, long before I began playing for the New York Yankees in 1985.

Although there might have been instances back in high school and the minor leagues, Dennis Eckersley was the first guy in the majors to call me a hot dog. I've heard it a lot since then, but he was the first. It was way back in 1980, my first full year in the majors and during my first go-round with the A's. Eckersley started a game for the Boston Red Sox and was in a groove. He was beating us 1-0 and had a no-hitter entering the seventh inning. We couldn't touch him, so our manager, Billy Martin, told me to walk to the plate and slow the pace. Billy said we could beat him if we slowed him down. So that's what I did. I walked up there and slowed him down.

I was at the plate one time for what seemed to be hours. One foot in the batter's box. One foot out. Raise a hand to call time. Straighten the sleeve. Adjust the pant leg. Reach down and tug on the shoelace. When I finally got into the box, Eckersley whizzed a strike right past me. Whoa, that was quick. I stepped out of the box and went through the same routine. Then I got back in, but I stepped right out when he was in the middle of his delivery. Time, please. I got back in and eventually drew a walk. He got riled and never regained his momentum. We came back to beat him 2-1.

After the game, Eckersley was furious. He said I was after "style points" and called me a "stylemaster" and a "hot dog." *Hot dog* stuck. I guess even back then Eckersley must have known I was good; all he was trying to do was compliment me.

Eckersley and I went at it quite a bit over the years. He'd strike me out and raise his fist in glory. I'd get on base and go out of my way to make sure he knew I was there. We had another big flare-up in '87 when I was with the Yankees and he was with the A's. I thought he was cheating, throwing spitballs. I said so, and he didn't like it. He called me a hot dog, and I called him a cheater. At least a hot dog plays by the rules. We had a couple of pitchers, Rick Rhoden and Tommy John, who were being accused of scuffing balls all the time. Nobody on the team had stood up for them. So when I saw Eckersley throwing those funny pitches all over the place during a 4-2 Yankees loss, I spoke out. I'm never one to hold anything back, especially when it comes to protecting my teammates.

A lot of opponents will say I'm trying to show them up. That's not true at all. There's a difference between being a hot dog and showing a team up. I don't show anybody up. This is a game. I have fun, but I play aggressively and play to win. So does someone like Eckersley. He's a pumped-up guy. Certain pitchers get pumped up after a strikeout, and he's like that. If you acknowledge that it's just a feeling he gets, a reaction to doing well, then you won't get mad at him. When I hit home runs, I get a little extra pumped. But it's not to show anyone up. It's just a reaction from being a competitive ballplayer.

Eckersley and I are a lot alike. Same with Tony La Russa, the A's manager since '86. When I was with the Yankees and we played against the A's, La Russa used to despise me. He was always mad at me because of the way I beat him, and I didn't care much for him because he always tried to intimidate me. It was his competitiveness versus my competitiveness, and sometimes it boiled over into bad feelings for one another.

I never had anything personal against La Russa or Eckersley, and that showed in '89 when I was traded back to the A's and suddenly we were all wearing the same uniform. We might as well have been brothers. All that stuff from the past was forgotten. It was nothing but our competitiveness shining through, and our desire to beat each other into the ground.

I've always seemed to be around showmen. Hey, I grew up in Oakland with a kid named Stanley Burrell, who's now known to the world as MC Hammer or just plain Hammer. I always liked watching athletes who were showmen. My favorite team was the Oakland Raiders. My first baseball hero was Reggie Jackson. My first manager in the big leagues was Billy Martin. When I broke into the majors, the A's owner was Charlie Finley. When I was traded to the Yankees, the owner was George Steinbrenner. I've played with Dave Winfield, Dave Parker, Jose Canseco, Dave Henderson, and, of course, Eckersley. Talk about showmen and hot dogs. For whatever reason, I've always found myself in the middle of lively and animated crowds.

I remember watching Billy Martin in my early days with the A's. He was definitely an entertainer. He'd get the fans going just by walking out on the field to talk with the pitcher. When he ran out to kick dirt on home plate and the umpire's shoes, the fans would really go nuts. I don't think he knew the impact of his dirt-kicking when he first started doing it. He was just upset at the umpires and wanted to stand up for himself. But it caught on with the fans in a hurry. It got to the point where they got excited every time he walked on the field. Billy realized this, and he tried to give the fans a show. After a while, he didn't hesitate going out there to kick and throw dirt because he knew the fans would appreciate him. That's what I call a good showman.

Like Billy, I march to a different beat. For example, I'm not one of those guys who places his cap and glove perfectly at the end of the bench so I can pick them up when it's time to go on the field. I don't always follow the company line. When I'm in the dugout, I'm always moving, always doing something. No way can I sit in one place for an entire inning. I've got too much energy. I've got to be on the move. I just seem to have more fun than most guys. Sometimes I'll be messing around on the bench so much that I won't notice it's time to go out on the field. It's amazing, but sometimes I'll take such a long time getting on the field that I'll hear a big cheer from the crowd when I finally do.

There are a lot of reasons why people call me a hot dog. Somewhere close to the top of the list is my snatch-catch. When I first came up to the A's, a coach named Lee Walls taught me to use two hands whenever catching a fly ball. That's all anyone on the team was permitted to do. Walls would yell at an outfielder anytime he made a one-handed catch, "Hey, two hands, two hands." I stuck with two hands. But eventually I got so good and confident with the two-handed catch that I wanted to add something different, an offshoot from the standard catch.

I had watched Willie Mays when I was young, and Willie would make those famous basket catches. That was real cool. I wanted to be different, like Willie. At the same time, I wanted to keep using two hands. And so, the snatch-catch. I followed all the traditional techniques of catching a ball, holding my glove hand up in the air and using my other hand as support. But just as the ball was about to reach the glove, I'd snatch it out of the air. I'd pull down the ball with a backhanded windmill swipe and slap my glove against my thigh—but I'd still be using two hands, just like Lee Walls had ordered.

I practiced the snatch-catch in spring training in the early eighties, but I never used it in a game until September 29, 1983. I remember it vividly because it was one of the most important catches I ever made. Mike Warren, a guy who won only nine games in his career, was throwing a no-hitter against La Russa's Chicago White Sox through eight and two-thirds innings. It was supposed to be a meaningless game because the White Sox had already clinched the division, and we were something like twenty-five games out of first place. The crowd was under ten thousand. But here was Mike Warren throwing the game of his life, leading 3-0 with Carlton Fisk his final obstacle for a no-hitter.

Carlton hit a one-ball, two-strike pitch to left field, right at me. The last out of the ballgame, the last out of the no-hitter, and I snatched the sucker out of the air. People looked out at me wondering what I had done and why I had done it. Afterwards, my teammates told me, "We would've killed you if you dropped that ball." They made a big deal out of it. But I had been working on it, and I wouldn't have tried it if I couldn't have done it. To tell the truth, that first snatch-catch was total instinct. And that's how most of my snatch-catches have been. I feel comfortable it's going to work every time. If I didn't feel comfortable, I wouldn't be doing it.

For the record, I've never dropped a snatch-catch. It just adds a little bit more flair, and people tend to like it. The only people who don't like it are the parents of the kids who try it at home. They'll come up to me and say, "Rickey, please stop catching the ball like that. My son tries it and gets popped in the head every time."

Well, the snatch-catch isn't for everybody. Not everyone can be a hot dog.

◇ **2** ◇

BASEBALL'S ANSWER TO SHOWTIME

'm in the on-deck circle. Bottom of the ninth. Two outs. Tie game.
Winning run on base. And there I am, posing for a fan in the stands.
Happens all the time. Hey, no big deal. The fan wants a picture, and
I don't want the fan to go away disappointed.

For some strange reason, baseball players have some sort of super-
natural power with the fans, especially the kids. It's amazing how the
slightest gesture can put a smile on a young kid's face. Even a simple
wave goes a long way. There are fans who come up to me years after
the fact and tell me they remember one game where I waved to them.
They tell me I made their day. If I can make someone happy by offering
a simple gesture such as a wave, I'll keep doing it. It's a nice feeling.

That's why I'll laugh and talk with fans throughout the game. Even
if it's the bottom of the ninth in a tie game. Sometimes all people want
is a "hello." I'll smile, I'll ask, "How are you doing?" or "How's your
day?" I'll see a kid pull on his mom and say, "Oh, did you see what
Rickey just did? He waved to me." If it's a thrill for the kids, it's just as
much a thrill for me.

There's another reason I have so much fun with the fans: it loosens
me up. The last thing I want to be is tense. Talking and laughing make
me relax. Other people try to relax in different ways. They'll meditate
or even smoke a cigarette or chew tobacco. I talk. Sometimes I go

overboard. Sometimes I'm out there waving and talking so much that teammates wonder if I'm actually paying attention to the game. They think the ball's going to come out and hit me in the head. No problem; I just tell the fans to let me know when the ball comes. In all seriousness, I'm able to focus on the game when it's time. It's become natural for me, almost a habit, to combine work with pleasure. I've been doing it so long.

One little girl, she's about seven or eight, sits down in the left-field corner at the Oakland Coliseum. I love talking with her. She's so cute. She's got a sign for everything I do. HELLO, RICKEY. HOW ARE YOU, RICKEY? GREAT HIT, RICKEY. OUTSTANDING STEAL, RICKEY. I love that little girl.

Back in the early eighties, when the Coliseum was bare and we'd often draw less than ten thousand people a game, I had a section in the left-field bleachers called Henderson Heights. Here I was, blessed with all the talent in the world, and I wondered, Why me? There were deprived kids, crippled kids, who weren't able to play ball or even watch ball. What could I do to help? I decided to donate a block of fifty tickets every game to underprivileged kids who wouldn't otherwise be able to enjoy baseball. It made me happy and proud to look behind me and see these kids having fun. I went out of my way to talk with those kids and make sure they were having a good time.

My funniest kid story is about a little boy who apparently is one of my biggest fans. One day a couple of years ago, the little boy told his mother he wanted a Rickey Henderson uniform. Socks, shoes, cap, Number 24 jersey, the works. So his mother went out and bought him all this stuff, a real A's uniform with all the Rickey Henderson fixings. The kid was so happy. He put on the uniform and went out and showed all his friends. Then he came back home and knocked on the door. His mother opened the door and almost fainted. This was a white kid, but he was all black. He had rubbed black grease all over his body and face. He had wanted to look exactly like Rickey Henderson. His mother sent me a picture of the kid with an A's uniform and a black face. I never laughed so hard. I showed the picture to the guys in the clubhouse, and they all thought it was as funny as I did.

It's an example of the power athletes have with kids and how kids can react to athletes. It's also a good reason athletes shouldn't abuse their power. A lot of players won't even acknowledge fans. They might be too tense about the game. They're afraid to communicate with fans because they think it disturbs their concentration. Hey, if it's two hours before the game, recognize the fans. That's what I try to do. I realize players have a job to do; the game is the priority. But give in a little. The fans pay to see you, and you've got to try and make them happy.

I know what it's like to be turned away by professional athletes. I got turned away so many times when I was a kid that I always told myself I wouldn't be that way if I ever made the big leagues.

The guy who turned me down the most was Reggie Jackson, my idol. I would stay after games for two hours waiting for that man. Everybody wanted to meet him, but I was a ballplayer and I thought it would be cool to meet someone who actually got paid to play ball. "Mr. Jackson? Excuse me, Mr. Jackson." All I ever wanted to tell him was he was my idol and I wanted to be like him. But all I ever got from Reggie was some cheap pen he handed me. No autograph, just an old itty-bitty pen with his name on it. Big deal.

I didn't come across Reggie again until my first spring training. I had signed after high school in '76 and played the second half of the season in Rookie League, so '77 was my first spring in Arizona. Reggie had already left the A's and was about to begin his first season with the Yankees, but their big league camp hadn't started yet. One day I saw Reggie in a tiny Arizona coffee shop. I was in there with three or four other young players. I was a pro, just like Reggie, so I was quite sure he'd finally give me my autograph. I was still in the minors and he was a superstar in the majors, but so what? I didn't know the difference back then. A pro's a pro.

He was sitting in the corner, and I told him who I was and asked for an autograph. He said he didn't give autographs. I was beginning to get upset. I said, "Hey, Mr. Jackson, I'm a pro, I'm with the A's." He didn't care. He refused to sign his name. My buddies went back to our table, but I wasn't budging. I told him, "One day, you'll ask for my autograph. I know that, Mr. Jackson. One day." I went back to my table really furious. He got up to leave, and we finished our meals. When we got up to pay our tab, the waiter told us it was already paid for. Reggie had picked it up. For that, he was still my idol.

By the time I got to the majors in '79, Reggie had won two World Series with the Yankees. He was bigger than ever. My first game against New York, I walked up to him. He was in the batting cage all by himself, putting on his big show. "Mr. Jackson, I made it to the pros, the real pros." When he was done, I reminded him about the coffee shop in Arizona and all the times he turned me down at the Coliseum. He said, "Yes, son, I remember you." Yeah, sure. During the conversation, he tried giving me advice. He told me to move way, way back when he came up to bat. He said, with his cocky attitude, that he hits the ball a long, long way, that I'd stay in the big leagues if I played way, way back. "No, Mr. Jackson. What's going to keep me in the big leagues is playing way, way in. Then I'm going to go way, way back and catch whatever you hit." I told him that.

When he came up, I rushed in about seven steps and caught his eye. He stepped out of the box and took a long look at me, a very long look. Sure enough, he hit a ball deep into the gap in left center. Uh-oh. I immediately hauled butt. I ran that ball down and grabbed it out of the sky. When he was slowing down around second base, he looked out at me and I looked back and smiled. "Hey, I told you so, Mr. Jackson."

A year later when I stole a hundred bases, I think he finally gave me my respect. More importantly, he gave me an autograph. An autographed bat. Yes, I finally got it. And guess what? Years later when he was with the Angels, he asked for my autograph. Just like I had told him he would. Without hesitation, I gave him my autograph. "Here you go, Mr. Jackson."

Although Reggie and I both played for both the A's and the Yankees, we were never teammates. The first time we wore the same uniform was with the '91 A's, when he came back as one of La Russa's coaches. La Russa already had a full squad of coaches when he hired Reggie, so Reggie became an assistant who could work with the team only before games. Now that was a change of pace for Reggie, going from a Hall of Fame ballplayer to an assistant coach. He didn't have to do it because he's a living legend. He handled it very well. Sometimes he held back because he didn't want to step on the toes of Rick Burleson, our hitting instructor. It was a tough transition, but it was also a start. People don't always start at the top, even Hall of Famers. But he got the opportunity to learn from a great manager. If he ever wants to become a manager himself, this was a good move. He knows the game as well as anybody, and his ideas always seem to be good ones. Sometimes I think he talks too much, but that's Reggie. He's always been that way.

When Reggie became our coach, he joined a team that already had big characters and big names. It was a team people liked to watch, a team that made people show up at the ball park early to catch batting practice, a team that put on a good show and provided good entertainment. Then again, I don't know if any successful team is boring. We've had a nice mix of everything: starting pitchers, relief pitchers, power hitters, average hitters, runners. People have come out to see us because we've been a complete package. Some people might think that package includes showboating. Well, I prefer to call it entertainment, and we've been more entertaining than a lot of other clubs. We're like the Lakers of the eighties—baseball's answer to Showtime.

It wasn't a fluke that we had the best road attendance in the majors in both '90 and '91. We drew more fans on the road than all the bigger-market teams like the Yankees, Mets, Dodgers, and Cubs. Every city we visited, people flocked to the ball park as well as the hotel lobby. It reminded me of my Yankee days. There's not a team in baseball that gets as much attention in a lobby as the Yankees did when I was there. The A's are close, but the Yankees used to get into a city at four in the morning and be forced to weave through a crowd of people in a hotel lobby. It was a big show, but it's always been that way with the Yankees, even in the down years. Because of the history, the tradition, the overall New York mystique, the Yankees will always be popular everywhere they go. With the A's, we get breaks in cities like Cleveland and Seattle, but people came out from everywhere when the Yankees came to town.

More and more, I'm beginning to get turned off by the lobby crowds. At one time, they were so innocent and players weren't hesitant to sign autographs. Now it's a sad, sad situation. The card industry has gotten out of control, and big card collectors and promoters pay off kids to work the lobbies all night long. There's no way these young kids should be at downtown hotels at those hours. They should be at home in bed. That's why a lot of players refuse to sign autographs; they know many of these kids are being used by card dealers who make huge profits by selling autographed items. It's very sad for the younger generation, the kids who want autographs just for themselves. Years ago, it was much more genuine. Players wouldn't think twice about giving a kid an autograph because they knew the kids weren't working for promoters like so many are today. Kids weren't in the lobbies at all hours of the night, either. Today, it all comes with the territory.

It's funny, but I was surprised the A's were getting as much attention as they were when I joined the team in '89. I didn't think the team had superstars, to tell you the truth. They had up-and-comers, guys who were still proving they could play. They had won the pennant only once, in '88, but they went on to lose to the Dodgers in the World Series. It was a relatively young team, and the players weren't as popular as they got to be over the next couple of years.

The foundation was young: Canseco, Mark McGwire, and Walt Weiss. Others like Eckersley, Dave Stewart, and Dave Henderson had come from other clubs, and they were emerging as stars in their own right. All of them had one good year together, and they were putting Oakland back on the baseball map. People were beginning to believe this was a good team.

When I was traded to the Yankees in '85, the Yankees already had their stars in place: Winfield, Don Mattingly, the proven names. There were more stars on the '85 Yankees than the '89 A's, but the '89 A's were still on the verge of proving themselves. If I had gotten to the A's in '90 or '91, then I would've joined a team of superstars. But not in '89. That all changed, of course, after we won the World Series later that year. I was traded back to the A's in June, and the club didn't miss a beat in winning the division, the pennant, and finally the world championship.

Now the A's have a lot of proven stars. People come out in waves to watch us. Jose and I are what you might call the biggest draws, the main attractions. Jose brings excitement to the power game, I bring excitement to the running game. It's a nice blend, but the team wouldn't have been so popular or successful without a great bullpen closer like Eckersley or a great starting pitcher like Stewart or a lot of other players who've contributed in so many ways.

I've been on a lot of great teams and a lot of bad teams, and I've played with a lot of great players and a lot of bad players. I've had different roles with different teams, playing in left field, playing in center field. I've been the leadoff hitter for each of my teams, but my role has changed from team to team and from year to year. I've been asked to concentrate solely on the running game, I've been asked to concentrate on the power game, I've been asked to do a mix of everything. When people think of Rickey Henderson, they first think of base stealing. That's only natural because my 130 steals in '82 are still the most in any season in baseball history, and my career total is an ongoing major league record that continues to grow by the game. But unlike most base stealers, I consider myself an all-around ballplayer. I take pride in my hitting and fielding. I've hit for an average, hit for power. I've won a Gold Glove. I've won an MVP and came close two other times.

When I broke in with the A's in '79, we didn't have a very good team. We didn't have great hitters or great pitchers. Dwayne Murphy was our best power hitter, but he was more of a line-drive hitter. Most of our guys were .250 hitters. My role was to spark the team and ignite rallies by stealing bases. We had to rely on fundamentals, doing the little things to win. When I got to the Yankees, they already had a great offense in place. I wasn't expected to run as much, so I started hitting home runs, fifty-two in my first two years. When I rejoined the A's, it was a much different team from the one I left in '85. Only three players—Carney Lansford, Tony Phillips, and Curt Young—were still around from those early years. They were a much better team, but they desperately lacked someone to get on base and set the table for the number-three, -four, and -five hitters. Every team I joined was missing a needed ingredient, and I tried to become the final piece of that puzzle. It wasn't always easy, but I feel I've adjusted pretty well to the teams I've been with.

The lineups have changed from season to season, and I've hit in front of a wide variety of number-two hitters, guys who would take pitches and allow me to steal, and guys who made it nearly impossible for me to steal. Murphy hit second for the early A's, but he was a free swinger and struck out too much. He was no second hitter; he was our home run hitter. Billy Martin batted Murph second because he knew I'd get on base and Murph would get more fastballs so he could hit more home runs. Joe Morgan also hit second with that team, but Joe swung at everything. So many times, I'd have a base stolen and he'd be fouling off a pitch. Willie Randolph was the most natural second hitter because he could hit to right field so well, giving me the opportunity to easily go from first to third. Lansford and Dave Henderson have hit second the last few years. Dave has complained that he can't find a good rhythm hitting behind me, that the pitchers spend too much time trying to pick me off. Well, sometimes I wish I had a guy like me to hit behind. I'd get a lot more fastballs. I've always followed the number-nine hitter, and some of those guys have been pretty weak over the years. I tell the guy who hits behind me to do only what he's capable of doing. If we understand each other's strengths and weaknesses, our relationship will be much better.

I love analyzing the game and the different players, especially hitters. I always thought I could be a pretty good batting coach. I love stealing bases, but I love hitting just as much. I keep an eye on other hitters and have a pretty good idea what they're doing right and wrong. I don't make it a practice to talk to other players about their hitting, but some people who know me well tell me I don't talk enough when it comes to noticing things in hitters.

Like everything else, I seem to have different ideas on hitting. The truth is, I don't think you need a hitting coach when things are going bad; you need one when things are going good. That's just the opposite of what most guys think. Most guys think they shouldn't analyze themselves too much when they're going good; they couldn't care less where they stand in the box or how they swing. When they go bad, they try to figure out where to stand, where to hold the bat, where to hit. I think it should be just the opposite. You shouldn't think too much when you're struggling, but you should think a lot when you're going good. If you think about what you're doing when you're going good, then you'll remember what to do when things are going bad. My theory on hitting coaches is this: When I'm going good, tell me everything about my swing. When I'm going bad, leave me alone. Let me step back and work it out on my own.

Sometimes too much advice can hurt a hitter. When someone's struggling, he often listens to everybody else's advice and uses everybody else's techniques, but then he'll be more screwed up than before. What he really needs to do is go back to basics. Nobody knows you better than you. Forget about everybody else. Burleson got mad at me in '91 because I wouldn't always listen to him. I didn't want to hear someone else's theory. I'm trying to work on my own theory. Whenever we get a new hitting coach—and the A's have had three since I arrived in '89—I sit him down in spring training and tell him certain things to look for. During the course of the season, just point out those things. But don't tell me to change the way I hit.

So many times when players analyze their hitting, they look at their grip, their stance, their swing, their follow-through, everything. Everything but their vision. Sometimes what a guy does with his body has nothing to do with his slump. It's the eyes. What is he seeing? More importantly, what is he looking for? If I have all my body motions working perfectly, but I'm having a tough time seeing the pitcher and the ball, I'm in trouble. I've got to know how to block out the center fielder, the middle infielders, even the fans beyond the center-field fence. Magic Johnson has been a great basketball player because he can see everything moving on the court, but it's different in baseball. In baseball, when a batter's standing in the box, everything that moves is a distraction, even the pitcher's arm.

In my last year in New York, Yankees executive Syd Thrift hired an optometrist from Southern California to teach us about eye contact. Bill Harrison was his name, and we'd visit with him when we traveled to Anaheim to play the Angels. He once told me something I'll never forget. Hitters are generally taught to follow the ball when the pitcher's in his windup, but Dr. Harrison taught me to look at the letter on top of the pitcher's cap. When the pitcher is about to release the ball, when his hand passes by his head, transfer the eyes away from his cap and onto the ball. The optometrist's reasoning made a lot of sense. If a hitter focuses primarily on the arm and the ball, his eyes move up and down with the pitcher's arm. He'll be distracted and pick up everything in the background. But a pitcher's cap is easier to follow because it doesn't move up and down like his arm. It's also closer to the area where the ball will be released. It's like a racehorse wearing blinders; his vision is focused just one way. Ted Williams was supposed to have better eyes than any other ballplayer, and I guarantee he blocked out everything behind the pitcher. The eyes play a big part in hitting, but I've got to constantly remind myself to use and train my eyes.

I play ping-pong, a lot of ping-pong. It's a fast-paced game on a little court, and it's great for hand–eye coordination. It teaches me to move my eyes quickly and accurately. A baseball field might be much bigger than a ping-pong table, and the sixty feet six inches between the pitching rubber and home plate might seem to be a long distance. But a hitter had better know how to use his eyes to pick up the ball when Nolan Ryan is firing one-hundred-mile-an-hour peas to the plate.

I have my own style, my own techniques, when preparing to hit. When I walk to the plate, I'm typically talking. Catchers think I'm talking to my bat, and they ask if the bat talks back. I tell them I sure as hell hope it doesn't. No, I'm not talking to my bat; I'm reminding myself what I have to look for at the plate. Even when I'm ready to hit, I'm still talking. I'm looking at the pitcher and talking: "Oooh, this guy dominated me last at bat, threw me a tough slider. But, Rickey, it's your turn. Let's go to work. Oooh, I'm gonna get ya. Look for the slider, look for the slider. Oooh, I'm gonna get ya. Might try to trick me. Look, look. Look at that ball. Okay, here it comes. Boom!" The catcher's scratching his head, the umpire's laughing. They're wondering what in the world I'm doing.

I have another theory that goes against the grain. I get criticized for not attending hitters' meetings. We have meetings before a series to study and analyze the opposing pitchers. Hey, I don't want to know about the opposing pitchers. I don't want to be in a position where I'm concentrating too hard on the pitcher's stuff. I'd get up to the plate and start trying to guess what the guy's going to throw. There's really only one thing I have to know: The pitcher's got to throw the ball across the plate if he wants to get me out. I already know that his curveball is going to break a little bit, his slider is going to come to me and dive, his fastball will go either in or out, high or low. Once I know that, all I have to do is go up there and look for the ball. It's that simple. Break it down any further, and I'm lost. I just want to see the ball, hit the ball, and run, run, run. My theory is, I don't want to know what the pitcher's got. Just let me know the basics, and I'll take it from there.

Baseball is a reactionary sport. Sometimes it's not as important to think as it is to react. It's just like being a kid again. When you're a kid, nobody tells you what to do on a baseball field. You just react on your own, let your instincts take over. If you start thinking too much, you've got problems. While those hitters' meetings might help some people, it's not necessary or beneficial for me to know every single detail about every pitcher who takes the mound.

Let's look at some other guys. Let's take Mark McGwire. In '91, I guarantee you, at least twenty people told him something new every day. He tried everything, and nothing worked. Man, just go back to basics. I didn't give McGwire any advice when he was slumping in '91 because so many people were messing with him and I was going bad myself. But I did tell him something very important in '90 when he was hitting a lot more home runs. For starters, I told him to make contact and don't overswing. I also told him he could be a better home run hitter than Canseco if he listened to me on only one thing. There's a reason for all those warning-track fly balls he's hit. It's his golf-stroke swing. He's been playing golf his whole life, since he was about four years old. All the talk about hitting a golf ball is to make contact with the ball when the hands and arms are close to the body, and to hit the ball almost behind the body. If you hit a baseball in the same location, you won't be utilizing all your power and your momentum. You hit it softly. McGwire puts his weight back, not forward. He's taken so many strike-outs on fastballs on the outside part of the plate because golfers aren't accustomed to going out and getting that outside pitch. Back in his rookie year when he hit forty-nine home runs, he had the same stroke, but he used his upper body and hit a lot of home runs to right center. Recently, he hasn't been hitting the ball out of the park to right field, and he rarely hits in that direction at all. It comes down to the upper body. Look at how Jose puts his upper body into the ball. He goes forward and gets it, while McGwire waits for the ball and hits it too far back in the zone. That's the difference between a warning-track fly ball and a home run. Just the slightest change could make a world of difference.

Dave Parker was hitting home runs in his late thirties because he continued to use his upper body so well. He flings his upper body through the ball. Lansford has an unorthodox stroke, twisting his body all around, but he's successful because he uses his upper body well. Same with Dave Henderson. When Hendu was going strong early in '91—his average in late May was .350—his hands were high and he was hitting everything. Later, his hands were lower and he started pushing the ball. He began taking a dive, and by the end of the year he was in a bad slump. He's usually a great second-half hitter, but he was just the opposite in '91. Another thing that affected Hendu was hitting all over the lineup. La Russa would hit him second, third, fourth, fifth, sixth. I guess Tony was trying to protect other guys in the lineup, but you mess up a guy doing that. Wherever you hit in the lineup, you're going to be pitched differently.

Canseco hits third every game, hurt or not. So he keeps coming up in similar situations. He doesn't have to worry about hitting fourth, fifth, or sixth. He's earned the right to hit third, but he shouldn't stop there. That's what I talk to Canseco about. I say, "Jose, what's wrong with you? You could knock in a hundred and sixty runs, just like Babe Ruth, Lou Gehrig, or Joe DiMaggio. You could do that, Jose." But he's got to know how to do it. He's got to say, "Hey, I'm the RBI man, I'm the money man. When Rickey's on second base, I can hit the ball hard, hit it out of the ball park, whatever. But when Rickey's on third, I've just got to make contact. I can't strike out." Don Mattingly isn't a big man, and he didn't strike out much anyway. But when I was on third base, Mattingly never struck out. And I mean never.

I've told Jose, "Jose, do not leave me on third base with one or no outs. Period. When you get two strikes, all you've got to do is tap the ball somewhere. I'm going to score. Even a short fly ball somewhere, I'm going to score. That's my job, to score. So don't go up there swinging with two strikes out of your butt and missing everything." We've got a bet going. He's supposed to take me out to dinner when he doesn't get me in from third with one or no out, and I'm supposed to take him to dinner if he does. I guarantee, he owes me a lot of dinners.

It's gotten to the point where he doesn't even want to know when I'm on third base. If I talk to him from the bag, saying things like, "Let's go, Jose. Bear down, buddy," he'll say, "Don't talk to me, Rickey, or I'll strike out every time."

Jose, like me, combines power with speed. I steal more bases, he hits more home runs. But we enjoy both parts of the game. Obviously, we're different types of players. He's an explosive power hitter, I'm an explosive base stealer. When stealing a base, I have explosive speed from the beginning, while he's a big tall guy who has to get going a few steps before he can explode. In '88, he was Mr. 40-40, the first player in history to hit forty home runs and steal forty bases in the same season. Everybody seemed more excited about his steals than his homers, but not me. I thought the forty homers were more impressive. See, I think a lot more players should be able to steal forty bases, but not everybody is capable of hitting forty home runs.

Jose has predicted he'll be Mr. 50-50 before he retires, and a lot of people say he's crazy because they don't think he should abuse his body by stealing fifty bases. I don't buy that theory. That shouldn't be a concern. To be a complete ballplayer, you've got to do it all. If you're afraid to get injured while running and just concentrate on being a power hitter, you're hurting the ball club. Jose would like to do both, but I believe the hardest thing in becoming Mr. 50-50 is hitting the fifty home runs. Fifty steals in one season has been reached a lot more times than fifty home runs. Stealing two bases a game is a lot simpler than hitting two home runs a game. Hey, you could steal two bases in one at bat. So Jose's got to think about hitting fifty home runs first; I think the base stealing part would be easier to pull off.

I get along with Jose. People still get on him for all his off-the-field hassles, his traffic tickets, his brushes with the law. But he's a good guy. So he drove faster than the speed limit a few times. So what. A lot of people get tickets, but he's Jose Canseco, so everyone knows about him. A lot of stories make him out to be worse than he is. I know how he feels; I'm often in the same boat. Jose's all right. We respect each other and leave it at that. In my mind, I don't seem to have too many problems with anybody, especially my teammates, and I try not to have problems with players on other teams. It just doesn't always work out that way, but I try.

The way I perform on the field has nothing to do with the way I treat people off the field. I like getting along with players on other teams, and I'll go out of my way to talk to opposing players before and during games. I know, I know, the baseball gods don't like opposing players fraternizing. But big deal. If somebody doesn't want to talk with me, that's fine. I won't bother him. But most guys are willing to exchange a few words. We're all in this together. A lot of us have been teammates elsewhere, and a lot of us are friends.

The only people you'll hear saying a nasty word about me are opponents I've just beaten. First of all, nobody likes to get beaten. Second of all, nobody likes to get beaten by a guy like me. You know, a hot dog.

U CAN'T TOUCH RICKEY

I haven't always been a hot dog, but I've always been a momma's boy. Always have, always will. There's no shame in that. I'm her baby, her pet, and she's my idol. She's been the greatest influence on my life and my career. Everything I've ever done, every base hit, every stolen base, every championship, every MVP, I owe it to my momma.

In a lot of ways, I'm a lot like Bobbie Henderson—my thinking, my personality, my athletic skills, even my physical appearance. I look more like Momma than any of my brothers and sisters—the build, the face, the complexion, the legs, the strength.

When she was a kid in Arkansas, she played football and ran track. She was a great athlete. She was always the fastest kid in her school. That's where I get my speed, from her. I've always been fast, from the minute I was born.

It was Christmas Eve 1958. The south side of Chicago. A typically cold, icy winter day. Momma was at home preparing for Christmas Day. My dad was out playing poker with his buddies. That's the way it was with John Henley, my natural father. Late Christmas Eve, I was ready to go. Time to be born. Let's get going. Momma felt some pushing and shoving, so she called my dad and told him to come home. My dad didn't want to come right away, because he was winning big. Imagine that. But he finally came back to the house to drive Momma to the hospital. He put Momma in the backseat of his Oldsmobile and sped off to the hospital in the snow and sleet.

Unfortunately for Momma, she didn't get to the hospital quite fast enough. By the time she got to the hospital, I was resting in her arms. Christmas morning I was born right there in the backseat of that Oldsmobile.

Like I said, I've always been fast.

My dad parked the car in front of the hospital and started running for a doctor. Momma yelled at him, "Forget the doctor." She said, "Just get me out of here." She didn't need a doctor. The work had been done. She did it all herself.

That's the way it's always been with Momma, taking care of everything herself. She's the strongest lady I've ever met. When I was two years old, John Henley left the family. I never saw or heard from him again. Momma was so strong. She had to be.

I was Momma's fourth child. I was supposed to be a girl because her first three children were boys. Even her fifth child was a boy. Alton, John, Tyrone, me, then Douglas. Not until her sixth child did she have a girl. And she had two of them, Paula and Glynnes.

I was a big-boned kid, a chunky kid. But Momma tells me I had cute, chubby legs. That's why she never let me wear long pants. She always made me wear shorts, always wanted to show off my legs. To this day she says I should've been a girl.

With Momma's husband taking off like he did, Momma packed up the family and moved back to Arkansas, a little rural town called Pine Bluff. We lived on my grandma's farm. That was a good time. It was the backcountry. A lot of cultivated land and pastures, with animals everywhere, mostly pigs, chickens, and rabbits. I used to ride the animals all over the farm, but they'd usually get the best of me. The hogs would throw me off every time I came around; a pony once rode me into a tree; and I once cut open my foot on some glass while chasing chickens around the coop. The chickens were my favorite. I could play with those chickens all day long. I'd chase them, then they'd chase me. Man, those chickens were fast. Put dozens of chickens together in one coop, and they run every which way. I had to be fast to keep up with them, but there wasn't a chicken on that entire farm that could outrun me. And I was teeny-weeny. I think that's when Momma realized I was going to be faster than most kids.

On the farm, Grandma was very protective of her grandkids. When Momma wanted to do something with us, Grandma wouldn't let her. She'd say, "You can go wherever you want to, but these kids are staying right here." There were five boys—my sisters hadn't been born yet—but there was no adult male to look after us, so Momma and Grandma took care of us the best they could.

Grandma supported us by working for a big white family. I was only a little kid then, but I was wondering if this was like the slavery days, living on the plantation and taking care of the white folks. I later found out it was only a job Grandma had; she was making money to help us survive. We learned a lot from Grandma. We learned to look after ourselves, to do our own jobs and chores. She taught us to cook and clean and take care of ourselves. With no father in the house, that was important.

With Momma set on bringing us to California, she went away for a while to find us a place to live and a job to support us. But she was just doing what was best for us. It wasn't easy. We didn't have much money in those days. Momma did meet a man in California, Paul Henderson. They got married, and Momma sent for the family. I was ten when she brought us all out to Oakland. Everyone came except my younger brother, Doug, because Doug didn't want to leave Grandma. Pretty soon, Grandma made it out and brought along Doug. In Oakland, the family continued to grow. Momma had Paula and Glynnes. The girls were born as Hendersons after the five boys had been born to three different fathers. The Henleys were me and Tyrone, but we all became Hendersons when Momma remarried. Paul Henderson adopted the five boys, and we became one big family. That was nice while it lasted.

As for John Henley, I never found out what he was all about. That's too bad. I always wanted to meet that man. I just wanted to know what he looked like in person, whether he was like me in any way, whether he appreciated what I had done, whether he had been an athlete, whether he was even alive. Early in my career, we hired detectives to look for him in Chicago. The detectives reported back to Momma, but they never did track him down. One day Momma found out that he had died. She waited almost a year to tell me. I was in the middle of a season, and she didn't want to interrupt what I was doing.

Because I never knew my biological father, I consider Paul Henderson more of a real dad than a stepdad. But he didn't stay around, either. He and Momma separated. He's in Kansas City now. He had been working at General Motors, but the plant closed down in the early eighties, so he moved to Kansas City for the work. Most of my life, there was no man in the house. Grandma raised us in Arkansas, and Momma raised us in Oakland.

In Oakland, we lived in a working-class area. It wasn't middle class, but it wasn't the projects, either. We never had much money, but that didn't seem to be a factor. There wasn't a reason to complain. Momma worked as a registered nurse and earned enough money to put clothes on our backs and food in our stomachs. I never felt like we were poor. Kids are usually happy even if they don't have money. Maybe if I knew then what I know now, I'd be upset. But as a kid, money wasn't an object, as long as I could play ball and have a roof over my head.

We've always been a close family, and Momma is the reason. She made sure we stayed close. Even to this day, she demands we all gather on certain days. We have some great get-togethers, especially on Christmas. She tells us to go nowhere else on Christmas except with the family. We always have a big dinner, a big party, plenty of eggnog. Every year, more and more kids join in. All my brothers have children, so kids are everywhere. Those parties have gotten so big that my immediate family no longer buys presents for every member of the family. We just draw out of a hat and buy one person one present. After that, we all take care of all the kids. And, of course, we all take care of Momma. Never forget the kids, never forget Momma. I used to spend a lot of money on presents; in '89 and '90, I spent most of my winnings from the A's playoff shares on Christmas presents. I was always one of those guys who has to get everybody something for Christmas. Brothers, sisters, cousins, aunts, uncles, all the kids. Hey, that's my time. I love shopping for my friends and family.

At the beginning of my career, I'd do anything for my family. My grandma told me to slow it down. She said it was getting to be a problem. I'd go overboard. She didn't want anybody to get to the point where they'd be depending on me. She said that was wrong, but I couldn't help it. Someone would say, "Hey, Rickey, I need two thousand dollars." I didn't ask questions. Okay, here you go. Grandma would call and say, "I told you, son, don't do that." You can get run over by that. She told me anytime I give something to somebody, friends as well as family, tell them to do something in return. Then they'll appreciate it more. When one person in the family makes a lot more money than everybody else, it's sometimes an uncomfortable feeling, but I'll help my family whenever I can. That's the way it should be. I have a twenty-six-acre ranch in the gold country of California, about twenty miles from Yosemite National Park, and there's plenty of work to be done there. So when I give something to somebody, I have them work at my ranch. My brother Tyrone lives there year-round and takes care of it for me. It's a great trade-off for both of us.

That ranch reminds me of my younger days on the farm in Arkansas. The outdoor life really suits me. I've played ball in major metropolitan areas, the Bay Area and New York, but I'm more at home in the woods, in the backcountry. The best thing about the country is the peacefulness. I feel an inner peace whenever I go to the country. It's away from the big city, away from fifty thousand people yelling all at once. It's just me and the wilderness. Sometimes I'll go fishing with Tyrone or a friend or another ballplayer. We have a six-acre lake stocked with bass, catfish, bluegill, perch, and crappie. I've taken Dave Stewart out fishing a few times. I love fishing, even when the fish don't bite. If I don't catch a fish all day, that's fine. I'm out there feeling the freedom. It was my stepfather who turned me on to fishing. He's an outdoorsman, always out in the wilderness. He's a hunter. I've never shot a deer, but I have hunted pheasants, ducks, and jackrabbits. Billy Martin used to take me quail hunting. But I'm not as much of a hunter as I am a fisherman.

Of all my brothers and sisters, I'm closest to Tyrone. He's only one year older than I am, and he used to take me under his wing when we were kids. He's the person who got me interested in baseball. He knew my favorite sport was football and that baseball was just a hobby—just like it became years later with Bo Jackson. I had to play baseball in the spring only because nobody else wanted to play football. I'd have to wait for the fall to play football, so I played baseball while waiting for football season. I first played baseball only because I was forced to by Tyrone. It was back in Arkansas. He was the only other athlete in the family, and sometimes he'd have nobody else to play catch with. So he'd throw a glove on me and drag me along. I didn't want to play, but he made me. And then he fired the ball at me. I'd get mad and fire it back. He'd throw it harder at me, and I'd throw it harder back at him. That's how I started playing baseball. I was forced to learn how to use my glove; otherwise, Tyrone's throws would've killed me. When I learned how to play catch, Tyrone got me on his Little League team—U.S. Brown Funeral Home. Nice name for a kid's very first baseball team.

Although Tyrone was a good athlete, he didn't pursue sports like I did. Tyrone was more of a pretty boy, the cutie of the family. He liked the girls. He was smart, too. Very, very smart. He had the brains in the family. A true genius, in my mind. He got an academic scholarship to the University of California at Berkeley, just a few blocks from our house, and he went on to study computers. He worked hard in college for a while, but then he got a girlfriend and said the heck with college. He was too much of a pretty boy. But I'll never forget him for pulling me into baseball, even though I despised it at the time.

After moving west from Arkansas, I quickly learned that the best thing about Oakland was the weather. It stayed warm year-round. There were no more cold winters. I could play outside twelve months of the year. And, conveniently, there was a huge park just a few blocks from our house, Bushrod Park.

My school, Washington Elementary, was situated on one corner of Bushrod. I used to run around Bushrod from sunrise to sunset, and often much later. It had plenty of room to play any sport I wanted. With two adjoining baseball fields and enough room to fit a full-length football field, Bushrod was a sports heaven. It was a few blocks from our house, just a short run. In fact, it was a sprint. I'd run as fast as I could to Bushrod, but I had a reason. I was racing the city buses. They were big buses, and they cruised pretty quickly. But they had to stop at every block. I didn't. I zipped right by them and beat them to Bushrod every time.

They've renamed Bushrod Park. It's now called Billy Martin Field. Billy grew up just across the Oakland border in Berkeley, and he played at that park every day during his boyhood. I love Billy, but it was called Bushrod when I grew up there, and it'll always be Bushrod to me. Nowadays, when I go by the old neighborhood, I don't see as many kids playing at the park. Back then, that's all we did, play ball. It's died down a bit. Maybe Proposition 13, which cut a lot of funding for public services in California, had something to do with it. Or maybe kids aren't as interested in playing sports all day. There are so many more options for kids today, some good, some not so good.

When I went to Bushrod, I usually found myself in a pickup game with neighborhood kids. I'd usually play with the older guys because that's where the competition was. I improved a lot faster by playing with guys two or three years older than me. Me and my buddies would be there all day long. You couldn't pry us away from that place. I'm still close to a lot of those guys today: Kenny Smith, Tony Wright, Fred Atkins. Fred and I have been especially close. We'd teach each other. We'd throw balls at each other's feet and dive for them for hours at a time to see who had the better instincts, the better hands. The guy who showed the better hands would get treated to a hamburger down at Sam's Hamburger Stand. I'm still best friends with Fred. He works with abused kids as an activities therapist at a youth center in Oakland. Looking back at Bushrod, it's a nice feeling because that's where I built some long-lasting relationships.

I'd hang out at Bushrod so much that Momma would get skeptical of me. How could any kid spend so much time at one place? I was a clean kid then, I didn't get dirty much at all. One day after I came home, Momma asked why I was so clean. She said, "If you're always playing, you should be dirty." She was thinking, "I know you didn't play ball. Where did you go?" She thought I might be doing something else. So every time I went to Bushrod, I made sure to get dirty. I'd slide on my legs, slide on my back, slide on my belly, anything to get my clothes dirty. I learned that a dirty uniform is a sign of hustle, even as a kid, and that was cool. Even if I didn't get a chance to slide in a game, I'd make sure I looked messy by throwing dirt all over me. That way, Momma knew I was really playing ball, and she wouldn't have to worry I was somewhere I shouldn't be.

Even when I came home dirty, Momma would often question why I played ball all day and did nothing else. She wanted me to stay home and do my share of the cleaning. It was tough to find time to do my chores because I was at Bushrod all day. One time, I was playing in a basketball tournament at Bushrod. Momma asked me to stay home and finish my chores. I argued with her and told her my team needed me, that I was the star of the team. It was a big tournament. But she told me if I played, I'd get a whipping. Momma then left the house to do some errands. When she was gone, I figured I could sneak over to Bushrod, play in the tournament, and be back by the time Momma returned. Well, she came home early. It was still only halftime by the time she got back. She sent my sister to Bushrod to bring me home. My sister told me, "Momma wants your butt home now." Oh, no. I was dead. I ran home and tried to explain about the importance of the tournament. She yelled at me, "Rickey, I don't want to hear about no basketball tournament." She whipped my butt like I'll never forget. Whew, boy, she whipped me that day. I could hardly walk. But she surprised me. She sent me right back to Bushrod to finish the game. I had to tell the kids I was walking funny because I cut myself on a fence coming back to the park.

From that day on, Momma realized I was happiest playing ball, any kind of ball. She knew I did her wrong that day, but she learned I'd sacrifice myself and get whipped if it meant playing in this tournament. That's when she knew that playing ball is what I wanted and what I loved. After that, she encouraged me to play. She stopped whipping me for being out at Bushrod all the time. She actually started coming out and watching me.

One of my biggest moments at Bushrod came when I won the trophy of trophies. In sixth grade, I was named Bushrod's Athlete of the Year. They'd give this huge trophy to the kid in the area who excelled the most in all the sports, football, basketball, baseball, track. I was the number one guy, beating out Lamont Whitehead and Kerry Bland, and I got the huge trophy. The thing was almost as tall as I was. I felt so proud. I was the king of Bushrod. That was my first trophy, my first MVP. I still have it. In fact, it's at Momma's house. I'd like to include it in my trophy collection, but Momma won't give it up.

If I wasn't playing ball at Bushrod, I was at Bushrod shooting dice. Aside from sports, that was about my favorite activity. The neighborhood kids would get together and shoot a lot of dice, and Bushrod would be where we'd go. We'd collect Coke bottles and cash them in for five cents a bottle. We worked hard for our money, and then we'd go off and shoot dice. We were big spenders. We'd go a dollar, maybe two dollars, a roll. Momma didn't like me shooting dice, and she'd break up a lot of games if she saw us playing. She'd always tell me, "If you didn't get nothing else from your father, you got his gambling habit." I definitely won my share in dice. Nobody was as good as I was. My buddies always told me I was lucky. I just told them I had lucky dice. I'm the same way today. Except I play cards, not dice. And I still win my share.

I haven't changed much since those days. To my old friends, I'm still the same Rickey. I try to be my normal, down-to-earth self. Fred and those other guys would say, "He's still the same Rickey. As a kid, he'd take all our money in dice games and never give it back. Now as an adult, as a successful baseball player, he still won't give us our money back."

We were out at Bushrod one day when an older man, a guy around thirty, showed up with a wad of bills. We had never seen him before, but he wanted to get in on the game. This guy was loaded, so I wasn't going to say no. I pulled out my lucky dice and went to work. After a while, I had won almost two hundred dollars off this guy. This was great. I was winning every roll. He was getting madder and madder. I finally won all his money, and he said he was returning to his car to get more money. Fine. Bring it on.

Well, this guy didn't come back with more money. He came back with a gun. He had actually gone to his car to grab a gun. We were all in shock. He yelled at us to line up against a wall. We were trying to tell him we were just kids having a little fun. He said he wanted all his money back. I was thinking, "Hey, baby, if he wants his money back, it's his. All of it. Money ain't that important. Take it all back, brother."

He took the money, but still wouldn't leave. He told us to drop to our knees. He was pointing the gun at us. Damn, this guy wanted to kill us. I dropped to my knees and started to pray, "Oh, Lord, please help us. Take us away from this crazy man." The guy told us not to move. He started to get back in his car when one of my buddies said, "Let's make a run for it." In a flash, we started running out of there. Forget that guy, forget the money, no sweat. We just wanted to stay alive.

Well, it didn't end there. The guy saw us running, so he got in his car and started chasing us through the parking lot. Then he got out of his car and chased us on foot through the ball fields. This guy was serious. Finally, he stopped. We all hit the ground. We knew he couldn't hit us on the run, but he could sure hit us if he stopped and aimed. As we all stretched across the ground, it became really quiet. The guy looked at us. He pulled back his gun, turned around, and walked away. Thank you, Lord.

One of my best buddies, a guy I shot a lot of dice with, was Louis Burrell. We were close. We hung out and played a lot of ball together.

Louis had a little brother who'd always follow us around. His name was Stanley. Stanley didn't run with us much, but he always seemed to be around when we shot dice. He wasn't much of an athlete. He was into other things. He'd always carry a radio and listen to music. He'd dance, he'd sing. But he was only so-so in athletics. If we didn't have enough players in our pickup games, we'd let him play second base. But mostly Stanley did his own thing, singing and dancing on the sidelines. It's a good thing he didn't pursue sports. It's a good thing he stuck with music, because he turned into a fairly popular rap artist.

A fairly popular rap artist named Hammer. As in MC Hammer.

Stanley was called Hammer long before the world knew of him as a Grammy Award winner. Stanley was called Hammer as a kid living in Oakland. Back in the days when Charlie Finley owned the A's, Stanley worked for the club. Charlie met him in the Oakland Coliseum parking lot one day when Stanley was entertaining a small crowd with his James Brown dance routine. Charlie took a liking to him and let him sit in his private box. One thing led to another, and Stanley became Charlie's right-hand man. Because Charlie spent most of his time in Chicago, he'd have Stanley sit in his box and give him the play-by-play of the games over the phone. He'd write out the lineup and have Stanley take it down to the manager. He'd have Stanley report back to him about happenings in the clubhouse. He'd have Stanley throw on a uniform and be a batboy for a day. Stanley did it all. He had a lot of responsibilities. He was Charlie's right-hand man, but he was just a boy. The A's front office was basically Charlie and Stanley. Charlie's front offices were always small, so Stanley was almost like the general manager. He ran the show and wore a hat with the initials of his job title, V.P. The players called him Hammer because he looked exactly like Hammerin' Hank Aaron.

I'd catch Stanley's act now and then, but I didn't go to many A's games back then. I was an athlete more than a fan. I didn't have time to watch games in person or on TV, and I couldn't care less about baseball. My team was the Oakland Raiders, not the Oakland A's. Every once in a great while, I'd get out to the Coliseum to watch baseball. But I'd go because Stanley was out there. I'd see those guys—Reggie Jackson, Sal Bando, Joe Rudi, Vida Blue—being so aggressive. Around the cage during batting practice, they'd be talking crazy to the other team, trying to rile the opponent. They all had big egos, and they were always talking it up. It worked because they believed in their words, believed in themselves. When they crossed the line, they knew what it was all about. They were all confident, and they won in an exciting fashion. They already had power and pitching, but they wanted more. They wanted excitement. They wanted to score a lot of runs, so they ran.

The A's have always been a running team, long before I began playing with them. In Charlie's early years, he wanted to emphasize the running game, so he made his players wear white shoes. That was his theory. He thought white shoes made his players look faster than they actually were. He also made sure he had guys who could run. He had Campy Campaneris, Billy North, Claudell Washington, Mitchell Page. He also went out and recruited world-class sprinters. He signed Matt "The Scat" Alexander and Allan "The Panamanian Express" Lewis. They could both run, but they couldn't play much baseball.

The designated hitter was Charlie's idea, and he also pushed for a rule to allow for a designated runner. Charlie's idea was to create a position where fast runners could come off the bench and substitute freely for slow runners. The baseball establishment laughed at the DR, but I think it could've worked. So many times, you've got slow guys, maybe a catcher, clogging the bases in a crucial situation. With a DR, the slow catcher could leave for a pinch-runner, then return to catching the next inning.

The most notable of Charlie's world-class sprinters was Herb Washington. Herb was strictly a runner, coming into baseball from the track circuit. He stole twenty-eight bases one year—and never got a chance to swing a bat. Herb was a pinch-runner, period. Charlie never got his DR rule in effect, but Herb was the closest thing to it. Charlie's substituting worked sometimes, though not always. It was Game Two of the '74 World Series against the Dodgers that Mike Marshall picked Herb off first base. That was the end of that.

Stanley got pretty close to the A's players, and he used to tell me about the A's, all the crap that happened with the team, all the fights those guys got into. Damn, they fought about everything. I knew a lot about what was going on around the A's, but I didn't much care. I'd say, "Okay, Stanley, fine. That's funny. But let's play ball." Whereas I liked to play sports and didn't like to watch them, Stanley was the other way around. He didn't play much, but he watched. And that's how he got himself his job with Charlie. After he got his job, he got his brothers, Louis and Chris, jobs with the A's—batboys, clubhouse boys, anything. It's the same thing he's done with his family now. His whole family works along with him, not only in the music business but the horse business. The Burrells have always loved horses; Louis and I have ridden together lots of times. Today, the family owns Oaktown Stable, the owner of the successful filly Lite Light.

Stanley's work with the A's helped him make it big in music. He got a boost from a couple of former A's players, Dwayne Murphy and Mike Davis, who loaned him some money so he could cut his first record. Now Stanley is known only as Hammer. His hit, "U Can't Touch This," became the A's theme song, and it's been played at the Coliseum when Dave Stewart takes the mound in the first inning.

Hammer is one of many musical acts to come out of Oakland. Oakland is like the capital of rap. Rap was popular all through the streets of Oakland long before it became popular on a national level. People like Hammer and Digital Underground, also of Oakland, really made rap take off. The list of Oakland musicians is long: Tower of Power, the Pointer Sisters, Maze Featuring Frankie Beverly, En Vogue, Sheila E, the Whispers. I like them all. I used to watch Frankie Beverly down at the Paramount Theatre in downtown Oakland. Frankie's so good, he used to have me down there every New Year's Eve.

I've always loved music, but I'm from the old school. I like musicians to harmonize. I liked Diana Ross, Michael Jackson, the Temptations, all of them at Motown. They used to really harmonize. I sat back and enjoyed that. Nowadays, it's mostly rap. They've got that same beat over and over, and sometimes I can't get it out of my head. Hammer has a different sound. I like it, but I don't like plain rap. I like jazz, something that's more mellow. In my day, musicians used to sing and jam, sing and jam. I don't see the same talent anymore. Nowadays, young kids come up and talk their way through songs. If you've got a good talker, a guy who can talk real fast, you've got a rap song at the top of the charts.

I can't talk about Oakland and exclude one of the bigger problems facing its youth of today. It's the subject of drug and alcohol abuse.

Back in my younger days, it wasn't like it is now. We weren't into drugs like so many kids are today. It was a different era. The kids I knew were far removed from the drug scene, the temptation. Sure, the grown-ups might have been into a little weed. That was the biggest high around. We thought that was dangerous, and it was. But it wasn't nearly as lethal as the crap going around today. The only thing kids got into was alcohol. We'd sneak off with a six-pack now and then or pay an older guy to get us a bottle from the liquor store. That was the extent of it. I'll say it now that alcohol is a bad thing, but we didn't do it often. And we didn't do it nearly as often as some kids are doing drugs today. When I was growing up in Oakland in the sixties and seventies, we never even heard of most of this stuff. After I went off to play minor league baseball in the late seventies, Oakland began to get hit hard. Around '86 and '87, that's when things got really out of hand in Oakland. Nowadays, it's just a damn shame.

So many of today's big-city problems are related to drugs. Drugs are too often the reason for gangs, drive-by shootings, and violence. What a society, man. Sometimes people can't even go to their jobs because these gangs get in their way. It's this turf against that turf, and innocent victims pay. Because it's tough for kids to make money these days, what are their choices? What do they turn to? Too many times, they turn to drugs. They sell drugs here, they sell drugs there. Pretty soon, they'll sell drugs on the wrong turf and get shot down in the streets. That's a big problem with our society. Our society teaches all this, teaches our young kids to take drugs and sell them. A kid thinks to himself, "Why should I make $3.95 an hour at McDonald's when I can make two hundred dollars on the streets?" That's ridiculous. It ain't nothing but a hustle, a fast-money game. You end up dead or in jail. You're killing and barely surviving. What's it worth? Once you start messing around with drugs, you start buying and selling with the big boys. Pretty soon, you're hooked and you're stuck. The big boys won't let you go anywhere. Your chances are not good. It's a big horror story.

I've known too many kids as good as me in sports who have stepped away from it. Maybe they didn't have someone to admire and take after. Maybe they were never taught about following the right path. Kids have to be taught to say no to the temptation because there's no benefit in the long run. It distracts from building the mind, and it'll wipe out any goals a kid might have in life. Kids must be told to go to other things in their spare time. Go to sports. That's what I did. If you're not an athlete, try something else. Play a musical instrument, learn a trade, read a book. Travel and learn about life and its rewards. Not its failures. The outlook in society has got to change. Politicians have got to do more. There have got to be more jobs so that people can make money honestly. After World War II, things could've gotten real bad if there weren't jobs. But people worked together and politicians created jobs and opportunities. We can't wait for a major war to create jobs. We've got to have our leaders act now. We've got to have our kids start leading normal lives.

Drugs are a killer. A kid might not see any harm at first, so he'll try it out. Suddenly he'll know how harmful it is, but it's too late. I'm amazed by people who use drugs and say it doesn't do anything to them. If that's true, then why do it? These same people snort cocaine and walk around with their noses bleeding and their skin burning. What makes these people sit back and think, "Oh, I could try it, it won't do nothing to me"? That's what freaks me out about all of this. I analyze it a lot. It comes down to this: You have to ask yourself, "What do I want out of life?" My answer is, "I want to enjoy life." One way to enjoy life is to stay away from drugs. If I had to choose between seeing the world or smoking up everything in sight, I'm going to see the world. I'm not going to smoke everything and say I had a great time. That's not a great time. Screw that. I'm going to enjoy life. I might be slow in that regard. I guess I'm fast on the field and slow off it. But that's cool with me.

Whenever I can, I tell kids about the dangers of drugs. I've tried getting kids to do positive things, whether it's telling them in person or giving them a ticket for Henderson Heights, the section at the Oakland Coliseum I used to buy out for underprivileged kids around the East Bay. By the time I got to the Yankees, I noticed that kids were tripping on drugs all over New York. Little kids were dying from overdoses or getting killed for selling drugs on the wrong turf. I felt it was necessary to take a stand. One year, Vince Coleman and I got together in an effort to teach kids to say no to drugs. For each of our stolen bases, we sent a kid to a drug-education camp. By that time, kids were losing interest in sports. Kids were quitting sports to do drugs. That's wrong.

I've been able to stay away from the drug scene. I've always wanted to be somebody. That's what my goal's always been. Maybe it goes back to what I was taught as a kid. My grandma always used to tell me to focus on sports and stay away from other things like drugs. I've always remembered that. Hey, I wasn't a complete angel. No way. I was a rough kid. I had my share of fights. People called me a bully. I didn't take crap from nobody. I wasn't afraid of nobody, which is why I got in a lot of fights. Other kids would hang out with me because they knew I'd take care of them. They knew I was bad. But that was kid stuff. People go through stages. We change. We grow out of certain things. We learn from our mistakes. When it came to drugs, I was fortunate to have people who cared about me, people who kept me focused on sports. My dedication to sports kept me out of trouble.

That way of life has stayed with me, being clean. Sure, I'll drink on occasion, maybe my birthday or New Year's Eve. I'll sometimes go out with my friends and drink, but I'm not going to sit and drink every day. To begin with, I hate beer. I hate the taste. That's why if I really wanted to be a big beer drinker, I don't think I could. I'm more of a juice man. I know ballplayers, outstanding ballplayers, who drink beer every day. There's nothing wrong with that, unless it's before a game. The only time drinking is wrong is when it's abused. Then it'll catch up with you, and bury you.

I'm fortunate in one way. My system doesn't adjust well to alcohol or certain prescription pills, not even aspirin. I try not to take things like Tylenol. I'll walk around with a tremendous headache before I take a pill. I've been in some serious trouble taking pills. I guess I have a gentle stomach. Doctors and trainers know they can't give me certain pills. One time the A's trainer, Barry Weinberg, gave me a couple of Naprosyn pills for a headache. Naprosyn is something people pop to kill the pain. But, oh brother, I went out there and played a couple of innings and got real sick. My eyes were bloodshot, and my whole head felt like it was going to explode. I told Barry never to give me any more of that stuff.

As a kid, I didn't take pills. I took home remedies. If I got sick, my grandma would give me a spoonful of sugar and a shot of whiskey. That was my cold medicine. I hated the taste, but she made me swallow it. She told me sugar and whiskey would sweat it out of me, and it did. That's real powerful stuff when you're a kid, but I take the same remedy today. Pills? Forget it. That's why Mike Norris, my very dear friend, once told me I have the ultimate body. My body can't take in a lot of alcohol or pills. Even if I tried smoking a cigarette, I'd get sick.

I grew up not knowing about heavy drugs. They just weren't

around. I didn't know about heroin until I heard about some big bust out of West Oakland, a guy getting caught with millions of dollars of heroin. Before that, I thought it was only used as medicine for older people. I didn't know it was so addictive. Same with cocaine. I didn't know anything about cocaine until after I got to the major leagues. I saw a lot of weed when I was coming up through the minors. But my early years in the majors, cocaine was everywhere.

Unfortunately, it got to Mike Norris. Mike's three years older than me. While I was playing in youth leagues in Oakland, he was over in San Francisco. I didn't know him personally as a kid, but I introduced myself one day on the field in one of my first spring trainings. I played in an A's intrasquad game and went up against Norris. I was still in the minors, but he was already a pitcher in the majors, one of the best on the A's roster. This game, he was throwing hard, blowing away everybody. He struck out the first five or six guys, and I was in the middle of the lineup. I walked up to the plate and wrapped the ball to straight-away center field. I thought it flew over the fence on a fly, but they said it bounced first. I was given a ground-rule double. Mike couldn't believe I could take him that deep. I didn't stop there. On the very next pitch, I stole third base. He looked over at me and kicked the dirt. From that day on, Mike was my friend and called me "Little Willie Mays." That's how Mike and I got to know each other.

In my first full season in the majors, 1980, I roomed with Mike in Oakland. He did his thing in his room, and I did my thing in my room. That was the year he was at his absolute best. He won twenty-two games and almost won the Cy Young Award. Within two years, Mike was having tremendous shoulder problems. I was no longer his room-mate; I had my own place by then. Mike's problems started with his shoulder injury. He didn't know exactly what was wrong, and he didn't want to go to the doctor. That's what started his downfall. He had a fear of going to a doctor and having an operation. Things just weren't right. One thing led to another, and he suffered the downfall. But his downfall was the result of waiting too long to take care of his arm injury. When he was on the mound, it was easy to see he was in pain. He knew he shouldn't have been out there, but nobody was as competitive as him. So he kept pitching.

Mike's record fell to 7–11 in '82. He turned to drugs. He hung around with the wrong people, and they led him in the wrong direction.

I always thought he was a great and intelligent person who knew what he wanted. But he sidestepped off his path and took another direction. He got burned. Mike's problem got big. He was out of the majors by '84.

I didn't find out until later that certain things were happening with Mike. It's just that drugs were all over during that era. It was the fad, the thing to do, the fast way of life. It was almost as if people thought nothing of it. Almost like my parents' era thinking nothing of smoking cigarettes, just because everybody else did it and the danger factor wasn't taken into consideration. It was a natural thing to do, and it was accepted in baseball.

Mike battled back. He realized his problem and tried to overcome it. He tried to fight his way back to the major leagues. And after seven years in obscurity, he eventually won the battle. The A's gave him a chance in '89, and his work in the minors that season earned him a spot with the big club in '90. He had a lot of success, posting a 3.00 ERA in fourteen relief appearances. He also won his first game since '83, beating the Angels in extra innings. I remember that game. It was the 12th inning at Anaheim Stadium when I singled to send Mike Gallego to third. Gallego scored on a groundout, and I scored on Jose Canseco's single. Mike pitched a perfect inning in relief, and we won 7-5. That's one of the best stories in baseball history. He was out of the game and came back at a late age, thirty-five years old. The odds were against him, but he came back and contributed to a World Series season. If he had come back and pitched poorly, that still would've been something to admire. But he came back and pitched well. He overcame his mistakes in the eighties to succeed in the nineties. He deserves all the credit in the world.

Cocaine changed a lot of guys in the eighties. Players seemed to miss workouts, or they'd miss entire games. Or they'd be there, but they wouldn't be in the right frame of mind to play. The drug took their attention away from the game. It got to a point of near disaster, but then the Pittsburgh drug trials came and changed things. People started thinking about the effects of cocaine. I don't see a big problem today. A lot has changed for the better. Now if someone's in trouble, the game doesn't try to destroy him, but tries to help him. Hey, if a player needs help, let's find a way to help him. Don't knock him down further. The first step is to realize that it's a disease or sickness rather than a crime.

Any trials like the ones in Pittsburgh in '86, the ones that brought together Dave Parker and Keith Hernandez and all those guys, are going to make a difference. Those trials brought the problem out into the open and addressed it. But I don't necessarily agree with the penalties assessed on the players. In fact, I don't think they needed to be penalized at all. I don't know if baseball should take the law into its own hands. Public figures shouldn't be penalized just because they're public figures. They shouldn't have been made examples of. At the same time, it was a learning process for not only the players involved, but anyone else who might have considered drugs. Perhaps the trials made Joe Blow on the street think twice before running with the wrong crowd. It's a shame, but sometimes the only way to get through to people is for a well-known public figure, like Dave Parker, to be made an example of. To me, that's a bad example, but sometimes it's the only way to get through to some people.

Look at Magic Johnson. AIDS was a problem long before Magic announced to the world that he had contracted the HIV virus. But a lot of people didn't concern themselves with the problem until Magic came out and gave his firsthand account. Because of Magic, more people are now talking about AIDS. It hurt to hear about Magic because Magic is perceived as such a perfect guy, but maybe Magic will make people focus more on what they're doing, focus more on being careful with their lives.

AIDS could happen to anybody, especially the professional athletes who seem to be chased around by members of the opposite sex. In a lot of ways, sex is like a drug. You abuse it, you pay. Magic's story has become a learning tool for athletes. Maybe more athletes will be careful now. Hey, everyone makes mistakes. There's always room for mistakes. But mistakes can be corrected by getting back on the straight path of life. God says we all have a path we must follow. Sometimes we'll temporarily jump off that path, and sometimes that path will turn crooked, with bumps and bruises. But we've got to jump right back on the straight path and continue with our lives.

The baseball commissioner during the Pittsburgh drug trials, Peter Ueberroth, resigned in '89. At that time, he declared the game was completely free of drugs. It was a nice thing to say, but it wasn't accurate. It was just like saying everyone in the airline industry is clean. It just can't be said. There's no proof, and there's no reason to believe it. He should've said there was a big change, a big improvement. He did help matters by opening people's eyes. He couldn't totally beat the problem, but he did a good job exposing it. I don't see nearly as much now of what happened in the early part of my career. It's not affecting baseball as much as it was then.

One of the debates in today's game is whether players should be drug-tested. Knowing everything I now know, the answer is no. That's too much a personal thing. Enough is enough. Baseball can go only so far when getting involved in players' personal lives. What players do inside their homes really doesn't have anything to do with baseball. If a player wants to jeopardize his own life, well, it's his life, it's his problem. Baseball doesn't involve itself with players' other personal illnesses or diseases. Baseball's got to continue to help players, not destroy them.

The question is asked all the time. When a player gets to the big leagues and earns a lot of money, how does he resist temptation? The answer is, he's got to go back to basics, what he was taught as a kid. Take that and apply it to the major leagues, no matter how much money or temptation is out there. This goes for anybody in any business. Think about what's healthy and follow what your eyes are telling you. If drugs or crime are ruining your life, you've got to tell yourself you won't let it. It's not easy. You don't fulfill your goals without a lot of hard work and dedication. It means staying clean and not running the streets. It means wanting it in your heart. It means believing in yourself. It means staying away from the wrong path. If you want to take that chance, it's your option. It's your life. You can do whatever you want to do. So if you want to take that chance and think it won't beat you, take that chance. But it'll beat you, no doubt about that.

I'd like to think I set a good example for kids, but I don't ever want to say what I do is right for everybody. I live my life the way I know how. What works for me might not work for somebody else. Just like in baseball. I do things on the field that nobody else does. I do things my way, nobody else's way. I play a different brand of baseball. That's pretty clear to see. But that's the way I like it. I'd rather do it my own way, the way I learned at Bushrod Park, the way my momma taught me. That's always the best way.

THE NEXT O.J. SIMPSON

I was bad in high school. Bad, man, real bad. Football, baseball, basketball, track. A four-sport machine. All-league, all-Northern California, all-this, all-that. I mean, really, I was bad.

Especially in football. I was being told I was the best running back to come out of the Bay Area since O. J. Simpson. Now that's bad, man. I was an awesome little football player.

Get this. My high school, Oakland Technical, for a long time had the worst football team in the Oakland Athletic League. An awful record, an awful team. Entering my junior year, the team had lost seventeen straight games. And we weren't any better my junior year, losing another eight in a row. We didn't have many real good football players, and we played some real powerhouses, schools loaded with monster athletes.

When I got the ball, there were never any holes to run through. Our offensive linemen got blown off the line on almost every play. But that didn't matter to me. I was through those big defensive linemen before they got out of their stances. I was in the secondary before they could blink. My first couple of steps were deadly, just like in baseball when I steal a base. I was like O. J. He was playing for the Buffalo Bills, and he didn't have a line either. He was a running soul. He had to create his own holes, just like me. The problem was, those bigger city schools beat us year after year. Against teams like Oakland High and Skyline, we didn't stand a chance.

That all changed. It was Halloween afternoon, October 31, 1975, my senior year. We had dropped our first five games of the season to extend our losing streak to thirty in a row. We were 0-5 on the season and 0-2 in our league games. We hadn't won a league game in four years, and the last time Tech won any game at all came over Berkeley in 1972. On October 31, 1975, we played our big rival, Oakland High, the top-ranked school in the league. It was on their turf, and it was their Homecoming Game. They wanted a pushover for their Homecoming opponents, so they picked us.

I was sick and tired of losing, sick and tired of being laughed at. I had only three games left in my high school football career, maybe my entire football career. I didn't want to lose anymore—especially because this game was going to be on TV. The local cable companies were just getting their foot in the door, and our game was the one picked that week to be shown on television. Some of Oakland High's players came out to the junior varsity game the day before, and they razzed us about how much they were going to destroy us. Some of our players felt scared. I held a little meeting with the team to talk about the importance of going out a winner. With only three games left in the season, it was important to start showing some positive signs, and fast.

We came out fired up. I took the opening kickoff at the two-yard line. I ran left, I ran right. I ran under, I ran over. I sprinted, I dodged, I shuffled. I shaked, I baked. A few seconds later, I was collapsing in the end zone, having run back the opening kickoff for a ninety-eight-yard touchdown. That got the team so fired up that we went on to pull off the major upset of the year. We beat Oakland High 24-20, and I was awarded the top honor—the Doten Pontiac Athlete of the Week. That night, we watched our game on cable TV, which seemed just as much fun as playing the game itself.

That day was a big thrill for me and the team, but we weren't done yet. We still had two games to go. After we beat Oakland High, we played Fremont at home. Fremont had a guy named Dallas Nelson, a big, tough dude—six foot three, 215 pounds, and mean as a dog. He'd yell the entire game, just yell and yell and yell. We ran a dive play to his side, and I ran over him for a touchdown. We won the game 16-12, and I scored both touchdowns and both two-point conversions. The next week, the final week of the season, we had McClymonds at home. I ran in two more touchdowns, and we finished the year on a high note with a 22-0 victory.

That victory over Oakland High, though I didn't know it at the time, was directly responsible for the turnaround of the program. That win gave us the confidence to beat Fremont and McClymonds and finish with a 3-2 league record, good for second place. Second place! And we hadn't won a game in all of my days at Oakland Tech until three games were left on the schedule my senior year. Finally our long-suffering coach, Wayne Brooks, was a happy man.

I was gone the following year, but the momentum from those last three games carried over. The team won a few more games, and more and more people became interested in playing. No longer was Oakland Tech the patsy school everybody scheduled for its Homecoming Game. They were playing competitively with all the bigger city schools, and it all started with that ninety-eight-yard kickoff return against Oakland High.

My high school had only three grades, tenth, eleventh, and twelfth. My sophomore year, a lot of guys went out for summer football. I wanted to work instead. You know, odd jobs, running a hot dog stand, whatever. First junior varsity game of the season, I was in the stands. After the game, I walked down onto the field and told the coach I wanted to play. He said, "What position?" I said, "Running back." He said, "We already have good running backs." I said, "I want to be the running back." I later went out to practice and became the number-one running back, and the guy whose job I took moved somewhere else, like wide receiver. By the second game of the season, I was the guy.

The next two years, I was on the varsity. I played both ways, running back on offense and linebacker on defense. I'd do anything: kickoff returns, punt returns, anything to be on that field. When you're a kid, you can go all day without getting tired. I loved running the ball, but I loved tackling just as much. I loved to hit, just like the Oakland Raiders. Everybody followed the Oakland Raiders then because they were a team that loved to hit. That was a great team during the George Blanda and Ken Stabler years, and I wanted to be a part of it when I grew up. They didn't have a great running back on that team, so I wanted to grow up and be the running back of the Oakland Raiders. I was a Raiders man, but first I was an O. J. man. I wanted to run like

O. J., I wanted to play like O. J., I wanted to *be* O. J. And I wanted to do it all for the Oakland Raiders.

By the time I was a senior, the college recruiters were all over me. They were especially on my trail when we started winning those games late in the season. I was named MVP of the team as well as first-team all-city running back and second-team all-city linebacker. I had rushed for 1,100 yards and scored at least one touchdown in every game. Scholarship offers were coming in every day, from UCLA, UNLV, Arizona State, all over the Pac-10, more than twenty in all. My first choice was Arizona State because I wanted to go to a college that would let me play both football and baseball. They had excellent programs in both sports. But it was football I wanted to concentrate on most. That was my favorite. Baseball was secondary. I would go off to college, win the Heisman Trophy, then get drafted by the Oakland Raiders. I had it all planned out.

Then came Momma. Momma said I should decide between the two sports. Actually, she's the one who made the decision for me. I was selected by the A's in the fourth round of the 1976 June draft, right as I was about to graduate from high school. The A's wanted to know what I was going to do, and so did the college recruiters. Go to college and play football? Or sign with the A's and go to the minor leagues? The A's tried to convince me baseball was the way to go, but I wasn't being convinced. So Momma and I had a long talk.

We went in the back room and talked and argued for hours. I wanted to play football, and she wanted me to play baseball. She said I was too small for football. She didn't want her baby to get hurt. I told her I had good enough size to be an NFL running back. Guys like O. J. and Marcus Allen have longer legs, but I was just as quick and had all their moves. We went back and forth on this, and finally I said, "Momma, I'll leave it up to you." She chose baseball. She said, "That's what I want you to do." She was thinking about my health. She was thinking I'd last longer in baseball than football. I was extremely upset. I started crying. But I said, "Okay, Momma. You made the decision. I'll go play baseball." But I told her, if I'm not in the big leagues in four years, I'm giving it up and going back to football.

My days as a high school baseball player were no less glorious than my days as a football player. I was all-city, just like in football. But the difference was, baseball wasn't my main sport. Football was. And I wasn't about to start off playing junior varsity baseball, even as a sophomore. Baseball wasn't important enough for me to start off on the JV. If I wasn't going to play on the varsity, I wasn't going to play. And I came oh so close to quitting on one of the first days of practice.

The varsity coach, Bob Cryer, went through some basic drills, then separated the varsity players from the junior varsity. It was tough to crack the varsity because Cryer had most of his team coming back. He didn't like sophomores playing on the varsity, so he sent all the sophomores down to the other field. Then he had batting practice. Toward the end, he asked, "Did everybody get to hit?" I said, "No, I didn't get to hit." He said, "I thought I told you to go to the other field." He was cutting me from the team. I said, "If I'm going to the other field, I'll quit." I was prepared to go out for the track team. So my buddy Fred Atkins, my brother Tyrone, and a fellow named Mobil Cox, who later got a scholarship to UCLA, told Cryer, "The kid's a good player. Let him hit." So Cryer let me hit, and I absolutely raked the ball. It wasn't too long before Cryer said, "Okay, I'll give you a chance." I remained on the varsity as a sophomore and hit .475.

I played mostly first base because the outfield was goofy for me. If you throw left-handed and can't pitch, there aren't too many options. You either play first base or the outfield. I played shortstop all the time as a little kid, but they don't let lefties play short in high school. I always wished I could play the infield, especially short or second base. Man, if I were right-handed, I'd have been a mean middle infielder. I've got the quick feet, the quick reflexes. I'd have been awesome on the infield. In football, it doesn't matter if you're left-handed or right-handed. Same with basketball. But baseball's an unfair game, so I was stuck at first base and the outfield. I preferred first base because it was closer to the action. Plus Fred Atkins played third base when he wasn't pitching, and we did a good job taking care of the corners.

As a junior, I played even more first base. By the time I was a senior, the outfield was getting more comfortable, so I played mostly in center. But it was still no piece of cake. I was okay running after fly balls, but I had trouble with anything hit directly at me. I also didn't have a very good arm. But I got by. In high school, it was always easy to get by.

Even though I excelled in baseball, football was still my first love. One day during football practice, Vida Blue came out to say a few words to the team and throw a few passes. Vida was a great baseball player, but I was even more interested in him because he had been such a great high school football player down in Louisiana. I could relate to Vida. Back in high school, Vida did it all. He struck out twenty-one batters in a seven-inning game and threw thirty-five touchdown passes as the quarterback of his football team. I liked Vida, but I didn't want to make the same decision he made. I wanted to go after football.

There was one major difference between baseball and football. Our football team played on the school grounds. Our baseball team played right on my old stomping grounds, Bushrod Park. Bushrod was Oakland Tech's home field even though it was a mile from the school; city schools don't always have complete facilities, so they have to find alternatives. We had our games at Bushrod, we had our practices at Bushrod. I was at Bushrod not only in the summer, but during the school year. I grew up at Bushrod, and I never left that place. It was my home park.

I always seemed to pop the ball whenever we played at Bushrod. I remember hitting a couple of balls over the fence in left field, which was 340 feet from the plate. I was barely five foot nine in high school, but I still had some punch. The object was to hit the ball over the fence, across the street, and into the big white house belonging to Gerald Price. The object was to bomb Gerald Price's house. It was quite a poke, but I bombed it once. With those aluminum bats we'd sometimes use, there was no telling how far the ball would go.

Our school hosted an annual Easter tournament at Bushrod, and I'll never forget the one my senior year. It was my most memorable baseball experience in high school. It seemed as if every at bat, I was pounding the ball. With Bushrod's two adjoining fields, I kept interrupting the game on the other field. I kept drilling the ball out there. One time, I hit a ball all the way to second base on the other diamond, the farthest ball I ever hit in high school. It kept rolling and rolling. I took an easy jog around the bases, sat down in the dugout, and they were still chasing the thing down.

A woman who helped organize those Easter tournaments turned out to be one of the most inspirational people in my life. She was one of Tech's counselors, Mrs. Tommie Wilkerson. Mrs. Wilkerson looked out for me. She kept me on a straight line. If I found myself threatening to steer away from the straight line, there would be Mrs. Wilkerson setting me straight. She gave me inspiration. She gave me incentive. In fact, she paid my very first salary. Nothing illegal, of course. Just something to keep me going. Every time I did something well on the field, Mrs. Wilkerson would reward me. She'd pay me in quarters. Every time I got a hit, a quarter. Every time I stole a base, a quarter. That was big money then. A quarter could take you down the street for a hamburger. A few quarters, and you'd be able to take a young lady to lunch. One day, I got five hits and five stolen bases and walked away with $2.50. That was hamburgers for a week. Mrs. Wilkerson also paid quarters to my buddy Fred. Fred pitched a lot and would get a quarter for each of his strikeouts. One game, he struck out eighteen batters and collected a bundle of quarters. Mrs. Wilkerson knew she had two pretty good players on her hands.

High school is where I met the woman I've been with for seventeen years, Pamela Palmer. One thing Pamela and I don't have—and it's not a big deal for us—is a marriage certificate. We've been together so long, a marriage certificate wouldn't make a lot of difference. We will get married some day. I always say we'll get married in February or November, just before the season or just after the season. I've been saying that for seventeen years. But we've both had personal goals we wanted to achieve. I wanted to do certain things in baseball, and she wanted to get her college degree. When we have Family Day with the A's, our third-base coach, Rene Lachemann, announces all the couples. When he gets to us, he'll say, "Here comes Rickey and his wife, Pamela." I'll say, "Lach, we ain't married yet." He says, "Yeah, you're married. You just don't know it." When we do get married, I'm going to say, "I do." She's going to say, "I do." And then we'll go back to living how we've always lived. Nothing will change. We respect each other, and we keep no secrets from each other. It's been that way since high school. We were close way back then, even though my main priority was playing sports.

Between football in the fall and baseball in the spring, I played basketball in the winter. That was the least of my sports, but I was still a pretty decent little guard. Nobody was quicker on the court than me. I was like Tim Hardaway. I drove by everybody. But mostly, I threw the ball to our center, a guy named Northern "Doc" Shavers. Doc's story is a sad one; he had some problems, but he was one of the best high school basketball players in the country and definitely the best in the state. I didn't play basketball as a sophomore, but that was the year Doc led Tech to the Tournament of Champions. In those days, at the end of every season, all the best teams in Northern California got together at the Oakland Coliseum Arena for the Tournament of Champions. Thanks to Doc and our big forward, Wolfe Perry—a guy who later went to Stanford and had a part in the TV series "The White Shadow"—Tech won the TOC. The next year, when I played junior varsity, the varsity lost in the TOC to Elk Grove, a team that featured a center named Bill Cartwright.

Doc also played in a big Christmas tournament in Southern California and knocked heads with guys like Bill Laimbeer, Roy Hamilton, and David Greenwood. The college coaches were drooling over him, people like Bobby Knight, Dean Smith, Al McGuire, and John Wooden. And this was back when Doc was a sophomore.

My senior year, I was a starting guard on the varsity. Doc averaged twenty-eight points and sixteen rebounds a game and was named an All-American, but Perry had graduated and we didn't make it to the TOC. When Doc got out of high school, he could have gone anywhere he wanted. He could have gone to UCLA. UCLA offered him a scholarship, but he decided not to go because UCLA wouldn't guarantee a lot of playing time. Hey, this was UCLA. You've got to go to UCLA. But he went to a couple of lesser-known schools instead, Evansville in Indiana and Jackson State in Mississippi. Evansville is the school that lost its entire basketball team in a December 1977 plane crash, but Doc, luckily, had transferred from Evansville to Jackson State before the disaster. At Jackson State, he played with Purvis Short and averaged twenty points a game as a senior. But Doc never played much basketball after college.

My fourth sport was track, but I didn't spend much time at that sport—all of one day. Our baseball team had a day off, and I walked out to the track and told the coach, Jim Brown, who was also the basketball coach, that I could beat any of his sprinters. He didn't believe me, so he lined up his best guys for a hundred-yard dash, and I beat them all, in a time of 10.7 seconds. It was a quick time, but it wasn't as good as I could have done if I had spent more than a few minutes in preparation. But at least I proved my point to Coach Brown. The next day, we played Skyline in a baseball game, and I hit a couple of home runs. I ended my senior year with a .465 average and—as the only player on the team with a green light to run at will—I stole thirty bases.

I've got some great memories of my high school years. Let me say this about my high school: We had a lot of people excel not only in sports, but arts and entertainment. We produced baseball players Curt Flood and Cookie Lavagetto and the former USC baseball coach, Rod Dedeaux. Other lesser-known big-leaguers include Joe Gaines, Len Gabrielson, and Jay W. Porter, and we had a bunch from the first half century, names such as Taylor Douthit, Lincoln Blakely, Bernie DeViveiros, Bud Hafey, Tom Hafey, and the elder Len Gabrielson. In basketball, we had Jim Pollard of the old Minneapolis Lakers and Wolfe Perry. In football, we had John Brodie, the great quarterback of the 49ers. But we also had actors such as Clint Eastwood—yes, Clint Eastwood—and Ted Lange, who played the bartender in "The Love Boat." We had the Pointer Sisters, every last one of them. Singer Tony Martin, poet Rod McKuen, Ron Dellums, the congressman. Even Huey Newton, the civil rights activist. That old school is packed with tradition, and I always dreamed about being one of the many famous people to come out of Tech.

Not only my high school, but the whole Oakland area had a long tradition of bringing along big names. Athletically, the stories I've heard go back to Bill Russell, Joe Morgan, Vada Pinson, and Frank Robinson. Having so many great athletes come before us was a reason for hope. If anything, we knew we had a chance. We knew scouts would come out and watch us because they had obviously been in the area before.

When I played Connie Mack ball in the summers, also at Bushrod Park, I played alongside some other people who later made a name for themselves, guys like Dave Stewart, Gary Pettis, and Lloyd Moseby. Now *that* was a team. It came as no surprise that we beat just about every team we played. We called our team the National Association for the Advancement of Colored People. Our sponsor, Clinton White, a good man and now a judge in San Francisco, was president of the local association, so we had NAACP stripped across our jerseys. That was pretty cool.

There's probably never been a Connie Mack team with that kind of talent up and down the lineup. We had ten guys on that team who got drafted. That team was so good, I didn't even hit leadoff. We had a short fellow named Johnny Cook who led off. Seattle drafted him. He hit left-handed and was so quick; no infielder could throw him out. Danny Liggins, our number-two hitter, was drafted by the Cardinals. He was just as fast as Cook. I hit third, and Fred Atkins hit fourth. The Yankees drafted Fred. Pettis and Moseby? They hit way down in the order. Moseby was our catcher, and Pettis our shortstop. Other guys drafted off that team were Cliff Weary by the Padres, Steve Moore by the Mets, and Gerald Price by the Braves—the same Gerald Price whose house we used to bomb at Bushrod.

That team was like an all-star team from all of Oakland. Our coach, Hank Thomasson, went to every local high school and rounded up the best guys from each team. And talk about fast. Cook and Liggins were both faster than me. Thomasson had us steal every time we got on base. But, man, he got me riled the way he talked to me. Before each game, he'd say, "Rickey, you can't steal no bases. I don't want you running nowhere." Then I'd get pumped up and steal five bases, and he'd say the same thing before the next game. He didn't know what I could do at first, but he learned. I guess he kept talking that way to motivate me. It sure worked. I proved him wrong over and over.

Thomasson was good to me. He was good to all of us. Some of us didn't have much money, and he did everything he could to keep us playing ball. Sometimes we had early games on Saturday mornings, and he knew I loved to sleep. So he'd come over to my house, all the way from across town, to give me a personal wake-up call. He'd walk in the house, get me out of bed, and say, "It's time, Rickey." He'd bring hot chocolate and glazed donuts, and then we were off and running.

While Pettis, Moseby, and I made it to the majors, it seemed as if a lot of other players on that Connie Mack team got hurt in the minors. Like Fred Atkins. I always thought Fred would go a long way in baseball. He was six-three and threw hard. I mean *hard.* Well into the nineties, just rushing the gas up there. And that was high school. A great hitter, too. Just a great all-around athlete. He would have made it all the way, but he lasted only one year in the Yankees' organization because he threw his arm out. After he hurt his arm, he didn't tell anybody. He kept pitching and eventually had to have an operation. He was afraid to go through the Yankees to have the operation, so he went through his dad, who was in the army. He ended up undergoing shoulder surgery by a doctor on the army base. After that, he didn't have the strength to lift his arm and had to quit. He could've continued playing if he had had arthroscopic surgery, but arthroscopic surgery didn't exist back then. Too bad. He was an awesome pitcher.

Dave Stewart is two years older than me, so I was really young the summer we were teammates. He was our number-one catcher. There wasn't a better catcher anywhere. He had a rifle arm. He was like Benito Santiago; he'd throw out guys from his knees. Yeah, nobody could run on Stew. He went to school at St. Elizabeth in Oakland, and he was like me, playing all the sports. He was also offered a bunch of scholarships to play football, but he chose baseball. He was a so-so hitter, but a great catcher. The Dodgers drafted him in the sixteenth round, but they didn't want him to catch. They made him a pitcher.

Stew excelled in both positions not generally played by blacks. I don't know what it is about that. Blacks are often drafted as pitchers and catchers, and a lot of them are turned into outfielders. Stew turned out to be a great pitcher, but there aren't many black pitchers in the majors. And there are hardly any black catchers. Maybe it's because of the old stereotype, about blacks not being able to hold a role of leadership. That myth was shot down in the NFL when black quarterbacks like Doug Williams, Warren Moon, and Randall Cunningham rose to prominence. But it hasn't changed much in baseball. Young black pitchers and catchers are out there, but the teams aren't letting them in. Or, if they do let them in, the pitchers and catchers are being turned into outfielders. It works the other way, too. There might be a great white outfielder somewhere, but he's being switched to another position, maybe first base or catcher. Maybe teams think he's not fast enough, so they take him out of the outfield. There are people on both sides who aren't getting fair shots because of their color.

When I was finishing my high school career and thinking about the pro draft, I almost didn't get a fair shot because of another reason, a different kind of prejudice—the way I hit the ball. I'm one of the very few people in the history of baseball who throw left-handed and bat right-handed. Think about it. If players hit one way and throw the other, they usually hit lefty and throw righty. Dozens of players are like that today—Wade Boggs, George Brett, Ozzie Guillen, Dave Parker, Kal Daniels, Kent Hrbek, Lou Whitaker, Von Hayes, and even my old pal Lloyd Moseby. The list goes on and on. But try to think of someone who throws lefty and bats righty. Some pitchers are like that, but that doesn't count because pitchers don't know how to hit anyway. Check the Opening Day rosters at the start of the '92 season. Only three non-pitchers in all of baseball threw lefty and batted righty, me and two younger guys, Brian Hunter and Mark Carreon.

I'm a natural left-hander. My momma's left-handed, and I got it from her. The reason I don't bat left-handed is simple. When I was a little kid, all my friends were right-handed and swung from the right side, so I thought that's the way it was supposed to be done. I thought every-body had to hit right-handed. When I first picked up a bat, I lifted it over my right shoulder. That's the way I learned.

Not many people have had that kind of combination in the big leagues, and scouts were skeptical of me because of that. They said I wouldn't make it my way. I was told I'd be a low-round pick because I had that unusual combination. They told me there were too many disadvantages for a guy like me to play baseball. First off, it was a disadvantage to be a left-handed thrower because you can't play four of the nine positions—catcher, second, short, and third. Then it was a disadvantage to be a right-handed batter because most pitchers are right-handed and throw breaking balls away from you. Also, you're a full step farther from first base than a left-handed batter. The odds just aren't in your favor when you throw lefty and bat righty.

There was another reason some teams were hesitant to draft me. They knew my first love was football, and I hadn't had my big discus-sion with Momma by draft day. It seemed the Dodgers were most interested in me. The Dodgers scouted me from day one. I remember them back in my junior year. The times they came out to watch me, it seemed like I hit .700. But the Dodgers had me going no higher than the fifth round. Their first four picks were Mike Scioscia, Don Ruzek, Max Venable, and Marty Kunkler. I have a feeling they regretted a couple of their picks, because the A's came along and made me their fourth-round pick. I was gone by the time the Dodgers could draft again.

The reason I was drafted by the A's was because of Jim Guinn. He was a Berkeley cop and part-time A's scout overseeing the East Bay. He was the one who signed Claudell Washington back in 1972, and he and I got to be real close. We'd spend a lot of time together talking about the future. He had talked to me about that righty-lefty thing and warned me that I might not go in the first three rounds. Not just because I batted right and threw left, but because I was too small and wasn't a great outfielder. But he had faith in me. He knew I was a pure talent, and he recognized my potential. He recommended to the A's that they draft me in the first round. The team's director of scouting back then was Syd

Thrift, but Syd had his eye on other people. He told Guinn that the A's would draft me only if I were still available in the fourth round. Guinn was worried that I might get picked up by another team, especially the Dodgers. But nobody touched me the first three rounds, and Syd kept his promise.

HEADFIRST

J ust because I was drafted didn't mean I was certain to play pro
baseball. I still had a lot of options, and I still didn't know what I'd
do.

I had the A's. I had college football. I had college baseball, but
college baseball wasn't as popular as it is now. There was no ESPN, so
it was never on television, and there weren't as many scholarships
available. I don't think there were more than a handful of college
baseball scouts talking to me. They were all pro scouts. Dr. Miles
McAfee, the coach at nearby St. Mary's College and now one of my
business associates, would have liked me to play for him, but he thought
I could get to the majors quicker through the minor leagues and recommended I sign with the A's.

Less than a week after the draft, Guinn came by the house with a
contract. I was still hesitant about letting go of football, and it didn't
help any that the A's signing bonus was only $10,000. This was back
in '76, when first-round picks were getting nearly $100,000 and fourth-
round picks were getting a lot more than $10,000. The year before, the
A's offered their first-round pick, Bruce Robinson of Stanford, only
$17,500. But that's the way it was with Charlie Finley. This was just
before he started selling off all his star players from the World Series

years, and he wasn't about to negotiate with any high school kid like me. He had Guinn tell me to take it or leave it.

Guinn spent a lot of time talking with me, trying to make me feel more comfortable about pursuing baseball. He said I could make up for the small signing bonus by quickly advancing to the big leagues. He also told me not to worry so much about the hit-right, throw-left thing. He reminded me that Cleon Jones was the same way, and Cleon was a .300 hitter a couple of years. With Guinn being so positive—and Momma being so forceful—I finally decided to sign the A's contract. I got the $10,000 signing bonus and was to report to the A's Single-A affiliate in Boise, Idaho, for a whopping base salary of $500 per month.

Even after I signed, I never gave up the thought of playing football. My ultimate goal would have been to play pro football and pro baseball. I wanted to be Bo Jackson before anyone ever heard of Bo Jackson. I wanted to be Bo Jackson back when Bo Jackson was in diapers. I was playing baseball in the summer, but I wondered all the time about playing football in the winter. One time, I thought I was going to get my chance. Al Davis, before he moved the Raiders out of Oakland, heard I wanted to be an NFL running back and had one of his right-hand men ask me about it. I told him I'd love to go out and play with the Raiders. I was serious, but Al Davis treated it more like a joke. I don't think it had ever occurred to him back then that it could be done. I could have done what Bo did, but it just wasn't acceptable at the time.

Bo took a different route than I did. He went to Auburn to play football and baseball. At first, everyone knew him as a football player. But he kept playing baseball, even after winning the Heisman Trophy. After his college career, he was drafted by the Tampa Bay Buccaneers. But he stuck with pro baseball, so Tampa Bay's rights expired after a year. Because he had signed with the Kansas City Royals, NFL teams didn't want to waste any more draft picks on him. Everybody passed on Bo, until Davis got him in the seventh round in '87. Bo then decided to go with two sports.

Davis had faith in Bo. He finally believed somebody could compete simultaneously in both football and baseball. Maybe my intention to play the two sports years earlier got Davis thinking it could be done. He took a chance with Bo, and Bo worked out. If I couldn't do it, I was happy to see someone do it. I'm glad Bo got the opportunity.

I've never regretted my decision to pursue baseball, even if it meant my football career was over. I would have done everything the same way. I think I could have been another Marcus Allen—I told him that, too—or maybe even another O. J. You never know what could have happened if I had taken another route. Look at the hip injury Bo suffered. Every time you step on the field, you risk injury. And that applies to baseball just as much as football. I don't think Bo has any regrets. I definitely don't have any. From the day I put on my very first big-league uniform, I never regretted the decision to sign out of high school. But, oh, man, there were times in the minors when I had second thoughts, and third and fourth thoughts.

After graduating from high school, I joined the Boise A's in midseason. Man, I was homesick for the longest time. I was still only seventeen. Momma had to come visit a few times. It took a while to adjust, not to the pressure of playing ball but to the pressure of going to all these different cities I had never seen before.

I played forty-six games, hit .336, and led the team with twenty-nine steals. But my defense was brutal, just awful. I got by playing the outfield in high school, but not in pro ball. Even though I played just half the season, I led all Northwest League outfielders in errors with twelve. The next year, at Single-A Modesto, I led all California League outfielders in errors with twenty. Most of those were throwing errors. I'd either charge the ball and boot it, or charge the ball, pick it up, and throw it away. I had just a terrible slice on my throws. They would start off dead on target, then slice ten feet out of whack.

I wondered if I'd ever get over that problem. But I worked and I worked and I worked. In the minors, because it didn't come naturally, I probably worked on defense just as much as baserunning. Lee Walls, a coach who stressed fundamentals more than anybody, helped me a lot with my defense. He'd hit balls to us over and over, and he'd give us drills like the ones for infielders. He'd toss the ball one way and make us dive, the other way and make us dive, but I had no problem with balls to either side; I could go and get anything because I had quick feet. My problem was still with balls hit right at me. I didn't like those. And because I didn't have an arm like Dave Winfield's, I had to charge everything. Guys with great arms could just wait for the ball and sling it back to the infield. Winfield never had to charge anything; he could wait for the ball and still throw you out. But I had to charge the ball, and that wasn't easy when the thing was coming right at me. So Lee worked on that. It took some time, but he was instrumental in helping me get over that problem.

I committed myself to becoming a good fielder, and the hard work paid off. By my third season in the minors, at Double-A Jersey City, I was making practically every play. I led all Eastern League outfielders in assists with fifteen and double plays with four. I was finally getting comfortable with my overall game by the time I finished up at Jersey City. But an incident early in the season really got me second-guessing my decision to play baseball.

We began the season on the road, so I barely had enough time after spring training to dump my things into my new apartment. Off we went on the road trip. When we got back, I returned to the apartment—and found nothing. All my stuff, gone. I had been ripped off. Everything I had brought from home—clothes, shoes, baseball stuff, money, all the necessities, like the things a kid brings with him when he goes off to college. They left me with nothing. The apartment was empty. I went downstairs to check on Darrell Woodard and Ray Cosey, a couple of my teammates, and they hadn't been hit. Just me. That was traumatic. I didn't need that. As a kid growing up, I wasn't accustomed to having anything stolen. Of course, I didn't have a whole lot to steal. I was never into breaking into houses, either. I guess it was happening, but I sure wasn't doing it. That wasn't me. All the stuff belonging to me was stuff I earned in the minors playing for $500 a month.

I didn't know what I was going to do. I considered going home. Enough with baseball. If this is how it was supposed to go, I didn't want any part of it. Hey, I was still a baby, just nineteen years old. But now I was a nineteen-year-old with nothing left, and the rent was due. I was thinking I had made a bad decision to play baseball. I called Momma and asked her if I should come home. She said, "Son, you have a job to play baseball. Stick with it." So I stuck with it. But I still had no money, so I called Charlie Finley and told him to send some money right away or else I actually would go home. Fortunately, Charlie sent me a few dollars to buy me some clothes. Things were back to normal, but it took a long time to get over that ugly experience. It was the worst time in my minor league career.

That first month with Jersey City, I hit about a buck-eighty-two. Nothing was going right, for me or the team. We were playing in a dump of a ballpark, Roosevelt Stadium, which they were about to blow up until the team came along, and they decided to rent it out instead. To top it off, I wasn't getting along with the manager, a guy named John Kennedy. He was acting like a fool to me. He was what I call a 'neck, a red-neck kind of guy; he actually had the red neck to go along with it. He didn't treat me right. He didn't treat anybody right. If you made a mistake, he'd be all over you. He'd take you out of the game. If you didn't run all the way to first base after a flyout or groundout to the pitcher, or even a walk, you'd be gone. It was miserable. Players were fighting with him every day.

One time I was up at the plate with a guy on first base. I check-swung at a pitch and hit a bullet to the first baseman. The first baseman was on the bag and got me out before I could even take a step out of the box. Boom, I'm out, just like that. The runner on first took a step off the bag, then returned. He was safe. I turned around and headed back to the dugout. No big deal. I was out by ninety feet. Nothing I could do there.

When the inning ended, I ran out to take my position in center field. When I got out there, I found out Kennedy was taking me out of the game. He waited till I got out there before he took me out. Now I had to come all the way back in from center field. I said, "Why did you take me out?" He said, "Because you didn't run to first base." *What?* Why should I run to first base when I'm out before I get out of the box? That got me fired up. I took my glove off and threw it at him. Then I stormed into the clubhouse. He came charging in after me and told me, "You'd better not leave till the blastin' game's over." I wanted to kick his butt right then and there. When the game ended, I went in his office and had it out with him. He was upsetting the whole team, and I tried to tell him. We left it at that.

Afterward, there I was again, on the phone to Charlie Finley. "Charlie, I've had enough of this. I want out of here, off this team." I told him to either send me up to Triple-A or back to A-ball. He knew I had already dominated A-ball, and he said he had no room on the Triple-A roster. Charlie didn't want me going anywhere, especially home, so he called Kennedy and told him to quit messing with his players. He told Kennedy to leave everyone alone, especially me. I guess he didn't want anyone messing with his star. After that, Kennedy didn't say much to me at all. He let me play. I ended up having a pretty good year, hitting .310 and leading the Eastern League with eighty-one steals.

For the most part, my days in the minor leagues were rewarding. The minors is where I learned the game, where I got some of my best advice. The minors is where I discovered guys like Ty Cobb and Maury Wills and Lou Brock; Lee Walls would bring in films of former players, and he asked us to focus on the guys who excelled in what we did. The minors is where I met Mike Rodriguez, the guy who taught me the headfirst slide. The minors is where I met Tom Trebelhorn, my manager at both Boise and Modesto.

Treb taught me so much about stealing. He used to drag me out to the park at one o'clock before night games just to teach me how to steal bases. He'd stand on the mound and imitate the pitcher, giving me every move in the book. He knew his stuff and was a workhorse when it came time to teaching kids how to play baseball. He took not only his work time but his free time to teach us. He was a real manager, a true teacher. He was just twenty-eight when I first played for him, but I knew he'd go on to bigger and better things. At thirty-eight, he began managing the Milwaukee Brewers.

Mike Rodriguez and I played at every level together, from Boise to Modesto to Jersey City to Triple-A in Ogden, Utah. Mike had knee surgery and never made it to the majors, but his slide did. He was like Pete Rose. He didn't have great speed; he was a catcher and third baseman. But oh, brother, he stretched singles into doubles and doubles into triples because of the way he slid. Whenever he got a chance, he dived headfirst. I had always wondered why he slid like that. He said he liked it, said it was cool. Meanwhile, I'd be popping into the dirt, feet first, with all my weight pounding on one leg. I stole a lot of bases in the minors, but my ankle would be bruised, my knee would be cut up, and my butt would be full of strawberries. I'd be constantly banging up my legs, and I'd be tired. He suggested I slide his way. I was hesitant at first, but he finally convinced me. We started practicing on the outfield grass after it rained. We'd put on some extra sweat shirts and slide out on the wet grass. Then I brought it into games. At first it was killing me. I didn't want to do it. But I eventually stuck with it, and now it's one of my trademarks.

That Modesto team was probably the fastest I've ever played on, and that includes Oakland's Billy Ball teams of the early eighties. Treb gave us the steal sign on a regular basis. I don't ever remember him flashing a red light. He'd just tell us to run. One day at Fresno, the team swiped fifteen bases, and seven were mine. Not in a doubleheader, in a single game. Every time I got up, I got on base. And every time I got on base, I stole. It was only the fourth time in the history of pro baseball that someone stole seven in a game. I ended the season with ninety-five steals, then a California League record. Darrell Woodard had ninety, Michael Patterson had thirty-seven, Ted Smith twenty-eight, and Rodriguez twenty-five. As a team, we stole 357 bases in 140 games. That's incredible.

Modesto won a lot of games, and we would have won the league if not for the Dodgers' team in Lodi and its funny-looking hitter, Rudy Law. Rudy bent way over the plate, and he spread his legs out so far. He barely stepped when he swung. But he hit .386 to lead the league. My .345 was good for third. I got to thinking about Rudy's stance more and more. My stance in high school was pretty low, but when I got to the minors I felt I was striking out too much. I quickly learned that I couldn't hit like Reggie Jackson, so I started developing an exaggerated stance like Rudy Law. I learned to stay down in my stance, and I started getting better pitches and making better contact.

It was at about that time I considered becoming a switch-hitter. I knew that if I could drag bunt, I could hit .330 or .340 regularly. It seemed that all the guys winning batting titles at that time swung left-handed: Dave Parker, Rod Carew, George Brett, Fred Lynn, Keith Hernandez. Those guys could get so many extra hits on simple grounders to the shortstop because they were a step closer to first base. Not only that, they were able to dump easy fly balls over the shortstop's head. Right-handers don't dump easy flies over the second baseman as easily as left-handers do over the shortstop, because the second baseman plays further back than the shortstop. Plus, it's easier for left-handers to hit the opposite way because they face mostly right-handed pitchers who deliver from the third-base side of the diamond. That's how Willie Wilson did it for so many years. He's a switch-hitter, and he couldn't hit a lick for power. So when hitting left-handed, he slapped that ball to left field and beat out everything he hit.

When I asked the A's about switch-hitting, they told me to forget it. Charlie Finley didn't want me switching anything in my game. My problem was simple: I had hit too well as a right-hander for them to start experimenting with switch-hitting. If I had struggled one year and hit about .210, then they might have listened to me. But I hit .300 every year in the minors, so they never let me try it. If I had started hitting left-handed at the time I became a pro, I probably would have developed into a decent switch-hitter. After all, I am a natural left-hander. Swinging a baseball bat and shaking hands are the only things in the world I do right-handed.

In the spring of '79, I broke camp with the A's Triple-A team in Ogden. I knew I was close to the big time, and I wanted to put on a big show to quicken the process. The organization was going in a different direction, as Charlie was giving a lot of younger guys the opportunity to play. I continued to have success against minor-league pitchers, hitting .309 in seventy-one games. In June, I got a break when Dwayne Murphy, Oakland's center fielder, fractured a finger and was placed on the disabled list. I had played center field throughout the minors and I was having another good year, so I was the guy they picked to replace him. One of my first thoughts was what I told Momma the day I signed, about how I'd give baseball four years before quitting and going back to football. Well, I signed in June '76 and got called up to the majors in June '79. So I made the big time with a year to spare.

Throughout the minors, I seemed to play in a lot of little country towns. There were times when I could feel the racial tension. There were times when the only blacks in town were the ones playing baseball. I approached those situations my way. I never tried to label people before knowing them. I didn't go into a town thinking the whole town was racist. I didn't grow up that way, and I wasn't taught that way. I always tried to treat people the same, no matter what their color. Whenever I did that, there was a mutual respect for one another. I treat you okay, you treat me okay. I always seemed to fit in well with people. Maybe a lot of that had to do with the fact that I was a star in every league I played in, and people seem to overlook race when you're the star. If they respect you as a player, they respect you as a human being, around the ball park and around town. They'll come up and introduce themselves. If you're an average player, it can be a different story. I sensed the average players having more problems than me. That's not right at all.

Utah had some towns that were 100 percent white, with the Mormon influence and all, but I didn't have many problems in Utah. Probably the biggest problem came after Ray Cosey and I threw a little party in our apartment, with a few guys and a few girls. Nothing out of hand, just a good time. The people in the complex didn't like it, and they wanted to kick us out. Cosey got all nervous and wanted to leave. I said, "No, I ain't going nowhere. You can't kick me out." In the next couple of days, I got called up to the big leagues, and Cosey went and stayed with Darrell Woodard. I felt they wanted us to leave because we were black, not because we threw a party.

When I came home in the winters during my days in the minors, I'd go home to Oakland and work odd jobs. I sure didn't make enough money in baseball to support myself. I was making only $500 a month, but I was spending $450 on rent and bills, so not much was left over for food. I couldn't go out and do much else with the rest of that money. Any way to save a dollar, I'd go for it. Everybody was like that in the minors. If it meant cutting each other's hair to save on the price of the barber, we did it. In fact, back in single-A ball, I was one of the team barbers, me and Shooty Babitt.

Back then, I didn't really care what my hair looked like. We did each other's, just to get it off our neck. I turned into a fairly decent barber, and I continued cutting guys' hair in the major leagues. I took care of Mike Norris for years. More recently, I've given Jose Canseco a trim or two. When we're on the road, he'll ask me to line his hair in the back. Lining is easy, but I'll do the whole job whenever anyone asks. You've just got to trust me. But not everybody trusts me. Like Dave Stewart. Stew has such short hair anyway, so he won't let anyone touch him.

One winter during my minor league days, I was a physical education instructor at Franklin Elementary School, working with kids. It was cool, but it was work. I wanted to play. But not necessarily baseball. In the winter, I always felt like putting on a football uniform and running through a defensive line. I was even pretty close to attending one of the local junior colleges one winter, just so I'd be able to play some football. Hey, I wanted to be out there.

I sometimes wonder what would have happened had I gone to college instead of signing. I was an average student, but I was pretty good in math, pretty good in anything to do with numbers. When it came to English, spelling, history, and other subjects, I'd sometimes have trouble. But I got into math. Maybe it's because sports is so number-oriented. It was a good way for me to get to know the young ladies during the breaks. They'd help me with other subjects, and I'd help them with math. If I ever decide to go back to college, I think I'd take up accounting. Pamela went on to study humanities and speech communications and earn a bachelor of arts degree at San Francisco State, but I'm the numbers brain in the family.

As a teenager, I learned an awful lot about life by traveling around the country playing baseball. I think you can sometimes learn more about life by experiencing it than by studying it in school. It all depends on the individual. You can learn about life through schooling, or you can learn about life through living. It all depends on your wants.

For me, I wanted to be an athlete, and in retrospect, the best way to be an athlete was to sign a professional contract out of high school. I don't regret that decision. After all, only three years after graduating from high school, I found myself in the show.

HOW WE SAVED THE A'S

The A's self-destructed while I was in the minor leagues. The day I signed with them they were coming off five straight division championships. They were a dynasty. By the time I made my way up to the big club, only three years later, they had the worst organization in all of baseball.

When I signed, in June of 1976, the A's still had most of their heroes from the World Series years: Vida Blue, Rollie Fingers, Joe Rudi, Campy Campaneris, Gene Tenace, Sal Bando. But within months, all but Vida were gone. Vida hung on for another year, only because commissioner Bowie Kuhn blocked his sale to the Yankees. Without any support, Vida and the A's went downhill in a hurry.

Charlie Finley did little to prevent the team's collapse. He cut his payroll so he could more easily sell off his franchise. The players he didn't trade or sell took the free agent route out of town. He continued making cutbacks by trimming his front office to a skeleton staff, and he even traded his manager—that's right, Finley traded Chuck Tanner to Pittsburgh for Manny Sanguillen and $100,000. By the '77 season, the A's were truly awful. They lost ninety-eight games and finished an unbelievable thirty-eight and a half games out of first place. Even the Seattle Mariners, an expansion team that year, finished higher than the A's.

The next year was almost as bad, with the A's losing ninety-three games. In those two years, Finley alternated managers just like George Steinbrenner has done in New York. He started with Jack McKeon, then brought in Bobby Winkles. Then Bobby Winkles left, and he brought back Jack McKeon. With all the big names of the early seventies gone—Vida was traded to the Giants before the '78 season—the new A's included names such as Dwayne Murphy, Mitchell Page, Tony Armas, and Wayne Gross.

If people thought '77 and '78 were bad, they had no idea—'79 was the worst of all. Finley was really eager to sell by '79. He had gotten rid of everybody by then, and he was ready to unload the team to out-of-town interests. He had a good argument. The team lost an incredible 108 games and drew only 306,000 fans. For one game against the Mariners, only 653 people bothered to attend. The Bay Area was no longer interested in the A's. Finley was looking for buyers, and he'd sell to anyone, from Denver to Timbuktu. While he waited for someone to step forward, he continued trimming his payroll. He cut down his minor league system and eliminated his advertising and promotion departments. There was going to be a sale, but this was going to be a fire sale.

After the '79 season, Finley got rid of Jim Marshall and hired a manager who excelled at getting the most out of his players. He had done it in New York, Minnesota, and Detroit. His name was Billy Martin.

By the time Billy came to the A's, I had less than three months of big-league experience, but I already had a good idea of what I could do on a baseball field. After being called up on June 23, 1979, I played left field for a few games, then played center through most of July until Murph recovered from his broken finger. When Murph got back, they asked me if I wanted to return to the minors and play center field or stay in the majors and play left. It wasn't a tough choice. I told them I'd live with playing left even though I hadn't played left except for a few times in high school.

In my major league debut, I went 2-for-4 with a double and stolen base, but we got beaten 5-1 by Texas. The man behind the plate that day was Jim Sundberg, a guy I've stolen more bases against than any other catcher. I went on to hit .274 with ninety-six hits in eighty-nine games and led the club with thirty-three steals. We were 22-50 before

I arrived and 32-58 afterward, so I didn't make a lot of difference right away.

But in 1980, my first full year in the majors, I made a whole lot of difference. I broke Ty Cobb's American League record with 100 steals, and I hit .303 with 117 walks and 111 runs. I was the leadoff hitter and instigator for a team that ran like crazy. That was the year the team stole home seven times. We could run, so Billy let us run. Even guys who couldn't run, like Wayne Gross, were able to run in Billy's system. Billy knew the team wasn't loaded, so he tried everything to win games, every trick in the book. And the tricks worked.

Most of the tricks came when we had runners on first and third. Sometimes, the runner off first, especially if he was slow like Gross, would run about halfway to second and fall down. He'd get in a rundown, then the runner off third would score. We'd also have delay steals, where the guy off first would take off after the catcher threw to the pitcher. If the pitcher threw to second, the guy on third would score.

Speaking of tricks, one time Billy made his lineup by picking names out of a hat. We were in that much of a funk. My name was the eighth he drew from the hat, so I hit eighth. Billy wanted to make a change that day, so I hit eighth and Jeff Newman hit first. We didn't score a single run. We lost 1-0 in the ninth to Kansas City. It was the last time in my career I batted as low as eighth. Billy tried everything. We'd bunt, we'd fake bunts, we'd pull back on bunts and slap the ball through the infield, we'd try the squeeze play, we'd hit and run, we'd run and hit, we'd do anything to compensate for all our problems.

One of our problems in '80 was that we didn't have a bullpen, no good relief pitchers. Billy had to keep his starting pitchers in for the whole game. Nowadays, starters work five or six innings, then get out of there so the bullpen can take over, from the middle man to the spot man to the closer. Back in '80, our guys finished nearly everything they started. That rotation, featuring Rick Langford, Mike Norris, Matt Keough, and Steve McCatty, threw an amazing ninety-four complete games. Langford threw twenty-eight complete games himself. Billy really had no choice. If Billy had had Goose Gossage in the bullpen, he would have used Goose Gossage. If he had had *anybody* in the bullpen to depend on, he would have used him. But he didn't, so he let his starters finish what they started.

Billy's maneuvering helped us win a lot of games. We went from fifty-four wins in '79 to eighty-three wins in '80, and we jumped from last place to second place. We didn't beat teams because we had a powerful offense. We beat them with trickery. If we couldn't knock home the run, we'd steal it. We'd run at every opportunity. Our aggressive style became known as Billy Ball. When people thought of Billy Ball, they thought of his wild, open-air style of managing. Billy was the publisher of Billy Ball, and I was the author. It was a marriage made in heaven. Oh, that was fun. That was an exciting club. I stole a hundred bases, Armas hit thirty-five homers, Norris won twenty-two games, and Billy was named the league's manager of the year. We even started putting people in the stands. We more than doubled our attendance, drawing 842,000 people. We were the talk of the town.

There was still this matter of Finley trying to sell the club. But interest was back with the team, and it became harder and harder for the city of Oakland to let go of the A's. They later lost their football team when Al Davis moved the Raiders to Los Angeles, but they weren't about to lose the A's without a fight. Finley continued talking with possible out-of-town owners, but the Oakland Coliseum came forward and told him he couldn't get out of his long-term lease. His only choice was to sell to someone in the Bay Area. Shortly after the '80 season, that's what he did. For $12.7 million, he sold to Walter Haas, owner of Levi Strauss, the blue jeans company based in San Francisco.

The Haas family was credited with saving the A's, but I truly believe the emergence of me and Billy brought life back into the club and made people fight harder to keep the A's in Oakland. If it hadn't been for me and Billy, the club could have been sold and shipped to Timbuktu. Billy and I brought excitement to the team and put fans back in the seats. Even if the team wouldn't have gone to Timbuktu, I'm sure it would have struggled a lot longer and continued to draw small crowds without me and Billy.

With the new ownership, the focus turned more to winning. The front office began to grow. No longer was there just a handful of people pulling the strings. We opened spring training in '81 with tons of confidence, a strong pitching rotation, and probably the best outfield in baseball. We jumped out to an 11-0 start and were 17-1 after the first three weeks. We were dominating everybody, just killing teams. In those games, I hit .350 and averaged more than a run a game. We leveled off after a while, but we never stopped thinking we were going to win the division.

Throughout the first half, there was constant talk of a players' strike. On June 12, it became a reality. This was turning into the A's best season since the early seventies, and it was turning into an MVP season for me. But the players' union decided to go on strike against the owners, and the walkout lasted for fifty days. I was just a kid at the time, and I didn't understand a lot about what was going on. I couldn't do anything about it. The veteran players were leading the fight. I supported them because I knew they were fighting not just for themselves, but for younger players like me who would get their due when the time came.

Throughout my life, I had never had a summer free of baseball. Ever since I was a kid, I played on some kind of summer team. So during the fifty-day delay, I enjoyed myself. That was a beautiful time for me, just a lot of relaxation and no worries. I thought it would be nice to have a break like that every summer. Sure, I had no money and I wasn't getting paid, but I was too young to care about something so trivial.

Because we were in first place at 37-23 at the time of the strike, we were awarded the first-half championship and would play the second-half winner in the divisional playoffs. We almost won the second half as well, but Kansas City beat us out by one game, so we were to play the Royals in a best-of-five series. The Royals had an overall losing record, but that's the way it was. They played well the final two months and got into the playoffs. Look at the Cincinnati Reds, who had the best record in baseball that year. They didn't make the playoffs because they finished second in the first half and second in the second half. We definitely deserved to be in the playoffs because we had the best overall record in the American League, 64-45.

Our series with the Royals was no contest. We absolutely dominated them. They scored only two runs off our pitchers. Norris threw a shutout in the first game, and McCatty and Langford won the next two. In the finale, a 4-1 outcome, I reached base four times and scored three runs to help clinch the series and set up the league playoff series between us and the Yankees.

Unfortunately, the Yankees swept us, but we had great chances to win each of those three games. I hit .364 in the series with two doubles, a triple, and two steals. But I didn't score a single run. We didn't have the timely hitting we had during the season or during the divisional playoffs.

We lost the first game 3-1. The Yankees didn't score after the first inning, but that was enough. They loaded the bases, then, oh, man, Graig Nettles hit Norris's two-strike screwball off the end of his bat. The ball hit something in left-center, then squiggled away from me and Murph. They scored all their runs on that hit. We had chances to come back, but didn't.

We led 3-1 midway through the second game, but the Yankees started hitting and Billy went to the bullpen. We couldn't hold the lead, and they walloped us 13-3.

The third game I'll never forget. We returned to Oakland and had Keough on the mound. It was scoreless through five innings, but both Murph and I went down during the game. Murph blew the heck out of his rib cage, and I toasted a ligament in my left wrist. Willie Randolph took Keough deep to the seats in the sixth inning, but it was still 1-0 in the ninth. Again, Billy went to his bullpen, and then the game got out of hand when the Yankees scored three more runs to put us away. The Yankees went on to lose to the Dodgers in the World Series.

Despite being swept, we felt we were in every game. We were so close to winning the pennant and going to the World Series, but we lost it. I was twenty-two years old, and I got a taste of the postseason. It was wonderful. Losing to the Yankees was a disappointment, but it made me hungry to win another championship and get back to the playoffs.

As far as my bid to win the MVP, well, that was also a disappointment. In fact, it was a disgrace. I finished second in the voting. The guy who finished first was a pitcher. A relief pitcher. Rollie Fingers won the award. Fingers had a nice year for Milwaukee. He had twenty-eight saves and a low ERA, and he won the MVP. That I didn't understand. Pitchers should never win that award. They have their own award, the Cy Young Award, and Fingers won it. But they also gave him the MVP. I played every day and was among the leaders in almost every category. Fingers was a relief pitcher who showed up every once in a while for one or two innings. Sometimes he'd come in and get only one or two outs. For him to win the MVP was embarrassing to everyday players who go nine innings of every game. Give me a break on that one. Non-pitchers can't win the Cy Young, but pitchers can win the MVP.

That doesn't make sense. Pitchers should never win the MVP. Give it to a player, an everyday player.

The only time they should even consider a pitcher for the MVP is if he wins thirty games and nobody in the league hits .300 or hits any home runs or steals any bases. But Fingers wasn't out there every day. He was out there fortysomething times. Because of the strike, we had 109 games, and I played 108 of them. I had a .319 average and led the league with 135 hits, 89 runs, and 56 steals, and I helped turn the A's from a last-place team to one that almost went to the World Series. Let me play fortysomething times a year. I guarantee you, I'll hit .400 or .500. Then will I get the MVP? That voting process needs to be changed.

The '81 season was significant for many reasons, not the least of which was a conversation I had with Lou Brock. It was at Fenway Park in Boston two years after his retirement. After one of our games with the Red Sox, he came down to the clubhouse to talk with me. I had wanted to meet him, and this was the perfect opportunity because I had stolen a couple of big bases that day. He told me if anybody had the ability and technique to break his record, it would be me. I didn't expect such a statement, such a compliment. I mean, a guy with his stature and experience coming up to a twenty-two-year-old kid and telling him, "You're going to be the one, the one who breaks my record." At the time I didn't know if I believed him. I didn't doubt myself, but it was such a monumental task. But just like that, I had a goal. Just like that, I saw that it was possible.

After the season, I met with Lou again. I had flown to St. Louis to meet with Richie Bry, an agent who represented Lou and later started representing me. Before that, I didn't have an agent. I used to deal with Charlie Finley myself, but Charlie didn't like that. So I went to St. Louis for three days to meet with Richie, and I ended up spending three days with Lou. We bumped heads, talked, and talked some more. He taught me so much. I tried to ask him every question in the book. We worked on stepping, leading, reading pitchers, everything. Back then, I was still sliding feetfirst quite a bit, so I incorporated a lot of Lou's ideas. I had slid headfirst a little, but I hadn't perfected the act and actually dumped it for awhile. One time I was about to slide but was hesitant over whether to go headfirst or feetfirst. After I fell over and hurt my leg, I realized I had to make up my mind which way to slide. Now I slide headfirst all the time, except when I slide into the plate. I still go feetfirst into the plate because I need the power of my legs to get by the catcher and his shin guards. Feetfirst or headfirst, I still feel very much inspired by Lou's actions and faith.

After our playoff loss to the Yankees, I thought all the time about getting another chance at the World Series. Unfortunately, the team began to slip after the '81 season. Just like that, the pitching staff fell apart. Guys who had completed twenty games had trouble completing any. Their arms got tired, messed up, and blown out. Billy took a lot of criticism for wearing out his starting pitchers, but it was unjust criticism. He got criticized by people who didn't understand what was happening. They didn't understand that Billy had no choice but to use his starters inning after inning. He had nobody in the bullpen to take over. It wasn't that Billy wanted the starters to pitch every inning; it was a case where we had no bullpen. Should he have stuck with his starters and won? Or should he have gone to his bullpen and lost? Of course, we wanted to win, and that's how we won. I agreed with Billy. Because of those starters, we had a chance to win almost every game. Billy was a smart pitchers' manager. He used what he had. It wasn't his fault we had no relievers.

The four starters, who had combined to win seventy-one games in '80 and forty-eight games in strike-shortened '81, won just thirty-five in all of '82. Norris and McCatty spent a lot of time on the sidelines with shoulder problems—Norris hurt himself even more by not showing up at the doctor's for treatment—and Langford and Keough pitched in pain and lost a lot more than they won.

Despite the pitching problems, the team continued to run. We were still a scrappy team without many hitters. And with the pitching about to fall apart, Billy decided right away that this team was going to run to new heights. From the first day of spring training, we set our sights on the big cheese, Lou Brock's season steals record of 118.

It was that first day in the spring of '82 when Billy came up to me and said, "Rickey, we're going to break the record this year." I snapped back, "Say what, Billy? Nah, can't be done." But he said, "You just get on base like you can, and we'll break it going away."

It's not that I didn't think I could do it; I had already done one hundred, so what's nineteen more? It's that I didn't know how I could do it under the circumstances. In '80 and '81, Billy hadn't given me the green light to run, believe it or not. I'd have to look in the dugout for the okay to go. He just wanted to make sure the green light wasn't automatic. But it all changed in '82.

Billy and I came to have an understanding about running. He knew I loved to run, and he loved to watch me run. He was a genius at figuring out what pitches were coming. He could pick almost any pitch in any situation. He'd figure a curve was coming and give me the green light. Boom, go, slide, safe. As easy as that. But in '82, Billy trusted me to run more on my own. I was so pumped up that when I left spring training, I knew it was over. I knew the record was mine. I had twenty-two steals in April alone, and another twenty-seven in May. I was averaging twenty-five a month, and my total through July was up to ninety-nine. I was running at every opportunity. I was running off everybody, especially Cleveland. I stole fifteen bases off Cleveland and was 13-for-13 off the Indians' catcher, Ron Hassey. Number one hundred came on August 2, and I had a full two months to steal the final nineteen bases.

The only question was whether I'd steal 119 at home or on the road, and that was an important question because the Oakland fans were turning out in record numbers. Billy Ball was attracting a new breed of A's fans to the Coliseum. The year before, despite the strike, we drew 1.3 million people, and that had never been done in Oakland, even in the World Series years of the seventies. In '82, we continued to draw even though we weren't winning. People were coming out to see me steal bases, and I was trying to give them a show. We ended up setting a franchise record by drawing 1.7 million fans—for a fifth-place team. Billy realized what was happening, and that's why he wanted so badly to break the record in front of the Oakland fans.

The schedule and Billy's desire to get the record in Oakland led to the funniest, strangest, and maybe most memorable play I've ever been involved in. I call it the okey-doke play because Billy tried to pull a fast one on Sparky Anderson. He tried to fool him bad.

I was up to 107 steals when we opened a gigantic twelve-game home stand on August 13. During the first ten games, I stole seven bases. I was at 114 when we entered a two-game series against the Tigers, the last two games of the home stand. I stole one base in the first game, so I needed four the next day to break the record at home.

We didn't have a very big crowd, maybe eighteen thousand, on the afternoon of August 24. I guess everyone figured I'd break the record on the road. But people had second thoughts after the first inning. First time up, I got a base hit. Then I stole two bases. Boom, boom! That was that. I now needed one to tie, two to win. Suddenly people started pouring into the stadium. They were coming in by the truckload. They knew they were close to seeing history. I didn't reach base in my next two at bats, but then came the wild eighth inning.

I was the inning's second batter behind Fred Stanley, the guy they called "Chicken" because he had such skinny legs. Chicken, our ninth hitter, walked off a right-hander named Jerry Ujdur, and there were immediate thoughts on our bench that Ujdur walked Chicken intentionally to clog the bases and prevent me from running. I didn't think much of that theory; I was just trying to get ready to face the guy.

Now I was up. I hit a sharp single to left, a rope. The crowd was going wild. By now, the crowd looked like it was twenty-five thousand. But it seemed I wasn't going to get the record like they hoped because Chicken stayed at second base after my single. There was nowhere for me to run. Ol' Chicken, he couldn't run a lick. He was oh-so-slow, a different story altogether. I hit that ball so hard, Chicken barely got to second base, let alone third.

That's when Billy took over. He wanted Chicken off the bases, off the bases right now. The wheels started to turn. A double steal? No way. If they threw out Chicken at third, I wouldn't have gotten credit for stealing second. I could have gone on to steal third and tie the record, but Billy didn't want that. He wanted it all now. This was our last hope. Why not break it now? But first Billy wanted to give me room to run.

Billy had Clete Boyer, our third-base coach, walk over to Chicken and tell him to steal third. Chicken said, "Steal third?" Chicken reminded Clete he couldn't run, that he'd be out by a mile. If they rolled the ball to third, Chicken would have been nailed. But Clete told him again to steal third base. Our first-base coach, Charlie Metro, came up to me and said, "Rickey, you stay here. Don't go anywhere." The Tigers' bench was close to the first-base line, and Sparky was trying to hear what was going on. He walked out of the dugout and wondered what in the world was happening. He looked over at Billy, and Billy had a big smile on his face. Now Sparky was really confused.

So here we go. Chicken had stolen eleven bases in his entire career, and he had no idea what kind of lead to take. He was out there at second base taking a tiny lead, and Clete and Billy were yelling at him to get off the base. Sparky was still wondering what we were doing. Finally, Sparky got hip to our plans. He jumped back out of the dugout, yelling, "Do not tag him! Do not tag him!" Chicken got his big lead, the biggest of his career, so Ujdur had to turn and throw back there. Chicken was a dead duck. He didn't know what to do, so he stood there, didn't move at all. While Alan Trammel, the shortstop, was holding the ball at second base, Sparky, getting madder and madder, shouted again, "Do not tag him!" Trammell didn't know what to do, so he threw to Enos Cabell at third base. Enos didn't know what to do, so he threw back to the second baseman, Lou Whitaker. The whole time, Chicken just stood there between the bases, not even a budge. Lou had the ball in his glove and was standing next to Chicken. Lou didn't know what to do. Finally, Lou tagged Chicken.

During all of this mess, I might have been able to go to second base. But Billy screamed at me to stay at first. Sparky was just steaming by now. He figured out we were trying to pull the okey-doke against him. "Y'all can't do that," he shouted at me. I looked at him and was thinking, "Sparky, I don't know what they're doing. This ain't my idea."

With Chicken out of the way, I could run now. There were two open bases for me, and Dwayne Murphy was at the plate. Well, if it's there, I might as well take it. I was into the moment now, and there was no way Bill Fahey was going to throw me out. Fahey was catching for the Tigers that day because Lance Parrish, their regular catcher, had flown home to be with his wife, who was about to give birth. Ujdur tossed over to first three times, then finally to the plate. A pitchout. I took off. Fahey threw to second, and I got under the tag. Yes! I've tied Brock. Hallelujah.

But noooooo. Durwood Merrill was the umpire, and Durwood called me out. A terrible call. I looked at him and said, "Whaaaat? No way." That danged umpire. The fans were going absolutely nuts, and so was my team. Here comes Billy. Here comes Clete. Here comes Metro. Here comes Murph. Right away, Durwood starts thumbing everybody. Billy, you're gone! Murph, you're gone! Metro, you're gone! Wayne Gross was out there; you're gone! You're all gone! Oh, Durwood, why ever did you do this?

I found out later. Murph told me he heard Durwood say, "You've got to earn it, not have some guy picked off on purpose." Chicken might have been safe, so I didn't think it was a bad thing to do. And I stole the base, fair and square. I was safe. I knew that, Durwood knew that. That argument went on forever. We lost the argument, but we won the game, 3-0. The fans went home disappointed, knowing the home stand was over and I'd have to wait for the road trip to break the record.

I wasn't laughing then, but when I think back on that play with ol' Chicken Stanley, I cry out laughing. Every time Merrill umps one of our games, we talk about it and laugh. He's actually a great umpire. He and I are always talking at each other. When he calls a strike on me that is no way a strike, I look back at him and he smiles. "That's a Hall of Fame pitch, Rickey. Nobody could hit that." I tell him, "I know I couldn't have hit it. It was two feet outside." He's funny. If I get in the Hall of Fame, I want him there with me, just so I can remind him about all those "Hall of Fame pitches" he's called on me.

After that okey-doke game, Sparky said the incident was bad for baseball and likened it to the 1919 Black Sox scandal. C'mon, Sparky. It wasn't that bad. Sparky thought Billy was trying to mess with his knowledge of the game. Billy didn't admit what he had done during the press conference after the game, but he explained his strategy to me on the plane to Milwaukee. Billy had good intentions. He wanted me to set the record in front of our fans, and so did I, especially because my momma was in the stands. It just wasn't meant to be.

Billy and Sparky were always bumping heads, but I always liked Sparky. I'd love to play for him some time, and I think he'd love to have me. The way he manages and the way I play would be an awesome combination. To me, he's another Billy Martin or Tony La Russa. It's exciting when managers like that go head to head. I remember when we played Detroit, sometimes Billy would have a strategy where he'd get all these pitchers up in the bullpen trying to make Sparky second-guess himself. Sparky would see a right-hander in the bullpen, then get a left-hander ready to pinch-hit. Then Billy would sit down his right-hander, and Sparky would have to sit down his hitter. It was a simple cat-and-mouse game, typical of what these guys did to each other. But nothing ever compared to the okey-doke play.

I had to wait until two days later to tie the record and three days later to break it. By then the incident back in Oakland was all but forgotten. When I stole second base off Doc Medich in County Stadium in Milwaukee on August 27 for number 119, I walked over to Murph and planted a kiss on his big shiny forehead, just like we had planned. It was Murph, our second hitter, who took all those pitches and gave me the opportunity to run. He often complained that he didn't want to bat behind me because he figured he was taking too many pitches. I told him he wasn't taking too many pitches; I told him he was missing too many pitches. I told him, "If you don't hit behind me, you won't get all those fastballs anymore." When I'm on base, pitchers usually throw fastballs to the next hitter to give the catcher a better chance to throw me out. Murph didn't realize he was actually getting some great pitches hitting behind me. After I broke the record, Murph was the first guy I wanted to embrace. I'll never forget that kiss I gave him.

The Brewers stopped the game and threw a nice ceremony for me. I was thrilled. It was something I set out to achieve, and I felt blessed that I could do it so early in my career. But I didn't stop there. The same day, I swiped four bases, all with Medich on the mound and Ted Simmons behind the plate. I brought Pamela and my momma along from Oakland so they could be with me. Brock was also there so he could be on hand when his record fell. For me, it was an honor to break the record in his presence.

I finished the year with 130 steals, but I could have had more. There must have been eight or ten times where I ran so fast that I slid right past the bag and was tagged out. Sometimes I just couldn't slow down and stop, which is one of the reasons why I also broke another record by getting caught forty-two times.

At the end of the season, Billy left the A's. He wasn't fired. I don't think the A's would have fired him, because he had become too much of a god. He left because he wanted to go back to the Yankees. Sure enough, a couple of months after the season, George Steinbrenner hired him for the '83 season. Billy was a die-hard Yankee, even while managing the A's. He always used to tell me how much he wanted to return to New York. He always rooted for the Yankees, unless we were playing them. He'd come up to me and say, "Rickey, my Yankees are losing. They need help. I've got to get back there." Whenever the Yankees fell into a funk, he'd go to Steinbrenner and ask to come back and manage the team. He told me his heart was with us whenever we played, but his soul was back in New York with the Yankees. He knew he'd get back eventually. The A's didn't want him to go, but after Billy tore up the office four or five times after games, the A's agreed to let him leave.

FROM SOUTH OF THE BORDER
TO THE HOUSE THAT RUTH BUILT

My first four seasons in the majors, I learned so much about the game. Not just from listening to other people, but by experimenting on my own. Three straight winters, I went off and played ball, either in Mexico or Puerto Rico.

I was dedicated to being the best I could be. I recommend it to younger kids coming up today. But kids don't seem to want to play winter ball anymore. Maybe they're spoiled. They think they make enough money as it is. Hey, get your butt down there. Forget sitting at home. Go learn. If you learn, you might get up here to the majors. The more you play, the more you learn and the better you get.

My first taste of winter ball came after my year in Double-A. I went to Mexico and played for Navojoa in the winter of '78–'79. I learned a lot down there, especially how to hit the curveball. I faced major league pitching, a lot of older guys, and, man, they threw nasty breaking balls down there. I mean junk. I got fed so many curves that I began hitting them much easier, and I continued to do so when I returned home.

The next two winters, I played in Puerto Rico, and I had a great old time. It was a better brand of ball, and the trips weren't as long. In

Mexico, we'd have some long trips, I mean fourteen-hour trips. That's too long. In Puerto Rico, I played for the team in Ponce, for an owner named Jose Cangiano. Jose Pagan, my Triple-A manager, recommended me to Mr. Cangiano. That man treated me like I was a member of his family. He called me Rickey Cangiano. He told the whole city I was his son, that I was Rickey Cangiano.

I'm the type of guy who loves to sleep, and I seemed to sleep very well down there. But Mr. Cangiano would come by almost every day and get me out of bed and bring me to lunch. I'd tell him, "I don't want to eat, I want to sleep." He said, "C'mon, my son, I've got to introduce you to this guy and that guy." He took me everywhere and gave me whatever I needed. If we went to San Juan for a game and I wanted to stay on the beach, he got me a condominium on the beach. He gave me cars to drive, anything I wanted. I was just a kid, but he loved me and took care of me. He told me all about the culture and taught me some Spanish words I needed to know.

My second winter playing for Ponce, I broke the Puerto Rican stolen-base record. In forty-eight games, I stole forty-four bases to break a record that had stood since 1949–50. The record had belonged to a guy named Carlos Bernier, who played a season with the Pirates in 1953. Bernier set the record in sixty games, but I broke it in forty-eight. It wasn't easy. Opposing teams didn't want me to break the record because I wasn't a native of the land, and even one of my teammates tried to prevent me from getting the record.

David Rosello was our number-two hitter and captain. He was winding down his big-league career—he played for the Cubs and Indians—and he thought the record should belong to a Puerto Rican. There were times he'd go out of his way to hit the ball if I were about to steal second base. I could have had more than fifty steals if we had worked together. I know Mr. Cangiano was on my side. He presented me with a beautiful ring for breaking the record.

The preceding season with the A's, I had broken Ty Cobb's American League record. So in that one year, I broke records in two different leagues and ended up with 144 steals. Not many players in the majors know that, except for the Puerto Rican players. At the beginning of every season, I ask the Puerto Ricans if my record is still holding up down there. They say, "Yeah, Rickey, you still got it." I might have it for a long time. Nobody can steal forty-five bases in such a short season.

We had a pretty good mix of American players on that team. We had me, Bobby Brown, and Joe Lefebvre in the outfield, and our pitching staff had La Marr Hoyt, Mike Griffin, and my A's teammate Steve McCatty. The pitching coach was Dock Ellis. I remember a story about Dock Ellis. One game I hurt my left knee sliding into the plate against the Santurce team. Gary Alexander was catching, and I slid right under him and blasted my knee into his shin guards. I was safe, but my knee fell out of whack. I was in pain, but the team needed me, so I played. On one leg. When I stood at the plate in my stance, I stood on my right leg with my left leg in the air. It hurt too much to put my left foot on the ground. That's how I swung, one leg up and pow! I even learned something from that experience. Ever since then, I've kicked high with my left leg just before hitting the ball. But back then, I had no choice. I'd hit the ball, then run to first base virtually on one leg. It got pretty ridiculous, so Dock Ellis came over and told me to knock it off. He said, "Young buck, you better shut your butt down. This ain't your league. You're in the big leagues. You don't need to do that type of stuff here." I said, "What are you talking about, Dock?" He said, "You'll ruin your career." He had been around a lot longer than I had, so I sat my butt down.

My leg was massively swollen. I mean, those doctors in Puerto Rico wanted to operate on it right there, but I wouldn't let them touch me. By spring training, it was pretty much healed, but I got it checked anyway. The team doctor looked at it and said in a real serious voice, "Well, Rickey, you've got twenty more years of playing time on that knee." I smiled and said, "Thanks, Doc. I'll remember that."

Another part of my game that improved in winter ball was my defense. The A's had begun playing me in left field, and that's where I played for Ponce. I learned a lot about the position playing every day in Puerto Rico. I was brutal in high school and the minor leagues, but I kept working at it. In '81 I earned a Gold Glove. Being a left-handed left fielder, I got that extra reach going to foul territory and into the corner. I went to the line really well to take away doubles, and I charged everything. I still made some errors, but I was daring. Some guys like Brian Downing of the Angels would go the entire season without making an error, but Downing would just wait for the ball to bounce into the corner and stop, then he'd pick it up. That was crazy, brother. That's turning a fly ball into a single. But that's how you prevent errors.

A lot of managers—Earl Weaver, Sparky Anderson, Gene Mauch, Billy—have called me the best left fielder in baseball, but all I've ever gotten to show for it was that one Gold Glove in '81. People don't always think about defense when they think of me because of my base-stealing abilities. But for me, being an all-around player means playing good defense. One thing with the Gold Glove, they don't pick one left fielder, one center fielder, and one right fielder. They pick three outfielders, period. It could be three center fielders or three right fielders, it doesn't matter. So even though I was called the best left fielder, I haven't gotten the Gold Glove except for '81. And maybe that was because they took the MVP away from me that year and gave it to Rollie Fingers. I dominated that season, so I guess they had to give me something. You never know with that award. If you look at the winners every year, each one of those guys had a good offensive year. It's tough on guys who don't hit well but are great fielders. They don't ever seem to win that award.

I could have won a Gold Glove in '80, my first full season. But they gave the Gold Gloves to Fred Lynn, Willie Wilson, and Dwayne Murphy, all guys who excelled in center field. Murph won Gold Gloves every year from '80 to '85. I guess they didn't want to give awards to two outfielders on the same team even though we had a great defensive outfield, probably the best in baseball, with my wheels in left, Armas's rifle arm in right, and Murph's all-around game in center. We had forty-five assists in 1980 alone. We took pride in not allowing runners to take extra bases on us.

A few years ago, Barry Bonds said he was the best left fielder in baseball. That didn't bother me. He's a guy with a lot of confidence. Saying that is a way to make yourself believe you're the best. Players do that. I say things like that. But I usually back it up with numbers and statistics. On defense, especially for outfielders, a ton of guys have good defensive numbers, good fielding percentages, so it's tough to back it up only with stats. It's a part of the game that needs to be judged by someone else. It's not always necessary to brag. But, Barry, if you say you're the best, then you're the best. It's better for players to believe they're the best than the worst.

A couple of things about Barry Bonds. I first met Barry when he was playing baseball at Arizona State. During spring training, I'd check out an Arizona State game now and then because it was the school I probably would have attended if I hadn't signed out of high school. Barry looked pretty good in college; he was a strong kid. But it was little Oddibe McDowell whom I remember hitting home runs when I was watching. As far as Barry, I guess he liked the way I played. He used to write little notes on his college books saying, "Rickey Henderson is my idol." After the Pirates signed him, I noticed he did a lot of things I did, as far as trying to be an all-around outfielder who could both hit and run. He tried adding a little of my style to his game; I even detected him trying a little snatch-catch now and then.

Barry and I got to know each other when he was playing at Arizona State. We went out after one of my workouts, and he ended up keeping one of my cassette tapes. It was a nice homemade blues tape that I had, with all the best songs from that time. We were kicking around in his car listening to that tape, but I forgot to grab the thing when he dropped me off. I ain't seen it since. He went back to school, and I left spring training. I never got it back. He's still got it. One day I'll have to talk to him about that.

One of the things Barry and I have in common is our knack for hitting a lot of game-opening home runs. I learned in my early years the value of leading off a game with a home run. It's not something you normally try to do. The main thing when beginning a game is to get on base. Sometimes that means hitting the ball hard. Sometimes that means the long ball. Man, those game-opening home runs can truly set the tone in a game. They put fear into pitchers. First swing of the game, boom! Out of the park. It gives your team a boost, a quick point on the board. Now the pitcher's got to be a little tentative and maybe even scared. He suddenly becomes a little more careful about what he's doing.

That's always a big thrill for me, unsettling the pitcher early in the game. I began the '92 season with fifty game-opening home runs, a major league record. Barry's done it twenty times. Depending on whether he hits leadoff or third in the order, he's got a good chance to catch his father, Bobby, whose record I broke. Bobby did it thirty-five times.

I was never really considered a power threat until my sixth big-league season. I never hit any more than ten home runs before '84. Then I started to go deep a lot. The sudden power display was partly due to a suggestion by my new manager. With Billy leaving after the '82 season, the A's hired Steve Boros to take over in '83. The nucleus of the team had changed, with Armas traded to the Red Sox for Carney Lansford, and guys like Davey Lopes, Joe Morgan, Dave Kingman, and Joe Rudi coming to Oakland to finish out their careers. In my first year under Boros, I stole another 108 bases. But in the spring of '84, he tried to get me thinking less about stealing bases and more about RBIs. He even talked about hitting me third in the lineup. I was hesitant at first to change my game, but I eventually realized he was probably right.

I entered that spring having lost my arbitration hearing. The A's won the case after arguing I wasn't a complete ballplayer, that I stole bases but didn't hit home runs. The arbitrator ruled the A's shouldn't pay me the money I wanted. I wasn't a power hitter, I was only a leadoff hitter. I didn't drive in the runs, I only scored the runs. That was his reasoning. That got me thinking. I thought I ranked among the top players in the game, but I wasn't getting paid like them. Power guys like Mike Schmidt and Dave Winfield were getting the big money, and the leadoff guys were way down on the scale. The big guys were knocking in one hundred runs, but I was scoring one hundred runs. Isn't that the same thing? Not according to the A's case in arbitration. Not according to the arbitrator.

First I heard it in arbitration. Next I heard it from Boros. Everyone wanted me to hit home runs. Eventually, I did decide to become a power hitter. That year there was a noticeable difference in my game. I nearly doubled my power output with sixteen home runs. It was a big adjustment. I was hitting balls out of the park, and it was a great feeling. But it was just the beginning. I wanted more, but I didn't want to eliminate my running game altogether.

As it was, I stole sixty-six bases in '84. That led the league, but it wasn't what I was used to. Obviously, the more home runs I hit, the fewer chances I had of stealing bases. Not only that, the team's style was very different, and we didn't emphasize the running game as much. Morgan and Kingman didn't like me running when they were hitting. Morgan hit second, but he was a free-swinger and didn't take many pitches. Kingman hit cleanup, and he was the same way. I didn't run in certain situations, but I ran if I felt the time was right. I tried not to let them take my game plan away, and I didn't want to take their game plan away. Hey, if I run and you swing and foul it off, fine. But don't get upset if I run and you swing and miss. Don't say that's my fault. It's not my fault. You shouldn't have swung if you couldn't have hit it. All that didn't bother me a lot. I adjusted. I've always been able to adjust pretty well to the type of team I've played for.

Those two years after Billy left, we finished in fourth place. Boros lasted all of '83 but was fired early in '84 and replaced by Jackie Moore. The team wasn't doing the things it had done in the playoff year, and management was getting impatient. In '84, they started talking about rebuilding with younger, cheaper players. They were in dire need of pitching. They started talking about trading some veterans, including myself. They thought they'd lose me anyway because I'd be eligible for free agency at the end of '85, and they didn't think they could compete with other teams. They figured they could trade me and get something in return rather than lose me for nothing to free agency.

I wanted to stay in Oakland, but most of all I wanted to play in a World Series. That was my priority. I was hoping the A's would work something out so I could stay, but they didn't seem like they were going anywhere. I began to imagine playing for other teams. It wasn't easy, because I grew up in Oakland and didn't want to move. But this was a business, and I had to think of my career first. Would I get to the World Series quicker by staying in Oakland? Or would I get there quicker by moving on? It was a safe bet I'd have to go elsewhere to fulfill that dream.

When I was a kid, I used to think about the Yankees quite a bit. I spent most of my childhood thinking about football, but when I thought about baseball I thought about the great players, the great teams. The Yankees were always a great team with great tradition. I always envisioned myself becoming a great player someday and playing for a great team. Even though I grew up on the West Coast, I wondered what it would be like playing for the Yankees. When Billy managed the A's, we used to talk about the Yankees all the time. Man, back in '82 he told me I'd someday play for the Yankees. He told me not to sign with anyone else if I ever became a free agent. He told me, "You deserve to be a Yankee." He made it sound like it was an honor to play in New York.

The A's didn't engage in much trade talk immediately after the '84 season, but things really heated up when Sandy Alderson, the A's general manager, and his staff went down to Houston for the winter meetings. It got to the point where I no longer doubted I was leaving the A's. I was so sure I'd be traded that I flew to Houston myself and checked into the hotel where all of baseball's executives were staying.

The A's talked to a lot of teams. The Dodgers were interested. They wanted me in the same lineup with Pedro Guerrero, but the A's wanted a half-dozen different guys in return, including Bob Welch—they've always liked Bob Welch—and their top pitching prospects. The Dodgers never liked parting with young pitchers, so that was that.

The Orioles also pursued me, maybe because I hit the Orioles better than any other team. If I played for the Orioles, I'd stop beating on them. But the deal fell through because the Orioles didn't offer enough pitching.

Then there were the Yankees. Billy had drilled into my head that I should be a Yankee, and toward the end of the meetings the Yankees made an offer that the A's liked. The Yankees were offering four pitchers—Jay Howell and their best prospects, Jose Rijo, Tim Birtsas, and Eric Plunk—plus an outfielder, Stan Javier. But the Yankees wouldn't complete the deal unless they could give me a long-term contract extension. They didn't want to give up all those guys, then lose me to free agency the following winter. At first, the A's gave the Yankees a forty-eight-hour deadline to sign me and complete the deal. That deadline passed, so the A's granted the Yankees a twenty-four-hour extension. Both sides were intent on making the deal.

During the negotiations between the Yankees and my agent, Richie Bry, I ran into Billy in the hotel bar. He told me, "Rickey, I'm going to talk to George Steinbrenner tonight, and you'll be a Yankee tomorrow. I'm telling him to sign you no matter what it costs." Billy sold George by telling him I'd be the most exciting Yankee since Mickey Mantle.

Two years after Billy told me I'd be a Yankee, he turned out to be a prophet. A couple of hours before the deadline, the A's got their five guys and the Yankees got me—for five years and $8.6 million—as well as a minor leaguer named Bert Bradley. Winfield and Schmidt were still making more money, but at least I was close. I was happy to be going to a team that could win the pennant right away, even if it meant being three thousand miles from home.

I left the Houston meetings a happy man. I knew I would soon wear the Yankee pinstripes. No more of those pullover A's jerseys with the stretch pants. The Yankee uniforms, far more traditional, had button-down jerseys and belt buckles, not real good accessories for a guy who slides headfirst. But that was the least of my concerns. I wanted to play for a winner, and the Yankees already had a stacked lineup: Dave Winfield, Don Mattingly, Willie Randolph, Ken Griffey, Don Baylor. Even though they were all great hitters, I knew I'd still be stealing a lot of bases. My 66 steals in '84, though subpar for me, were more than the entire Yankee roster combined, so they needed a guy who could run. Joe Morgan retired at the end of the '84 season, so I left the A's as the active leader in steals with 493. Yeah, I was the guy the Yankees needed.

And the Yankees were the team that I needed. I wanted to go where the legends played.

SAY HEY, RICKEY

Just because I was going to New York didn't mean I wanted to be the next Reggie Jackson. Unfortunately, nobody wanted to believe that but me.

By the time I joined the Yankees, Reggie had been gone for three years, and it had been four years since the Yankees had won an AL championship. The fans and the media were itching for another pennant, and they believed I was the guy who could bring a World Series back to the Bronx. They wanted a guy to take over where Reggie had left off, and they somehow figured I was his second coming. Well, they figured wrong. I had no problem with the World Series part. Nobody wanted to go to the World Series more than I did; that's why I liked the Yankees in the first place. But another Reggie? I'm sorry. That's where I had to draw the line.

Reggie was Mr. Publicity, off the field. He was a big showboat. He was flashy. I wasn't like Reggie. Sure, I was flashy, I had style. But there was one major difference: Reggie loved to be in the limelight twenty-four hours a day, the talk of the town. Whatever he was doing, on the field and off, he wanted everyone to know about it. When he arrived in New York, he proclaimed to the world that he was the "straw that stirs the drink." It was like Reggie was coming in and taking over. He got a lot of mileage out of that line, but he also got criticized by some of the people who had been in the organization for years.

Give Reggie credit, though. He lived up to every word he ever uttered. That's what made him, his ego. His ego made him do all that. But that's Reggie's style. He's an aggressive ballplayer, and if he couldn't play by his own rules, maybe he wouldn't have been so great. Same with me. To be successful, I've got to be free to do things my way.

But my approach is different from Reggie's. The truth is, I'm not the type of person who wants to be in the limelight every minute of every day. I need my moments alone, away from the ball park, away from the city, away from the media. I was coming from tiny old Oakland, where my private life was my private life. When I got to New York, all that changed.

I'll never forget my very first visit to the Yankee Stadium clubhouse. A lot of reporters will never forget it, either. It was at an off-day workout, and the team had already played ten games. I was coming in from Fort Lauderdale, where I had been playing for the Yankees' Single-A team while recuperating from a sprained left ankle. My flight had arrived late, and my new teammates were already out on the field working out. My first thought was to rush through the clubhouse and meet with the trainer to see if I'd be okay to work out. But when I opened the clubhouse door, I was swarmed by a mob of reporters. There were dozens upon dozens of people with notepads and microphones and bright camera lights. I wasn't expecting such a wild scene. I was a twenty-six-year-old ballplayer, and I hadn't ever seen anything like that. Back in Oakland, there might have been a handful of writers in the clubhouse. But this was different. This was like the World Series. The World Series on April 22nd.

I would have liked to have sat and talked with all those people; the perfect solution would have been to have a formal press conference somewhere at the stadium. But like I said, my flight was late, my team was on the field, and I needed to see the trainer. Hey, I was the new kid on the block, and this was my first day on the job. I wanted to impress my bosses. As it turned out, I might have impressed my bosses, but I totally turned off the press. I made my way through the crowd of reporters and blared out, "I don't need no press now, man."

That phrase came back to haunt me again and again. Anytime a reporter wrote something negative about me and needed ammunition, he'd go back and use that quote. I was surprised by it all, but I guess

I shouldn't have been. This, after all, was the big city, the number-one sports community in the world. But I don't think that, as a whole, the press stepped back and tried to realize where I was coming from. Yes, their job was to come and interview me, but my job was to see if I could play.

I talked to the press after the workout, but apparently that wasn't enough. I didn't try to show disrespect, but maybe they thought I did. Either way, it all proved to be very bad timing. It didn't help that Gary Carter—Mr. Microphone himself—was traded to the crosstown Mets the same winter. Those same reporters had been talking to Carter for the first ten days of the season, and Carter said all the right things. He wanted to be on TV, wanted to learn about TV, wanted to work the microphone. I wasn't that way. I wanted to come to the park and play ball.

There was another reason those first few days in a Yankees uniform were unforgettable. When I was traded, I envisioned playing for Yogi Berra, who was beginning his second season as the manager. I was really looking forward to playing for Yogi. He was a lifetime Yankee man, a living legend, a Hall of Famer. He was in his second term in charge of the Yankees after managing them to the World Series back in '64. The year before I arrived, Yogi's team won eighty-seven games but finished seventeen games behind the first-place Tigers. I really wanted the opportunity to play for him. Unfortunately, I never got that opportunity—unless you call six games an opportunity.

After my sixth game with my new team, after only the sixteenth game of the entire season, Yogi was fired. Sixteen games! Four and a half games out of first place! I never understood that move. I thought it must have been something else. It couldn't have been that he was managing poorly. We were 6-10 and had a lot of injuries. How could a guy be fired after only sixteen games? If nothing else, I learned an important lesson about New York and George Steinbrenner: Expect the unexpected.

I was upset when Yogi left. That was a sad day in my life. I'm still disappointed that George fired him. I feel guilty because I wasn't there to help out Yogi. I missed ten of his sixteen games, and I was just getting used to playing for him when George let him go.

The only bright side to Yogi's firing was his replacement—Billy Martin. I was back with my favorite manager. It was Billy who always told me in Oakland that I belonged with the Yankees, and now we had the chance to work together in New York.

I didn't know it would happen so soon, but I was quite sure Billy would return as the Yankees' manager. That's one of the reasons I didn't want to wear his number. There was some hype that winter about me wearing Number 1 on my uniform. But that was always Billy's number, and this was before his number was retired. I wasn't about to take his number when I knew he'd be coming back. Anyway, I've never liked single digits on uniforms. They don't look good. I know all the great Yankees—Ruth, Gehrig, DiMaggio, Dickey, Berra, Mantle, Maris— wore single digits, but I'd never wear one. Throughout my career, I've worn nothing but double digits. My favorite was thirty-two, because of O. J. Simpson, but I was never able to wear thirty-two in baseball. In the minors, I wore fourteen and twenty-four. When I got to the A's, Craig Minetto was wearing thirty-two, so they gave me thirty-nine at first before I settled on thirty-five. Just when I was getting used to thirty-five, I went to the Yankees and found out it belonged to Phil Niekro. So I decided to wear twenty-four.

As it turned out, there were a couple of ironic twists to my new number. Not only did I choose that number because of Willie Mays, but the Yankees ended up moving me to Willie's position. As a kid, I had never made it across the San Francisco Bay to Candlestick Park, but I liked Willie Mays a lot, the way he ran around so fluidly while chasing down fly balls. So here I was, all of a sudden, playing center field just across the Harlem River from the site of the old Polo Grounds, where Willie Mays played the first six seasons of his great career. The Yankees have had Hall of Fame center fielders of their own, people like Di-Maggio and Mantle. But when I got between the lines, life wasn't about history. As players, we have to eliminate what happened in the past. We can never try to follow in someone else's footsteps because each player is so different. I noticed and appreciated what those other players had done, but I didn't make it a point to copy anyone else.

I moved to center because the Yankees had nobody else to play out there, not since Mickey Rivers in the World Series years. They already had Ken Griffey and Dave Winfield to play left, so I played my first two and a half seasons in center.

The position was by no means new to me. I had played there a little in high school and a lot in the minors, and I played there most of my first month in the majors when Dwayne Murphy was out with a broken finger. But by the time I got to the Yankees, I hadn't played center in six years. There's a big difference between left and center. Center fielders come right at the ball and see true bounces. Left fielders get all kinds of wacky spins, balls that dance and hook every which way; it's a position where you need a quick reaction, almost like third base.

Although it might be tougher to play in left, center fielders run a lot more, especially at Yankee Stadium. That place is so incredibly vast, unlike center field in many other parks. To me, it always seemed much bigger than the actual dimensions. The reason? Our pitchers. They gave up an awful lot of hits, and I spent an awful lot of time running around the outfield tracking down doubles and triples. It would have been no problem playing center field if we had had a good pitching staff, but I always seemed to be tired when it was time to come off the field. When I got to the dugout, I was expected to motor up right away and start a rally. That was killing me, but that's the way it always was with the Yankees when I was in New York—a lot of hitting and no pitching.

The Yankees' offense was the best I've ever been associated with, even better than Oakland's offense of the late eighties and early nineties. I knew I wouldn't need to steal 130 bases on this team. I mean, it was probably the best offense in baseball. I can't begin to count the times we scored ten or twelve runs. And lost. We went through long stretches averaging six or seven runs a game. Hey, it was rare that a team could hold us to fewer than five runs. The problem was, we couldn't hold the other team to fewer than five runs.

If we had had guys like Dave Stewart and Dennis Eckersley during my five years with the Yankees, we could have won the championship at least four times. Instead, the best we finished was second, and that happened in each of my first two years. We ended two games behind Toronto in '85 and five and a half behind Boston in '86. George was always big on hitters, but not pitchers. He concentrated on beefing up his lineup instead of his rotation. Man, we used to cuss out George every day. "George, get us some damn pitchers." He'd say, "We already paid enough money on hitters, so the hell with the pitchers." He'd just tell us to score more runs. Well, we scored enough runs. But if he had picked up just two quality pitchers, we could have won it all. He didn't realize that if a team scores a lot of runs but gives up a lot of runs, it's going to lose a lot of games. It was so depressing, because just across town were the best pitchers in the game. We always had hitting, but the Mets always had pitching. Mix us up, and that team would have been unbeatable.

Our '85 team had a batting order that couldn't be topped, especially at the first six spots—myself, Willie Randolph, Don Mattingly, Winfield, Don Baylor, and Griffey. It took us a while to come together because of the numerous injuries during the spring. It seemed like we were all in pain coming out of spring training, with Mattingly just off knee surgery and Winfield having elbow problems. I was one of four guys who began the year on the disabled list. I missed the first ten games because of a freak injury I suffered against Boston, our biggest rival even in spring training.

The game was on St. Patrick's Day in Winter Haven, and both sides were going all out to win, which isn't usually the primary goal during spring training. I was on first, and Mattingly knocked a single to right field, a one-hopper to Dwight Evans. I was feeling pretty good and strong, and I knew I could go from first to third on anybody, even someone with a great arm like Evans. I was off and running, reaching second and cutting to third. I looked ahead at Wade Boggs, the third baseman. He was just standing there. I thought I had it beat. But he deked me. He faked me, making me think there was no throw coming. At the last second, he snagged the ball out of the air and tagged me out. I hesitated as I slid, and I badly jammed my left ankle. It wasn't the kind of start I had expected. It turned out to be the first time in my career I missed Opening Day.

It didn't help that I hit poorly when I finally got into the lineup. For me, it was still spring training; my strength was still at about 75 percent. I went 3-for-25 at the plate as we lost five of my first six games. After the White Sox swept us three games in Chicago, George canned Yogi and made Billy the manager of the Yankees for the fourth time. The move didn't go over too well with a lot of players, but we began to play better almost immediately after Billy arrived. Maybe it was because we were getting healthy, maybe it was because of the spark Billy Ball always brought to a team. For my part, I hit safely in Billy's first eleven games and raised my average to .304. I was up to .315 by the end of May, and those boobirds who at first had second thoughts about me now seemed to be cheering every move I made. I'd get thrown out at second and get a standing ovation. If I had a good month in May, it was nothing compared to June. I was named Player of the Month after hitting .416 with six homers and twenty-two steals.

The balls were leaving the ballpark like never before. When Billy came in, he brought along Willie Horton to be his bench coach, and Willie taught me a lot about the power game. I thought I could help the team more if I could hit the long ball. Lou Piniella was the official hitting coach, but his theories weren't for me. Lou was a big help to Mattingly; they had the same style. Willie was a home run hitter, so I wanted to learn from him. We had been extremely close ever since meeting each other in winter ball. Willie explained to me the difference between a power hitter and a singles hitter: A power hitter knows how to cock his bat back as the pitch is thrown. A singles hitter doesn't cock his bat. Willie said I'd never be able to knock a pitcher out of the park by just swinging the bat with my normal motion, just pushing the ball without utilizing my power. He taught me the cock-and-shoot method. To get that extra kick and have the ball explode, I'd have to hold the bat in front of me, then cock it back and take a longer swing, shooting forward to hit the ball. It might sound simple, but it made a big difference that season.

I ended up having the best year of my career to that point. I was the first American Leaguer in the 20-50 Club, hitting a career-high twenty-four homers and swiping eighty bases. I broke the Yankees' seventy-one-year-old steals record, belonging to Fritz Maisel, and only three catchers—Bob Boone, Carlton Fisk, and Rich Gedman—were able to throw me out. Maybe my biggest accomplishment was scoring 146 runs, the most in the majors since Ted Williams scored 150 back in 1949.

It was no coincidence that Mattingly had the highest RBI total of anyone in thirty-seven years. I scored 146 runs, and he drove in 145 runs. Did we have a system or what? I'd flash him signals to let him know when I was stealing, but I always had a good hunch when he was going to hit the ball. If he hit a home run, fine, I'd congratulate him at the plate. I scored fifty-six of the runs Mattingly drove in. He loved when I got on base. He'd sit at the plate all day and wait for me to get to third. Winfield used to get upset at Mattingly because Mattingly got all the RBIs. Every day, same thing. I'd get to first. Mattingly would wait. I'd get to second. Mattingly would wait. I'd get to third. Then he'd go to work. When I was at third, Mattingly didn't care if the pitch was inside, outside, over his head, down in the dirt. He never left me on third base. He hit the ball somewhere, anywhere, and I'd score. So many times it went like this: Okay, Rickey's on first, Rickey steals second, Willie bunts Rickey to third. Okay, Mattingly has himself another ribbie. Thank you, Rickey.

That's why Don's mad at the Yankees today. He doesn't have anybody like me anymore. That's why he hasn't enjoyed the same success. After I left, really, it's never been the same for Mattingly. If he were with another team, he'd end up getting back the glory he deserves. See, Don's a winner. In his heart and soul, he's a winner. But it hasn't been happening with the Yankees. Look at what they're doing to him. They suspended him a game in '91 for not getting a haircut. That was a joke, but that's the Yankees nowadays. Don thought his hair was fine, and it was; that's the style for a lot of guys. But the Yankees want that clean-cut image. They've never cared for any of that stuff like long hair or beards. Give me a break. Things are different for Don. He thrived on having players in his class around him. He looked around and wanted to be as good or better than everyone else. Now that he's all alone, how can he keep producing? Opponents pitch around him. And when they're not pitching around him, there's nobody on base for him to drive in.

He told me he's talked with the Yankees about trading him. I think he'd prefer to go someplace like St. Louis, closer to his home in Indiana. He thinks he needs a better atmosphere, and St. Louis has always had guys who can get on base. When I left the Yankees, he said he wasn't going to sign with them again. Then after he did sign right before the '90 season, he said he had made a mistake. Even though George gave him the big money, George never respected him. Don used to dog George about that. He said he didn't need the money, he needed respect. George didn't respect people unless they won a pennant for him, and the Yankees hadn't done that since the '81 strike season. That's why George had so much respect for Reggie. Reggie's Yankee teams won, Don's Yankee teams haven't. Everybody's great when you win. You lose, no matter how good you are, you don't get respect.

If Don wanted respect, he didn't need to go any further than me. I know that man well, and he's a tremendous player. My locker was always next to his because I was Number 24 and he was 23. When he and I were on the same field, we clicked together. We knew one another. He wants to win. He's a true player, a true Yankee. In my opinion, he's conditioned and programmed to be a Yankee. There's something special about that. There's not another team in baseball where there's such a special feeling when putting on a uniform. The pinstripes are a big deal, and Don fits the image. My best buddies in baseball are Lloyd Moseby and Dave Stewart, guys I've known since childhood, but my favorite all-time teammate is Don Mattingly. He's like my brother, like an old friend from childhood. I really look up to him. I don't have that feeling with many players.

Don does it all: a great team leader, a great hitter, a great fielder. I don't care what anybody says; I have never seen a guy play first base as well as Mattingly—Mark McGwire, anybody. They talked about Keith Hernandez when I was in New York. Hernandez had a good glove, but Mattingly can do it all as a first baseman and has perfect instincts. He'll go down to the dirt to get everything, and he's got a nice arm because he came up to the majors as an outfielder. He's so good, the Yankees once used him at third base, and he's left-handed! He knows how to play and where to play.

If someone other than Don had won the MVP in '85, maybe I'd have been more upset. I still think I had a better year. I carried the team in the first half, and Don carried the team in the second half; the second half was more on the voters' minds. I actually finished third in the balloting. George Brett somehow snuck in and finished second, and I still don't know why. I thought that was a bunch of crap. Including the disgrace in '81 when Rollie Fingers got the MVP, I lost out on two trophies that I had a pretty good chance to win.

On the other hand, it was great being back with Billy that year. Needless to say, Billy's different. I've always avoided getting close to managers. A lot of players and managers like to get close to each other, but that's not for me. I don't make it a habit to go up to a manager and reveal my personal thoughts. I became that way in the minor leagues, when the makeup of my teams—managers, coaches, teammates— changed drastically from year to year. At the major league level, it's never the players who get fired, it's the manager. They'll dump the manager before they dump the twenty-five players, so I feel comfortable getting close to my teammates. If I were buddy-buddy with my manager and then he got fired, I'd get really hurt. In this business, a player never knows where his manager will be one day to the next. So from a manager, all I want is respect. Leave it at that. I'll respect the manager, but I won't be all over him emotionally, and that went for guys I had in Oakland like Jim Marshall, Steve Boros, and Jackie Moore. Same with all of them: I didn't get close.

Only one man broke through my barriers. Only one man got close, and that was Billy. But even that took time. Back in Oakland, Billy immediately got close to Mike Norris, whose best season came in Billy's first year with the A's. Billy thought it was important to get close to me, too. He used to plead to Norris, telling Norris to ask me if he could just be my friend. He wanted to talk to me about things other than baseball, about anything. Norris came to me and told me what Billy wanted, and my reply was firm. I said, "No way. I don't want to get comfortable with no manager, and that includes Billy." But Billy kept trying. We finally did get close, but it took Billy three months of trying. When it happened, it got to be so strong, nobody could rip us apart.

We finally accepted each other thirty thousand feet above sea level, during a team flight. Billy, man, he used to live it up on those team flights. He'd sit in first class, drinking booze and eating smoked salmon and caviar, high-styling all the way. Players always sit in the back of team flights, with the manager and executives sitting in first class.

One time Billy got up out of his big lounge chair and called back to me, "Rickey, c'mon up here and join me." I was hesitant at first. I didn't want my teammates thinking I was the manager's pet or anything. Reluctantly, I went up there and sat next to Billy. You know what? I ended up staying with him the entire flight. We talked and laughed for hours. With everybody else on hand, it was a bold move by him to invite me up there, and it was a bold move by me to say yes. That's when we began forming a bond that never broke.

I found out that Billy and I had a lot in common. We grew up in similar neighborhoods, me in a lower-class area of Oakland and him in a lower-class area of Berkeley. We lived there in different eras, but our homes were only about fifteen minutes from each other. We even played at the same public park, Bushrod, the one they later renamed Billy Martin Field. Neither of us had much money, and neither had a father to rely on. Just like in my situation, his father left his mother when he was an infant. I don't think either of us got close to a father figure when we grew up, but we both got extremely close to our mothers. Both of us were forced to be tough kids, and both of us got into a lot of fights. We were both little guys and worked hard for everything we received.

He used to tell me stories about the old days at Bushrod, about the troubles in what was his own 'hood. He lived in an area with both whites and blacks, so he grew up with the black culture; he once had a black girlfriend. Maybe that's why he got along so well with players of all races. It was in his breeding.

Our relationship evolved into one where Billy looked at me as his son. He wanted a baseball player for a son, and it was as if I was a player in his mold. He was the ideal player, a hustler, a gamer, a winner. I think I play the game the way Billy played, aggressively. He dreamed of having a son in his image, and I was that son. As a father, you want your son to be like you in a lot of ways, or at least have the potential or intention to be like you. In me, he saw all the things he was, as well as the things he wasn't. He saw all the things he'd wanted to be, but didn't necessarily have the talent for. I know he put his whole heart into getting everything out of me, and I know I gave it to him. We were meant for each other. Whereas he looked at me as a son, I don't think I looked at him as a father as much as a guide and adviser. He taught me. I learned so much from that man.

When people think of Billy, they think of a fighter, a drinker. But those people never knew the real Billy. They never knew the side of Billy I knew. If Billy had only one shirt, he'd tear it off his back and give it to you. That's if he liked you. If he didn't like you, he would be a bulldog. And that's what people remember about Billy, the bulldog.

Sure, he had a temper, but mostly because he wanted to win so badly. His drinking was his biggest fault. That's something he liked to do, and nobody could change him. Sometimes it cost him. Because he was such a diehard Yankee, heart and soul, anytime someone would dog the Yankees, especially someone in a bar when he was having a good time, he would get upset. That's how he always got into all those fights, not because he was drinking and just wanted to pick on somebody. It usually had something to do with the Yankees.

Billy's brawls were legendary. He'd fight anybody, anywhere. A topless bar in Arlington, a marshmallow salesman in Minneapolis. He even went after his own players, like the time he and Reggie tangled in the Yankees' dugout at Fenway Park. The fight I remember the most, because I was there, was in '85 on the night of September 21. It was in the lobby bar of the Cross Keys Inn in Baltimore. We were in town to play the Orioles, and I had stolen three bases that day during a 5-2 victory. After the game, several of us went out to relax and have some drinks. When you're a baseball player in a bar, someone always has something to say to you. Well, someone was messing with one of our pitchers, Ed Whitson, and Ed was trying to get this guy off his back. Billy came over and tried to break things up because Ed was his player. Billy was just trying to stand up for Ed. Ed was really upset with Billy anyway because he didn't think Billy had been using him enough. A couple of days earlier, Billy had taken Ed out of the rotation. Ed had signed a $4.4 million contract the previous winter, but he was upset at Billy and getting really paranoid about being rattled so heavily by the fans.

So when Billy came over to help Ed that night, it fueled an even bigger fire. Ed looked at Billy and screamed, "This is because of you." Then Ed and Billy got into a shoving match, and they got madder and madder at each other. Ed is six foot three, but size never mattered to Billy. Ed kicked Billy in the midsection, and Billy got furious and went after him. Ed was pushed outside by the hotel's security guards. Of course, Billy followed. When they got outside, one thing led to the next and Ed charged Billy and knocked him down. Fists were flying everywhere during the scuffle, and it turned out Billy was the big loser. His nose was bleeding, his right arm was broken, and some ribs were cracked. He had to manage the next game with his arm in a cast.

After the season ended three weeks later, Billy was fired once again. He was the scapegoat, but he wasn't the reason we failed to win the division. If anything, he overcame many obstacles and was greatly responsible for us doing as well as we did. We won ninety-seven games, but all that did was prove that a powerful offense alone wasn't enough to overcome the Blue Jays. We were just too exhausted, both physically and emotionally. We kept scoring a lot of runs, but it didn't matter. We'd lose. We had too many problems down the stretch.

Not only didn't George get us any pitching, but he continued to pound us pretty good in the newspapers. George kept saying things the veterans didn't like. He lashed out at Winfield for the way he played late in the season by calling him "Mr. May." George was especially abusive during a mid-September series in which we lost three of four to Toronto. He told the press we were an "embarrassment," that we should be "embarrassed" to take his money. George had his own way of trying to motivate a team, and his latest speech was another perfect example. The players didn't understand his method of motivation, and they got sidetracked. They thought he was pressuring them rather than support-ing them. Well, that was true, but that was his way of motivating a team. He thought he was motivating his players, but his players took him the wrong way. The man wanted to win too badly sometimes, but he had the right to say whatever he wanted. He was the owner. If I owned a team that wasn't playing up to par, I'd lash out, too.

A lack of communication was always a big problem. The players didn't talk directly to George too often. When he made his controversial comments, he said them in the papers. I saw him in the locker room only once or twice, and he hardly ever called anybody in for a one-on-one chat. He talked to reporters more than us. He actually telephoned the papers himself, or else he'd wander through the press box to make sure the writers knew exactly what was on his mind. He liked to be in the headlines, but there was really no need to worry about George. It was nothing but a bunch of talk. The players are supposed to forget about things like that when they walk between the lines, but too many players got confused and weren't able to let his words go in one ear and out the other.

To me, George was like anybody else. You had to know how to read him. You had to eliminate what he said about you when you went out onto the field. He wasn't a bad guy. Sure, controversy followed him around, but I got along with George. In fact, I've had no problem with any owners because I've tried not to involve myself in their business. From Charlie Finley to George Steinbrenner, I've had owners who had wild ideas about the game. Finley was more of a baseball man, and George was more of a businessman. Sometimes George's emotions got the best of him, and he lost his business sense because he wanted to win so much. He didn't care what something cost. He went out and spent money if he thought it would help him win. Unfortunately, his plans didn't always pan out, and his players didn't always appreciate him. But the owner's job is to do what he knows best, and the players' job is to do what they know best. If you can separate those two, you'll be all right. A lot of Yankees couldn't separate those two.

Unfortunately, some guys got really mad after reading George's comments about Winfield and the team, and they let that affect them.

Then, less than a week later, there was the Whitson fight. With everything working against us, we lost eight in a row and fell six and a half games out of first. But in the final days, we still had a chance to overtake Toronto. We played them the final three games, and a sweep would have forced a tie. But the Blue Jays clinched the division with the second to last game of the season, beating us 5-1 in Toronto.

A few days later, George introduced Lou Piniella as the new manager and gave Billy a front-office job. Billy also joined the Yankees' television broadcasting crew, so I was able to keep in steady contact with him while he waited in the wings for his next chance to manage the Yankees. That was a good thing about George. Unlike other owners, when he fired his managers, he kept them in the organization and usually brought them back on the field. It wasn't as much a firing as it was a rotation. Billy wasn't the only guy who managed the team more than once. George also recycled Gene Michael, Bob Lemon, Yogi Berra, and Piniella.

Under Piniella in '86, we had another good team, another good offense. But we had the same problem: no pitching. Phil Niekro was released, and Whitson was mercifully traded to the Padres in midseason. Otherwise, we were left with virtually the same staff. Maybe George didn't get any pitching because pitchers didn't want any part of George. The Yankees had a bad rep. Pitchers thought they couldn't concentrate on their job if they played for the Yankees because of all the feuding, the confusion, the pressure. Too much pressure. We had pitchers as well as non-pitchers who couldn't deal with it, but maybe it was tougher on pitchers. Whitson couldn't deal with it, and other pitchers saw what happened to Whitson.

Don Baylor was traded a week before the season started, but not for a pitcher. For Mike Easler, a designated hitter. Later in the year, we traded Ken Griffey. Everyone thought we'd get Tom Seaver in return, but we didn't. In fact, we didn't get any pitcher in the deal. We signed Tommy John, but Tommy won only five games that year. Our biggest pitching acquisition was Britt Burns, but he never pitched an inning for us. He was sent home in spring training with a degenerative hip problem. Our best pitcher was Dave Righetti, who set a record by saving forty-six games. But we needed starters other than just Ron Guidry, guys who could keep us in games while our offense went to work.

For me, '86 was nearly as good as '85. I stole eighty-seven bases, another Yankees record. I passed Maury Wills and Campy Campaneris on the all-time list, and I became the youngest player to steal six hundred career bases. *Sports Illustrated* made me its cover boy in July with this title: THE BRONX BURNER, LEADOFF MAN EXTRAORDINAIRE." I scored another 130 runs and set another career high in home runs with 28. I remained in the 20-50 Club and set a league record with nine game-opening home runs. The only stat that dropped was my batting average, but something funny happened to me that season. For some odd reason, the umpires changed my strike zone.

I had struck out only sixty-five times the year before, but I fanned more than half that in the first two months of '86. The umpires were calling strikes on pitches they called balls a year earlier. Pitches would sail by me at eye level, and they'd be strikes. As it turned out, the umpires had gotten together and altered my strike zone themselves. A *Sports Illustrated* article written by Peter Gammons quoted umpire Jim McKean as saying my zone was no longer based on my batting crouch, but by where I was when I stood straight up. That's ridiculous. My crouch is small, yes, but there's no way I can hit pitches over my head. McKean said, "A lot of people have thought we should have done that years ago." Later in the article, I found the true reason for the change. Another umpire was quoted as saying, "He ticks everyone off. We're all sick and tired of his showing us up and slowing down the game by stepping out on every pitch. He told us, 'We're going to have a meeting,' and we just laughed. No matter what he thinks, the game wasn't created for him."

What kind of nonsense was that? Umpires have no right to change the rules of baseball just because they don't like the way somebody plays the game. George was even more upset than me. He stood up for me. He protested to the league president, Bobby Brown, and met with Commissioner Ueberroth. He issued a press release that read,

There is no way the Yankees will allow Rickey Henderson to be selectively prosecuted. If in fact the quotes are accurate, I believe that McKean will be told by President Brown, and higher, if necessary, along with those responsible for the supervision of umpires, that Henderson's strike zone shall be the same for any player in the game, be it Dave Kingman or Kirby Puckett. I was a member of a duly authorized committee appointed in the late 1970s to pass regulations concerning umpires and the standardization of their rule interpretations. At that time, the strike zone was officially adopted to be 'between the nipples to the knee when the batter is in his own normal stance.' If Rickey Henderson bats out of a crouch, then the strike zone should be called that way. There should be no different interpretation of his strike zone.

George sent tapes of the bad calls to the commissioner. He wanted the umpires to define my zone, and I wanted to know exactly what were balls and strikes. My body is structured differently than most guys'. My upper body is short compared with my lower body. I'm a short person anyway, but my upper body, from my waist to my neck, is particularly short. The umpires eventually got the message, and one day Ken Kaiser and some of them took me into their dressing room and measured my strike zone. They told me one very important thing: If I remained in my crouch well before the pitch and well after the pitch, then they'd call strikes based on my crouch. But if I was popping straight up in the batter's box, they'd continue calling strikes on the high pitches.

The situation improved a little bit after that, but a lot of umpires were still squeezing me with high strikes. One of the reasons I hit so many home runs that year was that I was forced to swing at high pitches. If they were going to call them, I was going to hit them. I drove some of those pitches nine hundred miles. I even amazed Piniella with some of those home runs. Some went way back into the bleachers in right-center. Lou had been a Yankee a long time, and he told me he had never seen a player hit a ball so far into those bleachers. I hit some no-doubters. Oooh, they felt good. I even amazed myself.

The power game was relatively new to me, and I was digging it. I was happy, I was styling. I began to show some flair after they left the park. I didn't think about it. It just happened that way. Opponents called it hot-dogging, but I wasn't always conscious of it. Yeah, the umpires might have been partly responsible for all those home runs. On the other hand, I ended up striking out eighty-one times and hitting only .263, the lowest average in my career. I even got thrown out of a game for arguing a called third strike. It was the only time I've ever been kicked out of a game. I usually don't get riled on the field, but I truly believed it was time to stand up for myself.

The controversy reached a boiling point in mid-June when we were in Baltimore to play four games against the Orioles. In the first two games, I had three hits and three RBIs and we won them both. Despite all the news of umpires calling high strikes, I didn't strike out in either game. In fact, I walked four times.

That got Earl Weaver steamed. He was quoted in the local papers the next day as saying that I was intimidating the umpires into calling strikes as balls. Earl said, "They don't know what a strike is when he's up there in that crouch. Every time a pitch is called a strike he complains. They're scared of him. They don't want to be showed up so they don't call any strikes. They call a couple of strikes on him, and he gets the owner to go to the commissioner. We throw him strike after strike and he walks down to first."

Now that was a strange twist. Here I was, wondering why I had such a massive strike zone, and Earl comes along and tells the world the umps are on my side. I couldn't believe it. I always killed the Orioles, I hit what seemed like .700 against them. Why would I want to duck pitches against the Orioles when I always beat them with my bat? Earl used to try everything to distract me, but he never succeeded. After reading Earl's comments, I went out in the next game and collected two hits, two runs, and two steals and broke a 2-2 tie against Scott McGregor with a home run off the left field foul pole. Earl didn't know what hit him. After we beat the Orioles for the third straight day, I told the press I had dedicated the game to Earl.

A quick note on Earl. Earl was a great manager, but he had me busting up all the time. Sometimes players have a team they simply dominate. For me, it's been the Orioles, especially in my early years. I don't care if I was in the worst slump of the season; when Baltimore came in, I was gold. I could do nothing wrong. Eddie Murray used to say, "Rickey, I see you're in a slump. But don't worry about it. We're here." I used to make Earl go to the back room and cry. He cried, man. He tore his hair out. He'd tell me he just held a meeting to tell his guys not to let me beat them. "Don't walk him. Don't put him on base. Don't let Rickey beat us. Whatever you do, do not let Rickey beat us." It didn't help. I'd beat them with the bat, I'd beat them on the bases, I'd beat them in the outfield. I remember one crucial game. The Orioles were down by two runs, ninth inning, a man on second base and two outs. A guy hit a screaming liner into the corner, an automatic double. But I was cheating toward the line. I shifted to jet speed, picked up the ball, turned around, and fired a seed on one hop to second base. Got him. Game over. Oh, man. Earl was fuming. He told his guys, "I told you. Don't let him beat us."

Back to that big June '86 series in Baltimore. After our victories in the first three games, I hit another home run in the series finale, but we lost and left town three and a half games behind first-place Boston. As luck would have it, we headed back to New York for a three-game series against the Red Sox. We actually played Boston six times over the next ten days. I had nine hits and four runs in the six games, but we lost four of them.

The series at Fenway got pretty heated, and Roger Clemens had some words saved up for me. He and some of the other players didn't like the way I was playing, and I heard it from all ends of their dugout. Afterward, Clemens told the press the same story I keep hearing whenever a team gets frustrated after a loss. Clemens said I was trying to show up the Red Sox, calling me "a fashion show." At least he didn't call me a hot dog. He had never seen a guy with my kind of ability. That was Clemens's first full season in the majors, and he went on to have a great year. He won the MVP and the Cy Young Award, but he also popped off a lot. I told him, "Shut your mouth and do your job. You ain't been in this game long enough to be mouthing off."

We swept the Red Sox the final four games of the season, but it was little consolation because they still won the division by five and a half games.

My first two years with the Yankees were a bittersweet experience. I put together back-to-back solid years, totaling 52 home runs—I had only 51 in my first six years with the A's—146 RBIs, 276 runs, and 167 steals. On the down side, we finished a disappointing second both years.

I think back to what people were saying after I was traded to the Yankees. They said New York would kill me, that I wasn't going to be able to focus on baseball. I was coming from Oakland, and they thought the pressure of New York was going to flatten me like it flattened other guys. The people who thought those things didn't know me. They didn't know that pressure has never been a factor in my life. Pressure affects some people. It affected Ed Whitson. But it never affected Rickey Henderson. I know my abilities and strengths, and I know how to use the skills I've been blessed with, whatever the situation. In Oakland or New York, I was the same person. I might have known more about the game, especially the power game, when I was in New York. But I was the same person.

I confess, it wasn't easy being away from my family most of the summer. Back in Oakland, I'd always look behind the dugout and see Momma. With the Yankees, I'd glance into the crowds looking for Momma. It was instinct to look for her behind the dugout at Yankee Stadium. I knew full well she wouldn't be there, but I wanted to make sure. I phoned her quite a bit, which is only natural for any mother's son. She knew it was in my best interest to be playing in New York, and she supported me. My younger brother, Doug, was living in New York at the time, and I still had a few friends from my days playing Double-A for Jersey City, so I made the adjustment in time.

New York fans should be given a lot of credit. They're the most knowledgeable in the game. They know baseball, and they know the difference between good baseball and bad baseball. They don't enjoy bad baseball. One day they'll cheer you, the next they'll cuss you. It all depends on how you perform on that given day. Some of our players couldn't accept that.

To tell you the truth, the glitter and glamour of playing with the Yankees was less intimidating than I had expected. In New York, I was merely a piece of the puzzle. In Oakland in the early eighties, I had been a big hunk of the puzzle. In a way, I was fortunate Winfield was in the middle of his long-standing feud with George Steinbrenner. That took some attention away from me and made it a lot easier on other guys to play ball. The press had something else to write about. I wasn't constantly asked to explain myself because they had all sorts of other wild stories to cover.

My focus was on baseball and the team. The sideshows were secondary to me, so those first two years went rather smoothly. Little did I know that all hell would break loose in '87.

BRONX ZOO, INDEED

The chosen phrase in the summer of '87 was "jaking it." Man, I hated that phrase.

That was a time of my life I will never, ever forget. I mean, never. That was a sad, sad time, the worst of my life. It got so bad, I was ready to quit baseball, just pack up and leave it all behind me. My heart and soul were shattered, and I figured it was more important to keep my heart and soul than all the money the Yankees were paying me. Oh, I was so close to giving it all up. For the rest of my life, I'm positive I'll never suffer as I did in the summer of '87.

It was the year I was going to put it all together, be the all-around player I've always dreamed of being. I hit for average my first year with the Yankees. My second year, my average was down but I hit twenty-eight homers. This was going to be the year I was going to be the consummate player: average, home runs, RBIs, stolen bases, everything. I wanted it all. I wanted the MVP. I had come close to winning two MVPs already, and I was just itching for an MVP trophy to call my own. That was my intention long before the season even started. I reported to spring training at 185 pounds. Solid steel, not an ounce of fat anywhere on my body. I had worked over the winter like never before. I had trained hard and felt strong and unbreakable. I had even spent a lot of time studying videotapes of my batting crouch so I wouldn't get called on high strikes anymore. This was going to be a perfect season. Damn, I was even working on my bunting game. I told Don Mattingly that winter to stay healthy because I was going to score 150 or 160 runs. Nobody had scored that many since Ted Williams in 1949, but that was my plan. I wanted to hit .330 with 30 home runs and 100 steals.

I was tired of finishing second, and I was determined to top off my MVP year by playing in my first World Series. I had done a lot of things, but I wanted to be in a World Series. I had heard so much about Ernie Banks and Billy Williams, Hall of Famers who had never been in a World Series but said they'd trade in everything just for the opportunity to play in one. I didn't want to be in their shoes. I remember when I got to New York, Willie Randolph told me, "Rickey, when we get to the World Series, they'll open up the city to you. They'll give you the damn key to the city." That's all I needed to hear. I wanted to bring the Yankees back to the glory years. The year before, the Mets won the World Series, not to mention the heart of New York City. They had taken our people, and we wanted to get our people back home, back to Yankee Stadium. George Steinbrenner even found some starting pitching that winter, picking up Rick Rhoden and Charles Hudson. It was all too good to be true.

I had my year all mapped out, all in my immediate vision. An absolutely perfect year for me and the Yankees. Well, for the first two months of the season, that's exactly how it was. Perfect.

I beat Jack Morris and the Tigers with a tenth-inning double on opening day and never missed a beat. I was absolutely killing the ball, hitting ropes all over the park. Everything, as I had anticipated, was clicking. I hit .400 and scored twenty-six runs in April and ripped six home runs in one nine-game stretch. Only the steals were down, and that's because there weren't any opportunities. I had pounded out too many extra base hits, eleven in my first sixteen games. Boom, in the gap. Boom, down the line. Boom, out of the park. Triples, homers, doubles. There were just no bases to steal.

I continued to pound the ball in May, and I even got my running game back in a groove. By the middle of the month, I had stolen twenty-three bases without being caught once. Counting the end of '86, when I reached safely on my final eight tries, I had run up a total of thirty-one straight steals. I was just one away from tying Willie Wilson's and Julio Cruz's league record for consecutive steals when I got caught in Oakland leaving first base too early. I got a bad jump, and I was picked off by Curt Young. Young's a left-hander with a goofy delivery, and I took off when he threw over to Mark McGwire. The relay to Alfredo Griffin caught me at second. Man, I still think about that one. Why did I do that, anyway?

The mistake in Oakland didn't put a damper on my road to the MVP and the World Series. I ran up an eleven-game hitting streak in May and finished the month leading the league in runs, steals, walks, and on-base percentage. Listen, I was bad. And there was a feeling of invincibility everywhere in the clubhouse. The Bronx Bombers were in rare form. Mattingly, Winfield, and I were in our third season together, and we were peaking. This time *Sports Illustrated* put Mattingly on the cover, but I felt like I was the leader of the team. I had MVP written all over me. One game against the Rangers, I even stole Mattingly's curtain call. He didn't want to acknowledge the cheers and take a bow after hitting a grand slam, so I took it for him. We ended May with a 31-18 record, in first place by two games. It still had all the makings of a great year. The pot of gold was there for the taking. We were rolling, I was rolling. I was having the time of my life.

Then came June. And July. And August. And everything went up in smoke.

Up to that point in my career, I was fortunate to avoid any major injuries. Except for the strike season and my rookie season, I had played at least 142 games every year. I had missed only nine games the year before, and that's impressive for someone who puts his body through torture. I'd sit out a game here, a game there, but I had never been seriously hurt, never even been on the disabled list.

That all changed in '87, but it was far more than just the injury that caused this season to go down as the very worst of my career.

At the beginning of June, I was out of the lineup for five games with soreness in my right leg. I had been told I should sit out two weeks. But we were in a pennant race, and I was brought back to the lineup for a night game in Milwaukee. I remained cautious. I had the leg all wrapped up, and I moved from center field to left field in order to limit my running. I felt fine through seven innings. We were losing 9-3 in the eighth when I led off with a walk against Teddy Higuera. I was trying to get something going, just trying to reach base. But then, for some wild reason, Lou Piniella flashed the steal sign. I couldn't believe it. Tom Trebelhorn, who had taught me so much about the running game in the minor leagues, was in his first full year managing the Brewers, and I've always wondered what he thought about that call as he sat in the opposing dugout. I probably shouldn't have been in the game that long. Not only was it one-sided, but I was trying to be careful with my leg. Remember, I had just sat out five games. It was no time to steal. I wanted to do things at my own pace, but the Yankees were looking for a championship and needed me doing the things I had done earlier in the year. I wanted a championship, too. We all wanted a championship and a World Series. But I wasn't ready. My strength was about 75 percent. But there it was, the steal sign. Nobody was holding me on first, so I got a good jump for second base. The pitch was fouled off. Okay, fine. Trebelhorn moved his first baseman close to the bag. That's the end of it, or so I thought. I got back to first, and Lou flashed the steal sign again. Uh-oh. Once again, I took off for second. The lead, the jump, the sprint—the pain.

Halfway to second, my leg collapsed. The pop was probably heard all over County Stadium, a sharp charge right up my leg. Oooh, this was serious. This was something I had never felt. I left the game right there and limped off the field and into the trainer's room. The Yankees placed me on the disabled list. They diagnosed the injury as a strained right hamstring. They said the cord of muscles from my butt down to my thigh had overexerted. They said I'd be back in two weeks. They had no idea.

Making matters worse, Mattingly had left the same game two innings earlier with back spasms and also went on the disabled list. It wasn't long before we dropped out of first place. The team left Milwaukee and returned home to play Toronto in a big three-game series, but the Blue Jays swept the series by outscoring us 22-3, knocking us two and a half games out of first. Without me or Don, we began to fall apart. Nothing was working. Pretty soon, Winfield and Claudell Washington fell to injuries, and we were really in sorry shape, hurting in every sense of the word.

As for me, the leg never seemed to improve. The Yankees thought I'd be back in two weeks, but I needed almost two weeks just to pick up a bat and take some swings. I was in such pain, I even missed seven games against my favorite team, the Orioles. I was much more careful this time, knowing what had happened in Milwaukee when I made a quick return to the lineup.

After missing twenty-two games, I still wasn't in top form, but I returned in the final days of June anyway. Things never got back to normal. I played every day for the next four weeks as well as the All-Star Game in Oakland, but nothing like I had in April and May. Something still felt out of place, and it showed in my performance. I stole only three bases and hit just .250 in those four weeks, dropping my season average below .300. I couldn't hit or run with authority, and I went eighteen games without a single steal, the longest dry spell of my career. In one game I even grounded into two double plays. That's not me. That's not Rickey. My dream of winning the MVP had been long forgotten.

I tried to tell the team doctor, John Bonamo, and the trainer, Gene Monahan, that I wasn't right, that my leg wasn't improving. They said my hamstring was just tight, that it should heal soon. It didn't. At the end of July, life really began to get ugly. Everybody seemed to be forming their own conclusions about me without checking with anybody who knew, specifically me.

The whole time, I found myself caught in the middle of a long-standing feud between George and Lou. Lou said some things in the papers, George said some things in the papers. I was confused. My teammates were confused. There were newspaper quotes from unnamed players questioning my injury, though not one teammate ever approached me man to man, so I've never known if those comments were legitimate or not. I received nothing but support from guys like Mattingly, Winfield, and, most importantly, our captain, Randolph. Those guys tried to tell the press that something was definitely wrong with me, but it never sunk in. As a result, there was tension everywhere in the clubhouse, and everyone could feel it. But nobody could feel what I was feeling, the sharp pain remaining in my right leg that forced me to play far below my standards.

The medical people were rubbing the leg and doing all they could on the outside, but this pain was inside, deep inside. The situation got so bad that I decided to work on the leg myself. After leaving the ballpark, I'd be up until 3:00 in the morning working with ankle weights to get my strength back. I also called Momma for advice. She was still working as a nurse, and she explained to me that internal injuries take much longer to heal than the other minor injuries I'd had on the outside of my legs.

I wanted to get better, but I realized I couldn't get any better by playing every day. I hinted over and over that the disabled list would be an acceptable option. Finally, during a close game at Comiskey Park in late July, I was in such extreme pain that I left in the seventh inning for a pinch-runner, a rare way for me to end a game, but the suffering got to be too much to bear. I had been playing in pain for a month, heavily favoring my leg just so I could be in the lineup. But the only thing I received in exchange was skepticism. I felt bad that entire game. One inning, I didn't even feel strong enough to go from first to third on a single to right field, and later I came up limping after bouncing into a double play. By the time I was replaced by a pinch-runner, I had absolutely no strength left at all.

A couple of days later, Lou actually wrote my name into the lineup. "Wait a minute, Lou," I told him. "I can't play. You see me. You see how I am." Lou thought I was healthy, but that's what he was being told. Believe it or not, the medical staff still said nothing serious was wrong with my leg. They didn't understand the severity of the injury. Everybody who examined me told me I was okay. It was clear that nobody was listening to a word I was saying, most of all Lou. When the press asked Lou about my health, he'd say, "Go ask Rickey."

Things seemed to worsen by the day. One day I heard that George was thinking about suspending me. Suspending me? For what? For being hurt? Unbelievable. He felt that if nothing was wrong with me I wouldn't play, then he could suspend me. But he didn't know firsthand that there was something wrong, something terribly wrong. George hadn't been told the entire story. He had received the medical reports from the doctors and trainers that I could play, so he naturally wondered why I wasn't out there. He was mad.

Fortunately, George himself stepped in. He wanted a second opinion, which was fine with me. I wanted the issue resolved more than anybody. I told George to spend some of his money and send me to a specialist, someone who could prove I wasn't, in Piniella's words, jaking it. Hey, this was New York. New York has some of the best doctors in the world. Let's go to one of them. The trainers could do only so much; they don't have the equipment for x-rays. Let's get a second opinion, a third opinion, a hundredth opinion.

George sent me to a specialist, and that's all we needed. What that specialist discovered pretty much cleared up any doubts anyone had about me. He put me through some extensive x-rays, which confirmed that I had torn a couple of inches of my hamstring. That's right, a tear. Not a pull, not a strain, not a cramp, but a tear. All along, it was torn. I had torn it back in Milwaukee in early June. And here it was, late July, and the Yankees were finally having me x-rayed and realizing the extent of my injury.

I had been limping around for a reason. I had been telling everyone I was in pain for a reason. No one believed me, not until the specialist's report circulated. Then suddenly everybody was in my corner, behind me 100 percent, the manager, the trainers, the doctors. It was amazing how such a seemingly minor miscommunication can turn into a huge mess. Everybody apologized. "Oh, I'm sorry, Rickey." I'm sorry, Rickey? Hey, I wasn't lying through all of this. I had tried to tell everybody all along. I had depended on people I thought knew about hamstrings. Everyone apologized, but the damage had already been done. It wasn't easy to get over. I still came out of it embarrassed and humiliated.

George flew to town in his Learjet to make one of his rare clubhouse visits. He wanted to find out the story for himself. He came into the trainer's room, patted me on my back, and asked about my problem. I was very honest and told him everything. He realized it was no hoax. He told me not to worry and to concentrate solely on getting better. That was the end of it. Just like that, I was on the disabled list. Just like that, I was able to rest the leg, which I should have been doing all along. No longer did anyone have any doubts about whether I was hurt.

From what I was told, the Yankees' medical staff was unable to detect the tear because of the thick muscle structure in my leg. George later admitted I wasn't built like other players. He admitted I have thicker muscles than most guys, making it difficult for the doctor or trainer to fully detect the exact problem. Why they didn't take x-rays right away, I'll never know. Maybe medical people are used to guys getting hamstring pulls and returning within a couple of weeks. I can't always do that. I'm a thoroughbred. I have a different body type, a running back's body type, and I guess I heal differently. My recovery schedule is different. I had to get on Monahan, the trainer, for this big mess. I told him, "Gene, there's one thing I hate about you. You should have known I was hurt, but you let the press dog the hell out of me." Here I was, busting my butt for him as well as the rest of the team. So why did he let the press dog me the way they did? He didn't stand up for me. That's the way it is. Trainers want to rush you out there as quickly as they can because the owners apply pressure to get players right back on the field.

Shortly after I went on the disabled list for the second time, trouble surfaced once again. With the team in Detroit and me back in New York, George revealed the entire story. Not to me, not to Lou, but, typically, to the media. He issued a press release on August 8 that covered a variety of subjects, including his problems with Lou and his general manager, Woody Woodward. The last part of the release went like this:

Now, as far as the Rickey Henderson matter is concerned, I was leaving that in the hands of our team doctor and trainer and general manager until Woody called me and told me that Piniella wanted to disable Henderson right away because he was "jaking it," his teammates were mad at him and he wanted guys who wanted to play and he would win it all without Henderson. I told Woody to get me the doctor's report—that I wouldn't disable a man as punishment—and despite what Piniella thinks, I don't think we can win it without Rickey Henderson. Woodward agreed on all counts. I said we should talk to Lou. We did, and Piniella told us he wanted Henderson traded as soon as possible. Both Wood and I agreed, "No way." We told him we were going to be sure that Rickey was okay and if not, then we were going to disable him. Woody said he would not affix his signature to any disabling papers as punishment. Dr. John Bonamo told us on Thursday that Rickey might be ready for the weekend in Detroit by Saturday or Sunday. Then on Saturday he reversed that completely and said Rickey's leg was sore with some swelling and told us the prognosis was not good. I went to the training room personally—told Rickey of our plans—patted him on the back and then told some writers that Rickey was indeed hurt, that he was not jaking it, and that we would disable him, but for the right reason. End of chapter.

Not quite end of chapter. I still had some unfinished business to clear up with Piniella. George had basically confessed that Lou had no faith in me whatsoever. He wanted me traded, gone from the team. It didn't make for good morale between player and manager. He thought I was putting on a big act, telling a big lie. He thought I wasn't hurt. Jaking it? That devastated me. I've never had a manager make those accusa-

(*Above*) Accepting the trophy for winning the Athlete of the Year award at Bushrod Park, 1968. That's Kerry Bland on the left and Lamont Whitehead on the right.

(*Right*) My senior picture at Oakland Technical High School.

(*Above*)The 1975 Oakland High School baseball team, with Coach Cryer standing at the far left and my buddy Fred Atkins standing second from right. Easy to find me? Right. Third from left, bottom row.

(*Right*) Here I am in '79, just twenty years old and a mean, green rookie.

(*Above*) Me and my all-time favorite manager, Billy Martin, discuss strategy at the '82 All-Star Game in Montreal.

(*Above*) Breaking Lou Brock's season record with my 119th steal in '82 at Milwaukee.

(*Below*) Posing with my Japanese connection, all-time homer champion Sadaharu Oh (left) and Tadashi Matsumoto, who led the Japanese league in steals a couple of times in the early eighties. One of my goals is to break the world steals record belonging to Yutaka Fukumoto, who has 1,065 lifetime steals.

(*Above*) Together with my good friend Dave Winfield after joining the New York Yankees in '85.

(*Right*) With my all-time favorite team-mate, Don Mattingly, during my first trip back to Oakland as a Yankee.

(*Left*) Two players who I hope will get into the Hall of Fame some day: me and Pete Rose at the '86 All-Star Game in Houston.

(*Below*) An All-Star cast in an All-Star mood: Dave Winfield, Willie Randolph, Don Mattingly, me, and Dave Righetti.

(*Left*) President Bush visits the Fenway Park clubhouse shortly after the '88 election.

(*Right*) Obliging the autograph seekers in '89 during my final Yankees spring training at Ft. Lauderdale.

(*Below*) The Oakland fans give me a warm welcome in my first game back with the A's after the June '89 trade. (*Martin E. Klimek photo.*)

(*Above and right*) As the A's new leadoff hitter, I was back on track, stealing 52 bases in 58 attempts in the second half of '89. (*Martin E. Klimek photos.*)

In the '89 postseason, I made it a point to torment opposing pitchers, including San Francisco's Scott Garrelts in Game 3 of the World Series. Nobody wanted to win the world championship more than I did. (*Robert Tong photo.*)

(*Left*) For obvious reasons, our division-clinching celebration was much more animated than our celebration after winning the Earthquake Series would be. (*Robert Tong photo.*)

(*Right*) My first World Series victory meant a trip to the White House and a visit with Barbara Bush

Here's my reaction to a memorable play against the Yankees in which I scored from second base on a routine groundout to the shortstop. (*Martin E. Klimek photo.*)

In 1990 I put together one of my best overall seasons to win my first MVP award. I swung well all year and continued to run at a record pace. (*Martin E. Klimek photo.*)

Stealing my
939th career
base to surpass
Lou Brock on
the all-time list.
(*Martin E.
Klimek photos.*)

My first reaction was to hug Lou, who had given me so much inspiration throughout my career. That's Momma sprinting onto the field from her seat behind the A's dugout.

Posing for a couple of baseball cards, one a "Dream Team" card and the other a "939" card with Lou Brock. *(Courtesy The Upper Deck Co.)*

tions. I knew Lou was given bum information, but I still didn't understand why he didn't believe my side. Why did he think I didn't want to play? Why would I bow out of an MVP season? Why would I agree to sit on the bench and allow somebody else to take my position? Why would I not play when there was an excellent chance to go to the World Series? None of Lou's thinking made sense, and his refusing to believe me definitely made matters worse.

When the team returned from the road trip, after going a disastrous 2-8 to fall into third place, I made it a point to meet with Lou. We kicked the press out of his office, shut the door, and decided to go at it man to man. I was mad. It was as if I was going to kick his butt, or he was going to kick my butt. Of course, it never got that far. I reminded him that he once told me he hadn't ever seen any player like me, that I was the best he ever had. But now I'm jaking it? I asked him to clear up the story and tell me who said all those things. At first, he said it was George's doing. I told him, "Get George on the phone right now and we'll have a press conference right here in your office." Then he conceded that he said those things, but under pressure. He said he didn't know what he was saying. He said he suspected I was really hurt, but that George had put so much pressure on him to get me out there on the field. He had no pull. He apologized, and that was it, end of the meeting. I said, "Okay, I'm gone," and I left his office.

Finally, management supported me. But this was mid-August. If management had supported me from the beginning—and I still feel strongly about this today—the team would have been much better off. If I hadn't made a quick return in Milwaukee, and if Lou hadn't asked me to steal that base with a 9-3 deficit in the eighth inning, I might not have torn the hamstring. If they hadn't messed with me, I could have been back at 100 percent much sooner. All I needed was rest. But I guess they couldn't afford to give me rest. They gambled with me and lost.

Unfortunately, it affected the team in the long run. We won for a while, but we were never really the same. There wasn't the same spark. There was a feeling that something was missing. By the time I returned to the lineup in September, I had been on the disabled list for five weeks. We were 16-17 without me. Remarkably, with a month to go, we were still only four games behind first-place Detroit, and we were relatively healthy, with Mattingly, Randolph, and Winfield back from injuries. I still wasn't at 100 percent, but I wanted to give it a try the final month.

In the end, it proved too much of a monumental task to overtake Detroit and Toronto. So much had happened, with all the clubhouse problems. George and Lou feuded right down to the buzzer, and we all knew Lou would be fired. Throw in all the injuries, and it was a lost season. We finished fourth.

It was ironic that it started as the best year of my career, yet ended as the worst. It was the worst I've ever felt in baseball. I had put so much effort into preparing for that season, and nothing turned out right. If it weren't for the injury, I would have done everything I had planned. But it was so bad, I didn't even lead the league in steals, the first time that had happened since I broke into the majors and played a half season in '79. I missed sixty-seven games, so Harold Reynolds got to be the steals champ.

People have asked me if the '87 season would have been different had Billy managed. The answer is a resounding yes. We would have won the division with Billy. Billy was one of the few people in Yankee management who understood what I was going through, who believed in me. He had always asked me how I felt, and I had always told him. He thought they should have handled it all differently.

That's one of the biggest reasons I respected Billy so much. He didn't care if we were on top of the world or beneath the world; he wouldn't force me to play if I was hurt. He'd just tell me to be honest with him. If I couldn't play, I wouldn't play. He's the only manager of the Yankees who was like that. Unlike Lou, he wouldn't have played me when I wasn't ready, and he would have been able to handle George because he had so much experience with George already. Lou didn't know how to handle George. With Billy, we could have accomplished a lot of good things. As expected, Lou was fired after that season. Once again, Billy was in control. I knew things had to improve.

Looking back at '87, they couldn't have gotten any worse. When spring training rolled around, there were plenty of reasons to be optimistic. Because I played the final month of '87, I knew I'd be healthy for '88. To make sure, I bought $10,000 worth of exercise equipment and worked on my body all winter. Billy knew I was strong again, and he put me back in left field full-time—Claudell Washington was better in center because he kept running into the wall in left. Billy predicted that I'd steal a hundred bases. Mattingly made a bigger prediction, that we'd finally win the championship. I thought the same way. It was a good enough team to win. This may sound repetitive, but we were more determined than ever. I was supposed to concentrate heavily on the running game because we had picked up another big bat, Jack Clark. That was George's doing, adding even more power but no more pitching. He said we'd have a better overall offense. We didn't need another slugger, we needed a pitcher. Still, we had Billy, and Billy was good at working with pitchers.

I had a solid year, hitting .305, but my home runs were down to just six. With Clark in our lineup—it was his first and final year in New York—I had made an effort to concentrate more on the running game. Randolph had really gotten on me for my home run stroke, and Billy, a running manager, told me to stop thinking about the long ball, so my game plan in '88 was to run. I stole ninety-three bases, breaking the Yankees record for the third time.

Keeping up to standards, I had another good year against the Orioles, which was probably the reason their manager began making excuses for my play. It wasn't Earl Weaver this time, it was Frank Robinson. Frank accused me of using an illegal bat and had it checked by the umpires. That was a new one, but Frank was just like Earl. Because I always beat up the Orioles, he'd do anything to distract me. All kinds of things happen to a manager when you dominate his team, so Frank checked my bat. He said he discovered black marks on the baseballs, but they didn't find anything wrong. I had never been checked for illegal bats before. I don't even think it's an advantage to load up a bat. You've still got to hit the ball on the money, and a loaded bat won't do you any good if you don't.

Once again, we jumped to a fast start in '88. After our great spring—we were 22-10 in exhibition games—I hit a home run in the opener and drove in the game winner the next day, and we went on to win our first five games. We finished April at 16-7, and I was on a wild pace to score 160 runs and steal just as many bases. Then, as always seemed to be the case in New York, we got sidetracked. Not only was there another series of injuries—Clark went down right away—but Billy got into more trouble with his drinking.

It was early May when Billy got into his much-publicized brawl at the topless bar in Arlington. After getting tossed from a 7-6 loss to the Rangers, he went out drinking, took on the bouncer, and got bounced out of the bar. He showed up at the next game with cuts and bruises all over his face. Later that month, Billy had more umpire problems. He kicked and threw dirt at a rookie umpire, and the league suspended him three games and fined him a thousand dollars. We were still in first place, so his job was safe. But then we started to lose a few games, and Billy didn't last through June. After we lost three straight games in the final inning at Detroit, Billy was gone. It was the fifth and final time he was fired from the same job.

In Billy's final game, I singled and scored in my first at bat and hit a solo home run in my second. Billy took me out of the game because I had a leg cramp, and we wound up losing 3-2 in ten innings. It was an eerie feeling. I missed two of those three Detroit games, and Billy was fired. I missed two months in '87, and Lou was fired. I missed the first ten games of '85, and Yogi Berra was fired. I felt bad. I've always wondered how things might have been had I been healthier in New York. It's almost as if I'm needed in every inning of every game. I just wished the team had played better when I was out of the lineup.

Billy's replacement was, well, Lou again. The problems from '87 were in the past, so I openly accepted Lou's return. It's a case where players shouldn't let management have a negative effect on them. The two sides should remain totally separate. When Lou came back, his job was to manage, mine was to play. So I didn't waste time worrying about him. Unfortunately, the three losses in Detroit knocked us out of first place, and we never got back on top for any significant length of time.

I played well after Billy left. Lou and I had a meeting to make sure we put to rest any talk of '87, and he assured me he wouldn't rush me back from any injuries. I continued to swing the bat pretty well the rest of the season. I was hitting .320 when Billy was fired, and I raised my average to .334 over the next two months, despite having a slew of nagging injuries. One game that I was sitting out, we were tied with Cleveland in the ninth inning, and Lou needed a pinch-runner. I volunteered. I ended up scoring the winning run in a 4-3 victory, and Lou thought it was a big deal that I volunteered. Hey, it was no big deal. I knew that was a time I could carry out that role without risking further complications. My priority was for the team to win games, and Lou's only choices were me and Joel Skinner. It was really no choice at all.

Things were running smoothly in Lou's first few days, but confusion returned at the midseason break as I was about to make my seventh straight appearance in the All-Star Game. I was chosen as one of the starters, joining Mattingly and Winfield on the American League roster for the game in Cincinnati. All three of us had been nursing minor injuries, but we were all healthy enough to play. George was upset. He wanted us to stay back and get rest. We all brushed it off as just another one of George's tantrums. Winfield and I got hits in the game, and we beat the National League 2-1. Although I knew George's spiel was no big deal, it once again affected some guys who thought it wasn't George's place to speak out.

We finished July a game out of first place, but we lost twenty games in August and virtually fell out of the race. Boston went on to win the division after beating us three out of four in mid-September to open up a lead of six and a half games. We ended up in fifth place, the lowest finish in my four years with the Yankees.

One reason '88 was such a disappointment had to do with a topic that's not usually talked about, but I talked about it. It's alcohol abuse. We had guys abusing alcohol on team flights, and it might have affected our play. Some of those flights, man, we'd get in at 5:00 in the morning and play that day. I didn't see how a body could adjust to that; I didn't think it was possible. It was wrong. Some guys were being abusive. I didn't see how you can drink as much as they drank on some of those planes—not all the guys, just some—and be ready to play the next day's game.

I discussed the problem with the press the following spring. I admitted that I did some drinking on the flights, but I knew when to cut it off. I knew my limitations. I was quoted as saying, "Alcohol doesn't leave your body overnight. You have to know when to party and when not to party." I didn't mention any names, but the papers came out with three pitchers involved, Neil Allen, Bob Shirley, and Tim Stoddard.

Some guys got upset and took exception, especially Dave Righetti, a close friend of the three pitchers who came up to me to talk about it. I told it like it was. I told him, "I was right there drinking with y'all, but I knew my limitations. I knew when to stop. I wasn't going to drink heavily if I knew we were going to be in at five in the morning. I had to go to the plate. All you pitchers, you didn't have to go out there every day." I also told him, "I don't feel we could be at our best as a team. I don't believe any team should do that. But the fact was, we were doing it."

As the '89 season approached, I knew I was down to the final year on my contract. I was going to be eligible for free agency the following winter, and the Yankees had to decide whether to re-sign me or trade me. Mine wasn't the only roster decision to be made. George started cutting expenses everywhere, and the makeup of the team changed drastically. George traded Rick Rhoden and Jack Clark, lost Claudell Washington to free agency, and released Ron Guidry and, early into the season, Tommy John. He also signed Steve Sax to play second base and forced our captain, Willie Randolph, to leave after thirteen great seasons in New York. To top it off, Winfield was lost for the season with a bad back.

The Yankees were beginning to fall apart. All the signs were there. I realized it even before arriving at spring training. Our new manager, Dallas Green—the sixth managing change of my Yankee career— ripped into me even before I got to camp. The comments weren't the kind you want to hear from the boss before you even start your job.

Before I get to Dallas Green, let me explain something about spring training. The deadline for players to report is written into the contract of every player and enforced by the commissioner's office. It's always the first week of March. If a player under contract doesn't report by the deadline, he can be fined. There are no other deadlines, period. However, teams can come up with their own dates for players to voluntarily show up. That's fine, but it's not mandatory. Teams can't force players to show up early.

With that in mind, a player is not late if he shows up after the team's voluntary date and before the actual deadline. I had never been late to spring training. I hadn't always been around when the other players showed up early, but I had never been late. As it is, spring training is too long. Even by showing up on the deadline day, players would still have more than a month to get ready for the season. The system is a holdover from the old days when players used spring training to lose weight and get in shape. Nowadays, most guys show up at spring training ready to play and don't need a full six weeks of training.

By now, my managers have all but stopped worrying about when I show up because they know I report in better shape than anybody. Other players might be able to use those first few days, but I'm already beyond that stage. If I reported to spring training out of shape, then when I reported would be a big deal. Call it what you want—Rickey Time, Rickey's rite of spring—but I've felt that way from the beginning, and people have come to expect me to report in great shape.

One manager who had a different view was Dallas Green. Dallas was different in a lot of ways. He wasn't a Yankee man like Billy or Piniella or Berra. He came from outside the organization when George named him the manager for '89. Of course, Dallas didn't last a full season with the Yankees. He wanted George to give him all the power to run the club. He didn't want any interference, but that ain't the way it works with George. George fired him in August.

Dallas seemed to take turns criticizing every player on the team, and I was apparently going to be the first in line. He didn't even wait until I got to spring training before he let me have it. He told the press, "Rickey Henderson is not going to run the Yankees in 1989. Dallas Green is. We sent letters to everybody about when to report. Maybe Rickey can't read."

As if that wasn't bad enough, he made a stupid reference about me and Margo Adams, the groupie who was in the news for her relationship with Wade Boggs of the Red Sox. The remark was uncalled for, but it proved to be just one of many criticisms he made about his players. He was more into tearing down players than building them up, and he never apologized for anything. Nobody agreed with his approach. Things were never right with that team. It was a bad scene. We ended up having a lousy time together.

It was frustrating from the very beginning. Even though I was going to be a free agent after the season, nothing was working for me. I was pressing like crazy to do well. I see myself as a sparkplug who gets a team going, but I never got started for the Yankees that year. I put together a ten-game hitting streak in May, boosting my average from .245 to .272, and I led off a game against the White Sox with a home run for the thirty-sixth time in my career to break Bobby Bonds's record. But I struggled over the next month. Then I heard the talk. The Yankees set the All-Star break as the deadline to sign me. There was also talk of a trade, though I never thought New York would let me go. In my first four years, we were 361-285 and averaged 90 wins a season. I produced when my legs were healthy, and we would have won more if I had been healthy more. But the Yankees had a losing record through the first two months of '89, and they were in the middle of a rebuilding process and looking for younger and cheaper guys. I had mixed feelings about a trade because I had built some strong ties with the Yankees, especially with Mattingly. I'd miss Mattingly.

Fortunately, I had a no-trade clause written into my contract when I signed back in '85. If I hadn't had that clause, they would have had the option to trade me anywhere. I could have gotten out of bed one day and found out I was being shipped to another city. With the clause, I had the authority to choose where I'd go if traded, and that clause proved to be very valuable.

The first word of a trade involved the San Francisco Giants. Syd Thrift, who was hired in the spring to run the front office but didn't even last the season, was the one who told me the Giants were interested. But the Giants wanted me to bat fifth and play right field. They already had a leadoff hitter, Brett Butler, and a left fielder, Kevin Mitchell. The move would have meant going back to the Bay Area, but I had to shoot that down right away. I had never batted fifth. I had never played right field. And I had never been in the National League. Were they kidding me? I was putting up the worst stats of my career, and now they were talking about bringing me to Candlestick Park? That would have been a goofy move and could have screwed me up even more. The Giants were offering Scott Garrelts and Candy Maldonado, but I suggested they take Jesse Barfield—he'd have been more suited to bat fifth and play right—and I decided to stay put and continue to take my chances in New York.

I had always wondered about playing in the National League. Several players who came over from the National League told me my style was more suited for the National League. I'm a good fastball hitter, and the National League was a fastball league with good, hard-nosed ballplayers. A lot of players who came over thought that the National League was better, that the pitchers challenge the hitters more. To me, baseball is baseball. I never thought the National League was any better. But this was not the time to find out. I told Syd that if I went to the National League, I wanted to start fresh, join a team before the season started. But don't send me there for just three months.

I had a good relationship with Syd—we had met when I signed out of high school and he was the A's chief scout—and he finally asked me where I wanted to go. I told him, "If I go anywhere, I want to go home, back to Oakland." I had talked to my momma, and she encouraged me to come home. She knew it wasn't working for me in New York. But Syd said he couldn't trade me to Oakland because the A's flat out weren't giving quality in return. So I told him I wasn't going anywhere.

Syd continued talking with the A's, but I never thought a deal was close until I ran across Tony Phillips during a rain delay in Baltimore on June 15. We were waiting to finish the final game of the series, and Tony dropped by because the A's were in town to play the Orioles the next day. Tony came down to the clubhouse and asked me, "Have you heard we're close to getting you?" I said, "No way." I knew the A's were looking for a leadoff hitter to replace Luis Polonia. Polonia was a slap hitter, weak in the outfield, and he wasn't the leadoff hitter they wanted, one who could start a big rally. I was more of what they were looking for.

A few days later, Syd told me he had arranged for a deal with Oakland. I said, "Fine, I'll go to Oakland." That was it, a three-for-one deal with the Yankees getting Polonia and two relief pitchers, Greg Cadaret and Eric Plunk. Poor Eric Plunk. He was also involved in the trade five years earlier that sent me from the A's to the Yankees. Ironically, the man who traded me to New York, Sandy Alderson, was the same man who brought me back to Oakland.

I learned a lot in New York. I learned to fit in. In my early years with Oakland, I was the whole show, but I was only part of the show in New York. There was Mattingly, Winfield, Griffey, Baylor, Randolph, Clark, Yogi, Billy, Piniella, George. Even on my final day with the Yankees, there was something brewing with George. He told me he was upset to hear I was traded, and to hear what the Yankees got for me. He phoned me long distance and told me he hadn't given his consent to the deal. He said, "Rickey, I don't know what they've done. I told them to get pitching, but I didn't tell them to trade you." He said he had been out of town and that by the time he heard about the trade, it was too late for him to block it. Even toward the end, I got along with George. I wasn't one of those guys who left the Yankees, then ripped George. He treated me right, and that's all I asked of him. But I still wanted to prove to him that it was a mistake for the Yankees to let me go.

When I was traded on June 21, I was among the leaders in steals, runs, walks and on-base percentage, but that was all overshadowed by a batting average that had sunk below .250. The day of the trade, I went from six and a half games out of first place with the Yankees to two games into first place with the A's. I had more than a half season to play, and the A's had a good chance to go to the playoffs for the second straight year. I could still be a free agent after the season, so the prospects were very bright in all regards as I headed home to Oakland.

EARTHQUAKE

When I rejoined the A's, I joined a team on a mission. These guys were out for revenge, and they had the same goal I had: not just playing in the World Series, but *winning* the World Series.

One year earlier, the A's had won the American League pennant for the first time since my childhood days in the mid-seventies when Reggie Jackson and those guys won three straight World Series. But in the '88 World Series, the A's were destroyed by the Dodgers in five games. Everybody called it a huge upset. Everybody but me.

There were definite flaws in Oakland's attack, and I should know. I was right there at the Oakland Coliseum, sitting behind the Dodgers' dugout and talking it up with some of their players, especially Mike Davis, an outfielder who had been my teammate with the A's in the early eighties.

The one thing the Dodgers did that the A's didn't do in that series was play fundamental ball. In every phase of the game, the Dodgers executed the fundamentals. They had a better strategy when it came time to score runs, plus they received some incredible pitching. But I think the A's made it easier on the Dodgers' pitchers. The A's were a more powerful team with the ability to hit a lot of home runs, and that might have cost them. It seemed as if everybody in the lineup was trying to hit a home run every at bat. Once the opposing pitchers realize that, it's easier for them to get guys out.

The A's downfall was not having a guy who could intimidate the Dodgers. They had nobody to provide spark, to get on base and start a rally. The only game they won was because of a home run—Mark McGwire ended Game Three with a blow off Jay Howell. Other than that, McGwire had no hits. Jose Canseco had only one hit, a grand slam in the series opener, but the A's lost that one in the ninth inning when Kirk Gibson took Dennis Eckersley out of the yard. Everybody said Gibson's home run—which followed a walk to my pal Mike Davis— was the difference in the series, but I disagree. The difference was the A's thinking about nothing but the long ball. They were simply out-played.

During the series, I sat with my good friend Fred Atkins. It was ironic. Fred kept telling me how the A's could have won the series if I were playing. Fred said, "Rickey, if the A's had you right now, they'd win it, because they don't have anybody to get on base and make things happen." He said that, honest to God. It didn't help the A's that they started four different players in left field—Dave Parker, Luis Polonia, Tony Phillips, and Stan Javier. Fred was right; the A's probably would have won that series if I had been out there. But I didn't give it much thought at the time. I was too concerned about making the Yankees champs to worry about how the A's could win the World Series.

But eight months later, that's all I thought about, the A's and the World Series. On June 22, 1989, I joined the A's in their mission to win the World Series.

There were some concerns about me returning to my hometown. Some people can't play in their hometown because of all the distractions, because of all the friends coming up and asking for tickets and asking to go out partying every night. But I never let any of that interfere with my job, not when I was with the A's earlier in my career and not when I returned in '89. I've always told my friends that the season is my time, that I'd hang out with them when the season's over. When the season's over, I've got four or five months to be with my friends. That's why I don't make it a habit to take care of thirty different ticket requests every game; that would take forever to set up, and it would only be a distraction. I've got a job, and my job's the priority.

If anything, playing in my hometown is an advantage rather than a disadvantage. I love Oakland. It's home, and I love my home. The Bay Area is where I want to live and raise my kids. This is my past, my roots. People who guided me in my childhood still live in the Bay Area. Plus, my family has the opportunity to come out to the ballpark and see me. Mostly, it's an opportunity and even a thrill for my momma. She's living out not only my dream, but her dream, and playing in Oakland gives her a chance to keep all her children together. I feel comfortable working close to home. Look at Dave Stewart. He was born and raised in Oakland, and he didn't do his best pitching until well into his career, when he joined the A's. If everything else were equal, I'd prefer to play in Oakland more than in any other city, so it was a bonus that the A's were a contender when I returned to Oakland two and a half months into the '89 season.

When I arrived, Tony La Russa didn't have to alter the lineup much at all. I replaced Polonia as the leadoff hitter and left fielder—I didn't have to play center because Dave Henderson was out there. Dave moved down in the order, and Carney Lansford replaced him as the number-two hitter.

I had known of La Russa only as an opponent, and he didn't like me because of the way I played against him and beat him. I'd always heard about how he was such a players' manager, but I didn't have any firsthand experience with the man. I'll never forget what Tony did my first day back with the A's. He sat me down in his office and told me, "Rickey, don't feel that you have to respect me." My reaction wasn't surprising. "Say what? Don't respect you? You're the manager. I've got to respect you." He said, "I want to earn your respect." I said, "Fine, Tony. Whatever you say." I didn't fully understand what he was talking about until after the season was over. But first, let's get on with the season.

My first game with the A's was June 22 at Oakland. It was a long day for me already, flying in from the East Coast, and then I found myself playing a four-hour extra-inning game against the Blue Jays. The game was nationally televised, so it was in the early evening, beginning at 5:00; I barely had enough time to learn the A's signs. I received a warm welcome from the Oakland fans, then went out and got a couple of hits, scored a run, and made a running catch in the eleventh inning to rob Ernie Whitt of extra bases. Fred McGriff ruined things by hitting a home run in the thirteenth to beat us 4-2. Even though it was a bittersweet debut, it was great being in an A's uniform for the first time since '84. I wore Number 22 until Ron Hassey agreed to give me number 24—in exchange for a couple of expensive suits.

I knew everything about that ball park, but I still felt like a rookie again. It was like I was coming up to the majors for the first time, as I had done with the A's exactly ten years to the month earlier.

Right away, my average went up. I did basically the same things I had been doing in New York, but the ball was suddenly falling for base hits. I felt I had swung the bat pretty well in my final three weeks with the Yankees, but the balls weren't dropping. With the A's, the balls dropped. I immediately put together a six-game hitting streak. In my third game, I was forced to learn the forearm bash, the A's way of shaking hands after hitting home runs. I homered off Dave Stieb, then knocked forearms with every member of the team. Man, it hurt. That first home run was important because I had a bet with the other Henderson, Dave, that the first guy to hit a home run after my arrival would be called "the real Hendu." But my homer off Stieb didn't change much; everyone was still referring to Dave as Hendu (and everyone still does). I continued hitting anyway. In my first seventeen games leading up to the All-Star break, I hit .413 with twenty-two runs, thirteen walks, eleven RBIs, eleven steals, and three home runs. My average, .247 when I left New York, shot all the way up to .282.

What did it all get me? A fine, that's what. Rene Lachemann, our third-base coach, fined me in Kangaroo Court. He said I was embarrassing the club. I was hitting .413, and all I got was a lousy fine for twenty-five bucks. But that was all right. I was having fun being back home with the A's, so I gladly handed over the cash.

I hit from the git-go, but there was one big problem in the early going. We weren't able to break away from the pack. Several guys were in slumps, and several others were on the disabled list, including Jose Canseco, Dennis Eckersley, Walt Weiss, and Bob Welch, and Canseco and Eckersley weren't due back until after the All-Star break. We lost the first two games I played and five of the first seven. The team had been flat before I arrived, coming off a road trip where repeated failures on offense led to six losses in ten games. The A's might have been better than the Yankees, but it took time for all the parts to come together. In those first seventeen games before the break, we were just 8-9.

We ended June a half game ahead of the Angels and ended July a half game back of the Angels. We had all kinds of injuries—I was probably the only healthy player in the lineup—and just couldn't shake those guys. We started winning after the break, but the Angels were just as hot. We were neck-and-neck all the way to September. I remember in late August when we trailed by a half game and were playing Minnesota. We were losing 4-3 when I opened the eighth inning with a bunt single, then stole two bases and scored on an infield hit. We went on to win 5-4 in ten innings. It was a big, emotional game for us, but all it did was keep us a half game out of first because the Angels also won that day.

Two days later, we beat Detroit and the Angels fell to Kansas City, shooting us into first place for good. We were 18-10 in the final month, and it was all over. The final blow might have come on September 20 when we beat the Indians 8-6. I opened the game with a home run, then in each of my next two times at the plate I walked, stole two bases, and scored on a sacrifice fly. After that, we blew away the Angels by increasing our lead almost by a game a day. The Royals made a surge and passed the Angels in the standings, but we still won the division by seven games.

One game in our stretch drive that stands out above the others was a 2-0 win over Nolan Ryan in Arlington. It wasn't that I had a big hit or big stolen base in the game. The thing that stands out the most is a strikeout. When Nolan fired a full-count fastball by me in the fifth inning, it was the 5,000th strikeout of his career. I wasn't disturbed or ashamed. I was honored. Hey, this man had struck out 4,999 guys before I got up there. He wasn't doing anything to me that he hadn't done to everyone else in the game. Man, Steve Carlton's the next closest guy, and Carlton retired with 4,136 strikeouts. It wasn't that Nolan was breaking a record or anything; he already had the record. This was just something their club drummed up to promote Nolan. It was a wonderful tribute to the man.

Afterward, opposing players came up to me and joked about it. "Hey, Rickey, I saw where Nolan got you." I'd say, "Well, thank you. I loved it." There were no hard feelings that I'd go down in history as Nolan's 5,000th victim. Maybe there would have been some hard feelings if this were my only mention in the history books, but I already had a lot of other records to go with it. This was an honor, a thrill.

As I stepped into the box, I asked Nolan's catcher, Chad Kreuter, "If he beats me here, can I have the ball?" I actually wanted to take the ball out to the mound and shake Nolan's hand on the spot. But Kreuter said, "No, I want it." He was a rookie, so I guess it was an even bigger thrill for him. I didn't pursue it because I didn't really think Nolan was going to strike me out. I had always made contact off him. I had his number. Before that game, Nolan had struck me out only three times in my career—he made it number four when I became the 4,998th victim in the third inning. As the game went on, the guys in our dugout were tripping off who would be Nolan's 5,000th victim. He entered the game needing six more strikeouts, so we knew it was going to be one of us. I just didn't think it was going to be me.

With 4,999 in the book, Nolan went into a cold spell, a cold spell for him, anyway. He faced five straight guys without striking out anybody. Walt Weiss, the number-nine batter in the lineup, grounded out to end the fourth, then I came up to begin the fifth. The count got to three balls and two strikes. I told myself I wasn't going to go down looking at the final pitch. So anything close, I was hacking. That next pitch was probably Nolan's best of the day. I don't think anybody on the planet could have hit it. He screamed a fastball—they clocked it at ninety-six miles per hour—barely on the outside and at the knees. It wasn't the hardest pitch he threw all day, but he spotted it so damn well. The umpire would have given it to him if I didn't swing, so I swung. And I missed. I missed bad. Maybe I tried to hit it too hard, I don't know. I do know that the field was immediately packed with players congratulating Nolan for his 5,000th strikeout. Kreuter ended up with the ball and ran it out to Nolan. But that was okay because we still got the win, and I still got to shake Nolan's hand.

The next day, I ran into Nolan and his family at a nearby restaurant called Black Eye Pea. In fact, he bought me lunch. He told me he didn't think I'd be the one. He said, "Out of your whole team, I could've bet the house you weren't going to be the one to strike out." He gave me one of his I-was-there T-shirts that commemorated his 5,000 strikeouts. I was more than happy to wear it around our clubhouse. Nolan is a great person, and it was an honor to play a part in his big day. I had hoped I could return the favor by setting the career steals record off him, especially because I had never stolen a base off him before. If I could do that, then he could come over and shake *my* hand.

The Rangers were out of the race in August, so Nolan's 5,000th strikeout was their final reason to celebrate. As for the A's, we still had a lot of baseball to go. We clinched the division on September 27 with a 5-0 win over Texas—my first champagne party since '81—and then waited for either Toronto or Baltimore to win the other division. On the final weekend of the season, the Blue Jays won back-to-back games over the Orioles for the right to face us in the playoffs.

I ended up tops in the league in walks and steals, tied for the lead in runs, and third in on-base percentage, and my average was almost fifty points higher in Oakland. The numbers weren't bad at all considering my slow start, but the real damage was going to be done in the playoffs.

That playoff series was one of the most emotional you'll ever see. It was also the most fun I've ever had as a baseball player. To this day, I vividly remember every game of that series. Maybe it's because I played such a significant role in each of the games.

Let's start with Game One. I was 0-for-2 but still made the key play of the game. It was tied 3-3 in the sixth when Jim Acker hit me with a pitch to load the bases. That's the last thing you want to do to me, hit me with a pitch. Lansford grounded a ball to shortstop that could have ended the inning, but I prevented the double play by knocking down Nelson Liriano at second base with a hard but clean slide. Liriano threw the ball away, and two runs scored. I got a great jump because the first baseman was playing in, and Liriano was surprised I got to second so fast. That gave us the lead for good, and we won 7-3.

In Game Two, I was 2-for-2 with two walks. After each of my walks, I stole both second and third and then scored. Through the first two games, I already had six steals. We won 6-3.

Game Three was our only loss. I helped the team to an early lead after walking and scoring the first run and then doubling, stealing third and scoring the second run. We led 3-0, but I didn't reach base again and we lost 7-3.

Game Four is remembered for Jose Canseco's deep home run into the fifth deck at Toronto's Skydome, but I hit a couple of two-run homers myself. One traveled about 430 feet to dead center, straight over Lloyd Moseby. We won 6-5.

Game Five was the finale, and I scored the first run after walking and stealing second. I later tripled in another run, and we won 4-3 to clinch the pennant.

I couldn't believe how enjoyable that series was, those five spectacular games. Don't tell me anyone ever had that kind of series. I was more excited about just being there than the performance I was having—and I was having a wonderful performance. Eight steals, a postseason record; Lou Brock set the old record in a series that lasted seven games. Seven walks. Eight runs. A .400 average. An on-base percentage over .600. In one stretch, I reached base eight straight times, another record. It wasn't tough to pick an MVP for that series. When it was over, I was so far above cloud nine that I had to ask my teammates what I had done. I couldn't even focus on my accomplishments until it was all over. To do so well at such a high level with the entire world watching is an unreal feeling, a dream come true for any ballplayer. And I was living it, for the first time in my life.

Unfortunately, the Blue Jays didn't appreciate my performance as much as I did. Kelly Gruber and Ernie Whitt popped off about me and Dave Parker because they didn't like the way we were beating their team, dominating their team. They didn't like it that Parker took forever to move around the bases after his home runs, and they didn't like the way I kept taking extra bases on them. In the second game, I stole a base so quickly that Whitt, their catcher, didn't even get a throw off. Because there was no throw, I slowed down to a walk before touching the bag. Whitt cussed me out and said I was showing them up by not running all the way to the bag. That wasn't the case. Like I've said, my legs are my game, and I'm going to preserve my body every chance I get. Sliding takes a toll on the body, and so does pulling up quickly, so I went into the bag slowly. Gruber didn't like any of that either, and suggested that if he were on the mound, he would start drilling me and Parker. When I hear that stuff, it makes me want to steal even more bases. That's one of the reasons I didn't stop running until the series was over.

Gruber and Whitt were just frustrated. They didn't know how excited I was. That was my first playoff series in eight years, since the strike season of '81. I was pumped. Like I told Joe Carter during the '91 season—Joe wasn't with Toronto in '89, and the '91 playoffs were his first—"Make sure you enjoy the playoffs, whether you win or not. Get fulfillment out of it, because nobody ever knows if you'll be back there again." I hadn't been there for eight years, and that turned out to be the greatest time in my baseball career.

There was nobody on the A's who wanted to go to the World Series more than me. Most of my teammates had played in the '88 World Series, and they were out to seek revenge against the National League because they had been embarrassed by the Dodgers. I wasn't around in '88, so the World Series was brand new for me. I wasn't going to be satisfied unless we won it all. Some people say just getting to the World Series is good enough because nobody remembers the playoff teams that lost, but everybody remembers the teams that went to the World Series. Well, I say people remember the team that won the World Series a lot more than the team that lost the World Series.

Our opponent was the San Francisco Giants, which was nice because I'd be able to stay at home the entire time. My home in Hillsborough is actually much closer to Candlestick Park than to the Oakland Coliseum. When we began the series with the first two games at the Coliseum, I sensed the Giants were one of those teams just happy to be there. We proved we weren't that way. We never missed a beat, playing the Giants even better than we played the Blue Jays. I went 5-for-8 in the first two games, and we outscored the Giants 10-1. I was the frontrunner to win another MVP trophy.

I was sitting in the john, taking care of business, at 5:04 P.M. on October 17, a half hour before the start of Game Three. Whenever people meet someone from the Bay Area, they always seem to bring up 5:04 P.M. on October 17, and they ask where you were and what you were doing. I don't like that question because I always have to give the answer. Anyway, I was sitting in the john when suddenly there was a tremendous amount of shaking in the clubhouse. My immediate thought was that the Candlestick crowd was getting ready for the game. I'd been through many California earthquakes, and this one wasn't like the others. This one kept going. That's why I thought it was just the crowd whooping it up. I was getting my mind into the game when one of the clubhouse guys came racing into the room and told everybody to clear out, that there had been an earthquake. I opened the door of the stall, and there was mayhem, guys running every which way and dust from the air vents being blown all around. I was told again to get outside. An earthquake. An earthquake! By then I was a believer. And, oh brother, I rushed outside with everybody else.

When we all got out to the field, we had no idea how serious this was. We soon learned. With most of the stadium's power knocked out, we watched news reports on portable televisions that some fans had brought along. We watched in horror as they showed scenes of the Bay Bridge, a connection between Oakland and San Francisco that had collapsed, and the Marina District, a section of San Francisco that was burning down. At Candlestick, where 62,000 people had gathered, all seemed to be well, but it didn't take long to realize there would be no game on October 17. The players began to escort their families out of the stands. I had many family members there, and I brought them down to the field. Right away, we walked up the right field line and straight to the parking lot. Forget the clubhouse. We all left in our uniforms. The team had chartered some buses from the Coliseum, and most of the players piled in and returned to Oakland, but I wasn't on board because I had come straight from my home. The drive didn't take the normal twenty minutes. It took almost the entire night, and that was just getting out of the parking lot.

I was one of the lucky ones. The earthquake was measured at 7.1 on the Richter scale, but everything in my house was intact, the lights, the TV, the shelves. Not a single dish in the kitchen had fallen. Others weren't so lucky. Dozens of people were killed, and the financial losses were in the billions of dollars.

There was talk of postponing the World Series several weeks or even canceling it. Some players even said they wouldn't mind if they didn't play another game until spring training. I never felt that way. The community needed an uplift because it was being torn apart emotionally as well as physically. We were the answer. The community truly needed us. Canceling the World Series would be just another reason to feel sorry. By playing, there was reason to cheer, reason to rally around each other, reason to feel proud again. The city of Oakland needed us even more than San Francisco needed us. Oakland was much harder hit than most other areas in northern California. The Bay Bridge collapsed on Oakland's side, and Oakland's downtown was in shambles. The city had taken a pounding. To top it off, Oakland was in financial ruins already, and this certainly didn't help matters. Because of that, we were part of the medicine, the cure. The commissioner, Fay Vincent, made a wise decision when he announced that the World Series would be delayed only ten days.

It wasn't easy to get back into the spirit of baseball. In fact, I had missed the first workout after the quake because bad phone lines made it impossible to get through to the A's offices. I never knew about the workout. I took some heat for that, but I had been spending my time stocking up on necessities like food, water, and batteries just in case something else happened. Other players didn't have to worry as much because they weren't permanent residents of the Bay Area; they lived there only during the season.

Once we worked out a couple of times, I realized that the team was as hungry as ever to win the World Series. La Russa did a good job forcing us to stay together as a unit. While the Giants continued working out at Candlestick, he packed up the whole team and chartered a flight to Phoenix to spend a couple of days working out under the sun at our spring training facilities. The Giants didn't think it was necessary to go anywhere, but that was the best thing that could have happened to us. It kept us close, and it kept us focused on baseball. Plus it was fun. I had spent spring training in Fort Lauderdale, so this was my first trip to Arizona since I was traded to the Yankees. The fans in Arizona got a big kick out of our presence because they had never seen big-league baseball in October.

The delay between Game Two and Game Three allowed me to give my legs a rest, so I was feeling quite strong when we returned to Candlestick on October 27. The team quickly proved we hadn't lost our strokes. We crushed the Giants 13-7 and closed it out the next day with a 9-6 victory. Four games, four wins, fifteen days to do it. A lot of people think the earthquake lessened our moment of glory, but I believe the earthquake made the World Series much sweeter than if we had swept the Giants under normal circumstances. The earthquake made the games more meaningful to the people in the Bay Area. We had lost a lot of spirit from the tragedy, and we were bringing the spirit back to the people through baseball. It wasn't much of a consolation, but at least it was something to take people's minds off the disaster.

There was no question that we were the best team in baseball, and there was no question that nobody was as happy as me. I had been close to winning many times, but this was my first World Series. Not only was it a sweep, but I hit a whopping .474. In my nine postseason games, including the five playoff games, I had a .441 average with fifteen hits, twelve runs, eight RBIs, and a perfect 11-for-11 in steals. I was coming off a playoff MVP, and I could have been the MVP in the World Series just as easily. In fact, in my own eyes, I was the MVP. But the award went to our ace pitcher, Dave Stewart. It was incredible that we had so many guys doing so many great things—Dennis Eckersley, Carney Lansford, Mike Moore, Dave Henderson. But the MVP was between me and Stew. Stew felt he deserved it, but I thought I deserved it. I thought I did it all in those four games. I remember that before the last game, some writers told me all I needed was a couple of hits and the trophy would be mine. They agreed that Stew and I were neck-and-neck, so Stew came up to me and said, "Rickey, I want you to go out there and go 0-for-0, get four walks but no hits." I said, "Sorry, Stew, I can't do that." Parker was there. He and I were playing dominoes in the clubhouse, and I told him I wasn't going to walk at all. In fact, I told him, "I'm hitting the ball over the fence in my very first at bat." He said, "Right, Rickey, now take your move." I said, "Watch and see." Sure enough, Don Robinson got behind in the count, and he threw a 2-0 pitch that I skyrocketed out of the park. I took a peek at Parker while rounding the bases, and he was falling off the bench cracking up. Just like Babe Ruth himself, I called my shot.

I ended up getting more than a couple of hits; I fell one double shy of hitting for the cycle. In fact, I was robbed of a cycle in my last at bat when Matt Williams backhanded a ball on the third base line and threw me out. It had double written all over it. I still homered, tripled, singled, and scored two more runs, so naturally I was thinking the MVP was mine—that is, until I walked into the clubhouse and saw Stew holding the trophy. "Oooh, Stew," I said, "that was for me." Stew didn't even pitch in that final game, having beaten the Giants in the first and third games, but he got the hardware. I think I would have been more disappointed if I hadn't known Stew so well, having grown up with him in the same neighborhood. Yeah, I was happy for Stew, but I think they at least should have given the award to both of us.

That year was an unreal year for me. I had experienced the entire spectrum of ups and downs, starting all the way at the bottom with the Yankees and rising all the way to the top with the A's. I finally proved I could play with money on the line. I never made it to the playoffs in New York, so I never got that chance. Me, Mattingly, and Winfield always thought we could do well in the postseason, but we never had the pitching to get us there. I would do the same kinds of offensive things in New York, but our pitchers would lose the game in the late innings and no one would remember a thing. Deep down, I think the Yankees knew they had made a mistake by trading me. I think George Steinbrenner wished he had blocked that trade.

After the World Series, I walked into La Russa's office and reminded him of what he had told me my first day back with the A's, that he had wanted to earn my respect. Nothing made me happier than telling Tony face to face how much I respected him. He earned my respect and then some. Tony was as good to me as Billy Martin had been.

Unfortunately, Billy never managed again. His time in '88 proved to be his final go-round. On Christmas Day, on my birthday, two months after the World Series, Billy passed. All my family was with me at my condominium in Oakland, having our Christmas dinner. Someone from the family heard the news on the radio coming over and told us that Billy had died when his truck skidded off an icy road in upstate New York. I said, "Nah, you're crazy." We turned on the TV and found out it was true. I was stunned. I was heartbroken. He was such a big part of my life. We had been through so much together. What a big loss this was. Billy was special, a special human being, a special manager. He had taught me a lot about the game, a lot about life. I respected him as a person, not just as a manager.

After we got the word about Billy, we said our prayers, cried a little, and tried to go on. I was devastated, but I tried to think back on what my grandmother had told me before she passed earlier in the year. She was so close to me, but she told me not to cry or feel bitter when she died. She told me to enjoy myself. That's the way I try to be when people close to me pass. Sure, I had my moments when Billy died. That's only natural. But you try to go on with your own life. That's what we all tried to do after we heard about Billy. We carried on with the day. The room was full of kids, my nieces and nephews, and it was still Christmas Day.

George Steinbrenner helped set up Billy's funeral at St. Patrick's Cathedral in New York. Mike Norris and I had planned to be there, but we couldn't get a flight because of snowstorms on the East Coast. Instead, we attended the service his sister arranged in Berkeley, at a church and then at her home.

Had Billy not passed, he would have gotten a chance to manage the Yankees for the sixth time in 1990. I have no doubts about that.

MVP

When I arrived at spring training the following season, I was the recipient of a playoff MVP trophy, a World Series ring, and a new contract. I had avoided free agency by signing a four-year deal with the A's worth $12 million. I wanted to stay in Oakland. This was the team, the city, that gave me new life, so I gave the A's first crack at signing me, fully aware that the Dodgers and even the Yankees were also interested and willing to sign me for much more money. In retrospect, I almost wish I could have been a free agent the following year. Before I signed, I was skeptical because I had a hunch that the market would take off even further because of baseball's billion-dollar television contract that was going into effect in 1990. Sure enough, a lot of other guys, guys who seemed to be only average players, were signing contracts for three million dollars a year. After I signed, La Russa made me a promise that made me feel much more comfortable about the contract. He told me, "We'll take care of you" if I kept up the good work and continued to sink from the top of the salary charts. I kept that in mind throughout the upcoming season.

By the end of spring training, I knew I was going to be the league MVP. Before the '89 playoffs, I told Dave Parker, Dave Henderson, Rene Lachemann, even my buddy Fred Atkins, that I'd win the playoff MVP. And in the final game of the World Series, I had called the home run before it happened. Now I was predicting an MVP year. I had never predicted an MVP year, but I had a strong feeling about 1990.

Six months later, I was putting the finishing touches on my best all-around season. I had done in '90 what I would have done in '87 if that season hadn't been interrupted by the hamstring injury and all the controversies with Lou Piniella. I finished April at .338 and never dipped below .320. I combined all the facets of my game, collecting sixty-five steals and twenty-eight home runs. I was even second in the league in slugging percentage, and that was virtually unheard of for a leadoff hitter.

In May, I became the American League's all-time steals champion. I tied the sixty-eight-year-old record belonging to Ty Cobb on May 26 and broke it three days later. That was a real honor, breaking a record of a guy who played before Babe Ruth. Luckily, I swiped both bases in Oakland. I remember back in '82 when Billy Martin's plan for me to break the season record at home backfired, and I didn't want that to happen again. Ironically, I had a very good chance to break Cobb's record at the same park where I ended up breaking Lou Brock's season record—Milwaukee. I began an eight-game road trip needing six steals to match Cobb's record of 892. It was a long shot, but I've certainly stolen six bases in eight games before. As it turned out, I bagged four steals on the trip and returned to Oakland trailing Cobb by just two.

The funny thing is, I still almost failed to break the record at home. After tying the record by taking third base uncontested against Cleveland—no throw, no slide—I went into a pivotal game against Toronto on May 30. The last game of the home stand was the following day, but it had a good chance to be postponed because there was a flow of rain showers that had already wiped out another game that week. I began the sixth inning with a double and then noticed the catcher calling for a breaking ball. This was my chance. I took third uncontested. Again, not even a throw. I lifted the base out of the ground, lifted it to the skies, and later presented it to my first pro manager, Tom Trebelhorn.

If people thought I'd be slowing down that season at the ripe old age of thirty-one, they were mistaken. Only five catchers threw me out stealing. Twice I scored from third base on pop-ups to infielders, one being Cal Ripken, Jr. and the other Harold Reynolds.

My most memorable baserunning play came against the Yankees, when I scored from second on a routine grounder to the shortstop. That's right, all the way from second base. We were down 1-0 in the eighth when I doubled off Jeff Robinson. Lansford, the next hitter, hit a grounder to Alvaro Espinoza. The game easily could have been over if I hadn't scored. It was late in the game, a do-or-die situation. I got a great jump off second. When I got to third, I looked back at Espinoza and noticed him double-pumping. That's exactly what I was looking for, having watched him do that when I was with the Yankees. I hesitated briefly, but when he double-pumped I decided to keep running. Don Mattingly knew I was going, but he had to wait for Espinoza's throw. Plus, because Mattingly is a lefty, he had to make a backward turn before relaying home. Carney was out easily, and Don's throw home was on the money. It was one of the very few times I've slid headfirst into home. Bob Geren was blocking the plate, so I slid around him and caught the plate with my hand. The umpire shouted, "Yes, you're in there." I was so jacked, I pumped my fists all the way back to the dugout. That tied the game, and I won it in the eleventh when I drew a bases-loaded walk off Eric Plunk.

That win was our sixth straight over the Yankees, and we went on to beat them in each of our twelve meetings that season, becoming the first team in history to sweep a season series from the Yankees. I think I might have beaten them at least four times myself. Twice at Yankee Stadium, I hit a pair of home runs. One game I distinctly remember. My first three times at the plate, I looked bad. Guys in the Yankee dugout, especially Mel Hall, were all over me. They were laughing it up because they knew how much I wanted to succeed in New York. My fourth time up, Mike Witt was blowing the gas by me, and I wanted to get him so bad. He fell behind, and he was coming in with more gas, so I swung hard and, *ka-boom*, took him to the triple deck in left field. That tied the game at two-all. Next time up, Lee Guetterman tried to rush something by me on the outside, and I took him to the monuments over the wall in left center. The ball bounced over the monuments and into the bleachers, way out there where the ambulance parks—farther than the three-decker. After that, the Yankee fans were really behind me. They shouted things like, "The Yankees should've never traded you," "When are you coming back?" and "They should've traded George instead." The next day, second pitch of the game, Tim Leary fired the ball behind my back. I stared back at him. "C'mon, man, there's no need for that."

And there was Mel Hall, out in right field, still laughing away.

As the season wore down, the batting title was in my grasp, but I got cheated out of it. George Brett won it after sitting out several games down the stretch so he could preserve his average. I didn't think that was right. I was among the hitting leaders all season on a team that stayed in first place month after month. George is a great hitter, a Hall of Fame hitter, but he didn't start hitting until the second half with the Royals already in last place. George was trying to become the first player to win batting titles in three separate decades, so he was getting the sympathy vote. George didn't catch me until mid-September, and by September 25 he was leading me .330 to .320. After that, he started sitting out to preserve his lead. There were times I could have sat out to protect my average. But I played, and I played hurt. My right thumb had been sprained in early September, and I was in pain every time I picked up a bat. That's the reason I didn't break the career steals record that season; sliding headfirst could have damaged the thumb even more. People have dogged me about sitting out when I'm hurt. Hey, I was hurt that entire last month. But I was in the lineup till the very end. Cecil Fielder made me a special pad to protect my thumb so I could play, and I played.

We were running away with the division, and the biggest thing left for me, aside from the upcoming playoffs, was securing the MVP trophy. Fielder was hitting forty-seven, forty-eight, forty-nine home runs, and I figured I'd have to play every day to win the award. I had a choice between trying to win the batting title by packing it in, or winning the MVP by playing out the season. I definitely didn't want to pack it in, and the MVP was more important than the batting title anyway.

With the bad thumb, I could barely swing the bat as it was, and my decision to keep playing backfired on me when George asked out of the lineup four of the Royals' final five games. He wouldn't play against left-handers, and he sat out most of a series against the Angels because they were throwing guys like Chuck Finley and Mark Langston. He couldn't hit lefties like he could hit righties.

With all the things stacked up against me, I still could have won the batting crown. The last day of the season, George was out of the lineup for a game in Cleveland. He did put himself in later, but he singled and right away took himself out. By the time our final game started, I needed to go 3-for-3 to pass George. I didn't want to take a walk, so I was going to swing at anything close. The day before, Jim Abbott had walked me on four pitches, and I cussed him out all the way to first base. I yelled at him, "You know what's at stake. Try to get me out. Don't just give me ball four like that." That really fired me up. I can imagine what Billy Martin would have done if he had seen that. His head would have blown up. On the final day, I needed a miracle. But I struck out in my first at bat—on a pitch about two feet out of the zone. Now I needed to go 4-for-5. I singled my next at bat, but then grounded out. That was that. George beat me by four points, .329 to .325.

I still respect George because he's still a great hitter, but I do think he should have battled me game by game. I would have played if I were in his position. If you're going to win it, you're going to win it. Julio Franco could have sat out to preserve his lead over Wade Boggs in '91, but Julio said, "Forget it." He kept playing and ended up hitting a lot higher than Boggs. There's the famous story of Ted Williams entering the final day of the '41 season hitting .400, but refusing to come out of the lineup to preserve his average, then getting six hits in a double-header to end up at .406.

A bigger prize than the batting title, of course, was the MVP. I had a chance for the MVP in two other seasons—'81 and '85—and if I didn't get this one, I don't know what I would have done. That would have been too much to take. If I didn't get this one, I probably wouldn't have thought about another MVP the rest of my career—I would have just given it to someone else if I won it. Fielder ended up hitting fifty-one home runs, but I still felt my season was better. Well, the third time for me proved to be the charm. Both Cecil and I were named on all twenty-eight ballots, but I finished 31 points ahead of him, 317 to 286. It proved my point that the game had changed. When I broke into the majors, the MVP went only to the power hitters, never to the little guys who helped the big guys get the pitches to hit. Now here I was, Rickey Henderson, MVP of the American League. The biggest individual honor for a baseball player, and I was the guy. Not winning in '81 and '85 made this MVP much sweeter.

As for Fielder, he now knows exactly how I feel. He finished second in the MVP voting again in '91. First I beat him. Then Cal Ripken beat him. He thought he should have won both times. I know how he feels. I went through the same thing myself. I deserved it twice before. I had finished third and second before finally finishing first. There's one thing I can say to you, Cecil. The third time will be the charm.

With the regular season over, we still had this matter of the postseason. After becoming the first team in twelve years to win three division titles in a row, we swept past the Boston Red Sox in four straight playoff games. Wasn't even in doubt. They had the best team average in baseball, but our pitchers gave them only four total runs. Dave Stewart won the MVP after twice beating Roger Clemens. Stew had dominated him so much over the years that Clemens went bonkers in Game Four. He fell apart and turned goofy when things weren't going his way in the second inning. He was on course for another loss to Stew when he started cussing out the plate umpire, Terry Cooney. Cooney ejected him, and then Clemens's behavior really got out of hand. I had never seen anyone carry on that way on a baseball field. It was a pretty ugly display, so it was a good thing that was the final game of the series.

I had a good series, hitting .294, but I really took off when we played the Reds in the World Series. The press had made a big deal of me going against Lou Piniella, who had left the Yankees that season to manage the Reds. It was hard to forgive him for that big mess in '87, but it had been three years now. I had tried much earlier to let it rest. Anyway, he was the opposing manager, not an opposing player. Players play against players, not managers.

In the World Series, I hit .333 with two doubles, a homer, three walks, and three steals. Unfortunately, nobody really did anything in that series except me. The Reds did to us what we did to the Red Sox. A four-game sweep. Boom, boom, boom, boom. The Reds had all the parts working, and we didn't. Oh, we had our chances. We had a chance to beat them in the second game, but Canseco didn't catch Billy Hatcher's ball in right field, which would have kept us on top 4-3. Hatcher got a triple and scored to tie the game, and the Reds won in the tenth inning. La Russa criticized Canseco for not catching it, but I didn't have a problem with that. The thing that got me was that he didn't retrieve that ball after he missed it. I can't blame a guy for not catching a ball—yeah, I think he should have caught the ball—but he didn't retrieve it after missing it. He should have gone out and gotten it. It was a big game. It was a close game. Bob Welch was throwing good out there. I was thinking, "C'mon, brother, go after it. We're up next. Catch the ball, it's still a close ball game." It shocked the club. It shocked the club bad. In the clubhouse after the game, the club was so furious. Oh, brother, we were out there busting our butt.

After that, we flew home for the third game but never got over our first two losses. The momentum never changed back to our side. We lost the third game, and Jose didn't start the fourth game because he was slumping and hurting. He was going bad. We needed a change. We lost anyway. We were outscored 22-8 in the four games. It turned out to be a bad series, a bad way to go out. We had a good team, a great team—we had six guys place in the top twelve in the MVP balloting—but we just didn't do the job. We went all the way and couldn't pull off the nitty-gritty.

There wasn't a man in baseball who put up the numbers I did during my first year and a half back with the A's. In 221 games, I hit .313 with 37 home runs, 117 steals, and 191 runs. In that time, the A's were 158-95 while the Yankees were going 108-146. In Oakland, I was healthy and happy. When I'm healthy, I'm happy. When I'm healthy, nobody needs to worry about Rickey Henderson. My heart is out there, every day. Tony La Russa will say the same thing. Tony used to tell me all the time how wonderful everything was during '89 and '90. In fact, he told me every day. It got to the point where I almost stopped believing him. I told him, "Hey, you don't have to tell me no more." But he kept telling me, over and over. That's how it was. With me, it always comes down to health. When I'm healthy, I can do practically anything on a baseball field, have practically any kind of year imaginable. But if I'm hurt, I sometimes need to take a few days off to recover. The manager might not want to give them to me, and I'll go out there when he needs me. But when my body is at 70 percent strength, I ain't the same Rickey Henderson. In New York, there were times when the managers told me to play at 70 percent strength, and they knew full well I wasn't at 100 percent, but they'd be critical of my play because I wasn't producing at my top level.

With La Russa, I proved to the critics that I could play for any manager. In New York, it seemed that my numbers were always better with Billy Martin managing. That might be true, but it wasn't just because Billy was managing. It was because I was usually healthy when Billy was managing. People forget I did put up great numbers when playing for Piniella, but I was healthy at the time. When I had a serious injury and played for Piniella, I didn't put up great numbers, and it showed in the results. I'll give my heart and soul to any manager, but people have to realize that I'm not the same base-runner, defensive player, or hitter when my body isn't running on all cylinders.

I think people would better understand my thinking if they made this comparison: A pitcher will never pitch if his arm is sore. Even if the doctor doesn't detect anything, he will not pitch if he feels the slightest bit of tightness in his arm. His arm is his bread and butter. My bread and butter are my legs. If a pitcher ever felt in his arm what I've felt in my legs, he would never go out and pitch. But I've gone out there and played with sore legs because I consider myself very much a team player. People take that away from me sometimes. They downplay the fact that I do play hurt. I've played hurt, and I've been criticized for it. I've been told I don't hustle. I've been told I don't want to play. Hey, I don't want to sit down. I'd rather go 0-for-40 than sit down. Sure, 0-for-40 would hurt the team, but it definitely wouldn't be for a lack of effort. When I'm on the field, I always try to give my best. Sometimes it might not appear that way. Maybe it's because I'm favoring an injured part of my body. Maybe it's because, as some people say, I make the game look easy. Whatever it is, that's the way I play. And I have no regrets about the way I play.

I'm convinced nobody on the A's had any regrets about the way I played in '89 and '90. But '91 was a different story altogether.

12

"I'M THE GREATEST"

When I stole my 939th career base and passed Lou Brock on the all-time list on May 1, 1991, I grabbed the microphone and told the world, among other things, that I was the best base stealer who ever lived. In fact, my exact words were, "I'm the greatest of all time." Little did I know in this so humble world of baseball that honesty isn't always the best policy.

Getting the career steals record was a dream of mine ever since Brock talked to me that time in Boston in the summer of '81. When he singled me out as the guy who could break his record, I immediately made 939 my long-range goal. As the years passed by, I realized I was going to break the record with plenty of room to spare. I had nearly five hundred steals before my trade to New York. I stole my seven hundredth base in late '87, eight hundredth in early '89, and nine hundredth in mid-'90. I figured '90 would be the year, but the thumb injury limited my headfirst slides and I finished the season three shy of the record.

For obvious reasons, most career records are established in the final years of players' careers. Hank Aaron was in his twenty-first season when he broke the all-time homers record. Pete Rose was in his twenty-third year when he set the hits record. Even Brock was in his final year when he broke Billy Hamilton's steals record. In fact, Brock was in his final month.

All those guys had deadlines. They had to do it in a hurry or not at all. When I was zeroing in on the record, I had no deadline. I still had half my career left. When it happened, it happened. I had hoped it would happen in '90; that would have been icing on my MVP cake. But when it didn't, I didn't worry about it because I had a lot more years to go. That's what has made the record even more unique. I've taken extra pride in pulling it off so quickly. Aaron and Rose each played hundreds more games than the guys whose records they broke, Babe Ruth and Ty Cobb. But when I broke Brock's record, I did it in one thousand fewer games than Brock. These other record-breakers, all great athletes, needed at least twenty years to set their records. When I set my record, I had less than twelve years in the majors. I was only thirty-two years old.

I got off to a slow start in '91. A contract dispute between me and the A's proved to be a distraction during spring training, and then things got out of hand when I was injured in April. I had played only three games before a calf injury sent me to the disabled list for two and a half weeks. Typically, I heard the same foolish things I heard in '87: that I wasn't really hurt, that I just didn't want to play. Some people just never get the point.

When I returned to the lineup on April 27 against the Angels, I was one steal from tying Brock and two from passing him. It was a super opportunity for me because a couple of old buddies, Dave Winfield and Dave Parker, were playing for California. In my second game against the Angels, I was drilled in the back by Jeff Robinson. Tony La Russa wanted to take me out of the game, but I had no intention of leaving. Whenever I'm drilled by a pitcher, it's payback time. It's like this: "You hit me with your pitch. Now I'm determined more than ever to steal a base off you." I knew Robinson wasn't going to beat me, and I think he knew it, too. Whenever I close in on records, pitchers are extra careful in keeping me close to the bag, so Robinson stepped off the rubber a bunch of times. But once he went to the plate on a one-ball, two-strike count, I was off. And I was safe. Number 938. I got a huge cheer from the crowd at the Oakland Coliseum, so I blew kisses, genuflected left-handed to the good Lord—people say I genuflect backwards, but if I were right-handed I'd genuflect right-handed—and pulled out the base to present to the A's owner, Walter Haas, as a token of my appreciation for being so good to me. Number 939, the record-breaking base, I was going to keep for myself.

The night I tied the record, Brock came over to my home and we discussed the game. Poor Lou. Back in '82, he had gone out of his way to be there when I broke his season record; it seemed like he was with us for days before I finally broke it and let him go home. This time it got even worse. He had accompanied the team earlier in the season, then left when I went on the disabled list. He came back after I returned to the lineup in late April. He joked that he was going to charge me for all his parking fees, and I joked that I would rent out an apartment for him. I didn't want him to wait much longer than he already had, and I was determined to set the record against the Yankees, who came to town after the Angels for a two-game series.

Anticipating the big day, I printed a bunch of certificates with a superimposed photograph of me and Lou stealing a base together. It read: "I was there when Rickey Henderson broke Lou Brock's all-time stolen base record of 938 with steal number 939. Compliments of Rickey Henderson." I handed them out to my teammates and the press and got the stadium people to hand some out to the fans.

With the Yankees in town, I knew it would be a nice present for George Steinbrenner if I could steal the big base against my old team, and I had plenty of good chances. In the first game, I singled to open the sixth inning, and I think two of my teammates, Dave Henderson and Jose Canseco, were a little too kind to me. They expected me to go, and they took five strikes between them. But when I break a record, I want to do it only if it helps us win a game. For me, the time wasn't right. Finally, when Jose had a two-strike count, I took off. I forced the second baseman to cover the bag, opening a hole on the right side. Jose hit a beautiful single through the vacated area, and we had runners at first and third.

For a brief moment, I considered taking home. Wouldn't that have been something? Breaking the all-time record with a steal of home? But I immediately came to my senses and remembered we were down 2-0. Plus, a left-hander, Harold Baines, was batting, and you don't steal home with a left-hander at the plate. As it turned out, Jose stole second, but I didn't budge off third. It would have been too risky. Baines eventually got me home, and we scored four runs in the inning and wound up with a 7-3 win. No steals by me, but there was still one more game against the Yankees.

Man, I really had to work hard for that next stolen base. I was still smarting from the injury; because I favored the calf, the pain was moving to my knee and thigh. I just didn't feel good not being 100 percent. I wasn't comfortable reading pitchers, so my timing was all goofy and I wasn't getting good jumps. I wasn't running well at all, and the press was letting me know all about it. I stole only two bases in my first five tries of the season, and then Matt Nokes made it 2-for-6 when he threw me out in the first inning of that next Yankee game. Nokes made a big deal out of throwing me out. I saw him high-fiving everybody in sight over in his dugout. Oh, man, he was over there pumping his fists like crazy. That burned me up inside, knowing I was hurt and knowing he couldn't throw me out if I were healthy. I decided I couldn't let Nokes get out of town before beating him first. Even if my leg had been broken, I wasn't letting him out of town. And even if I didn't get him this time, I felt like I would have waited until we got to New York later in the month so I could break the record off him then.

Luckily, I got another chance against Nokes. I reached base in the fourth inning when Alvaro Espinoza couldn't field my grounder at shortstop. I moved to second on Dave Henderson's single. Now it was time for my specialty, stealing third base. With Tim Leary looking back from the mound, I knew he had no chance to pick me off. Back in the first inning, Leary had thrown over to the bag four times, stepped off the mound a couple of times, and thrown pitchouts to the plate. These guys did not want to go down in history as the pitcher and catcher who allowed the recordbreaking steal. But when I got to second base in the fourth inning, I knew they couldn't stop me.

Just to make sure, I called for a pair of my new-age mirrored sunglasses, the same kind Tony Gwynn wears when he hits in day games. I wanted to wear them because of the bright sun and because the pitcher couldn't read my eyes when I was on the base paths. There were newspaper reports that I wore them only because I had an endorsement and that I was under contract with the company—I read where I was paid as much as $30,000—but that was all a bunch of bull. I had no contract with any sunglass company. I wore them because they worked, and because they were cool.

We had runners on first and second when Canseco came up and flied out to shallow center field. Baines then got up and took two balls. Second pitch, I headed for third. Next thing I remember, I was lifting the base from its socket and showing it off to the crowd. Then I started hugging everyone from Lou Brock to Frank Ciensczyk, the equipment manager, as forty thousand fans roared and celebrated. Right away, my momma raced down to the field and threw her arms around me, kissing and squeezing and not letting go. I had all my family in the stands, and Pamela came down with Momma to be with me. I wanted Mrs. Wilkerson, my favorite high school counselor, to come down, but she preferred to stay in her seat. Tony La Russa and Dave Stewart were alongside me as the A's held a big ceremony right on the spot.

This was supposed to be a big-time thrill because people said Brock's record was one that would never be broken. It was supposed to be an event, a happening, a wonderful feeling of joy, something I'd be anxious to tell my grandkids about. I had set out to break the record a long time earlier, and I had done it. My first three years back in Oakland, I accomplished something big every year: the World Series in '89, the MVP in '90, and now the career steals record in '91, and this one ranked right up there with the World Series and the MVP. But when it happened, it wasn't as positive as it should have been. It didn't have the drama or joy for the world that it was supposed to have. The record wasn't the main focus. The press wrote about things other than the record. First of all, there was still a lot of negative talk from spring training. And I was getting ripped because of the injury that took away from my running game. Also, there was that very memorable speech I made after breaking the record.

During the ceremony, I said a few words to the crowd. As it turned out, people resented some of my words. People resented me saying, "I'm the greatest of all time." For a lot of people, that's all they thought I said. I'd turn on the tube, and all I'd see was that one line, that five-second line. How about the rest of the speech? I talked for over a minute. Most people never knew I thanked many of the people who helped me along the way. I didn't call myself the greatest, period. I said a lot more. Here it is, the entire, uncut version that you probably didn't see on the evening news:

It took a long time, huh? [Pause for cheers] First of all, I would like to thank God for giving me the opportunity. I want to thank the Haas family, the

Oakland organization, the city of Oakland, and all you beautiful fans for supporting me. [Pause for cheers] Most of all, I'd like to thank my mom, my family, friends, and loved ones for their support. I want to give my appreciation to Tom Trebelhorn and the late Billy Martin. Billy Martin was a great manager. He was a great friend to me. I love you, Billy. I wish you were here. [Pause for cheers.] Lou Brock was the symbol of great base stealing. But today, I'm the greatest of all time. Thank you. [A lot of cheers.]

That's how it went, word for word. I didn't hear one boo. Just cheers, and a whole lot of them. I didn't think anything of it. But later in the day, Nolan Ryan threw another no-hitter, the seventh of his amazing career. I thought that was great. In fact, after I became his 5,000th strikeout victim, he was the guy I had wanted to get my record against, just so he could shake my hand afterward. But after he threw his no-hitter, the press created an image of me and Nolan, Mr. Ego and Mr. Modest. Even though we played in different games in different cities, we were linked together because we each did something historic on the same day.

Nolan's a great pitcher, the greatest at what he does: the greatest at striking out people, and the greatest at throwing no-hitters. It just so happens that he didn't tell anybody that day. People were saying he's a wonderful human being and that he's modest because he didn't call himself the greatest this or greatest that. They said he didn't even give a speech. Well, of course not. He didn't know he was going to throw a no-hitter. But I knew I was going to steal the base, and people came to the game expecting me to say something after I did.

So beforehand, I thought about making a speech. I even ran it by Lou Brock and asked for his thoughts after I tied the record. He didn't see anything wrong with the speech. I had achieved the all-time record. That means I was the best. I had the right to say it, and I didn't see Lou too disappointed when I said it. But after Nolan's no-hitter, people suddenly got all over me. It was a bad time. Hey, I didn't know Nolan was going to throw a no-hitter and take away the publicity. I guess I should have faked it, broken down in tears and told the world how modest I actually am. Well, that ain't me. I'm different from Nolan. We grew up in different areas, we live differently, and I assume we'll always be different. I don't think that should be a knock against a guy. If we were all the same, all clones, how exciting would that be? I liked the way

Muhammad Ali called himself the greatest, and I wanted to use the same line.

Granted, my timing wasn't too good. Maybe I would have made a different speech if I had known everything would have turned out the way it did, but I have no regrets about the speech. I don't care how much people dig into me, I'll never regret it. I have to stand by my actions. Any other speech wouldn't have been from my heart. It wouldn't have been how I felt. I don't want to lie. I want to be honest. And I actually felt that day that I became the greatest base stealer of all time. If I'm not, who is? Yes, I am the greatest. My definition of the word "greatest" is doing more than anyone else. There's nobody in the major leagues who has done what I've done. I can say that now. I didn't try to hurt anybody by saying it. If someone steals more than I do, then I'll move over and he'll become the greatest. But nobody's done that yet.

The A's gave me a tremendous ceremony. They presented me with a statuette of myself holding up the record base. They gave me a huge commemorative plaque containing spikes, batting gloves, and a base. They even gave an award to my momma. They also gave me the keys to a '91 Porsche 911.

I remember when Walter Payton broke Jim Brown's NFL rushing record in '84, he got a Lamborghini. When Vida Blue had his big year for the A's in '71, Charlie Finley presented him with a Cadillac. So I had hinted to the A's that a Testarossa would be a nice reward for bringing the all-time steals crown to Oakland. But Sandy Alderson said that a $150,000 Testarossa wouldn't be a good public relations move considering that I was having a contract conflict with the A's that spring, so he came up with an alternative. He suggested a $75,000 Porsche with the other $75,000 going to various charity groups in my name. Hey, that was fine with me. I would get a car, and groups like the Oakland schools' sports program would benefit. The other charities that I chose, mostly in the East Bay, included the Alta Bates Sickle Cell Program; the Mother's Wright Foundation, which had been seeking a homeless shelter; Interplast, the group of medical volunteers who work with Third World nations; Children's Hospital in Oakland; and the Spanish Speaking Foundation, which concentrates on the East Bay Hispanic community.

I picked up the car a few days later. It's black with a license plate that reads "SB 939." I went from a medallion that reads "130" for the season record to a Porsche that reads "SB 939" for the career record. I guess that's a product of inflation.

Looking back, the weight of stealing the recordbreaking base was finally off my back. Lou could finally go home, and I could concentrate more easily on the games and sleep better at night. Lou had warned me that those final two bases—938 and 939—would be tough. I didn't believe him at first, but he was right. They were probably the toughest two bags I've ever stolen.

The night I broke the record, I went next door to the Coliseum Arena to watch an NBA playoff game between the Warriors and the Spurs. Then I went home and opened a bottle of champagne that I had received in 1976 as a gift for my high school graduation. I'm not much of a drinker, but I figured this was a good enough time to finally pop that bottle. Sure enough, that Dom Perignon was way too potent for me.

I received congratulations from all over. George Steinbrenner sent a personally inscribed box with a gold-plated hat and ball. Magic Johnson sent a basketball with a scribbled message: "To the greatest base stealer of all time—Magic Johnson." Willie Randolph sent a telegram. MC Hammer sent a cake. Yeah, a cake. Hammer had it sent to my locker, a cake covered with yellow carnations shaped in the form of a base. Even the Hall of Fame called to ask for the fluorescent batting gloves I wore that day—they didn't want the mirrored shades. (Other items the Hall of Fame has taken over the years include the shoes I wore in '80 when I became the first American Leaguer to steal 100 bases in a season; the shoes I wore in '82 when I broke the season record with my 119th steal; the base I stole in '83 that made me the first major leaguer with three 100-steal seasons; and a cap and bat from my Yankee years.)

There is one congratulatory offering I waited for but never received: a call from the President. Hey, I was pretty disappointed. I didn't get a telegram or a call from President Bush. I always thought this sort of thing warrants some kind of note of congratulations from the President. But nothing. Maybe if I had been playing with the Texas Rangers, George Bush, Jr., the owner, would have gotten his daddy to fly his helicopter down for a few minutes to say a few words.

As for Matt Nokes, well, he threw me out one more time in the same game. That was it. No more, man. The next time in New York, my leg was feeling better. I went up to him and said, "Matt, you will not throw me out ever again. I'm going to get you." He chuckled. I chuckled. Then I went out and stole three bases off him in the first two games. He was getting mad at his pitchers, just like Rick Dempsey used to when I stole so many bases off the Orioles. Frustrating the catcher works in my favor, and I wouldn't mind if I keep frustrating Nokes for the rest of my days.

My running game started getting back on track after that series in New York. I stole ten in a row and twenty-seven of twenty-nine. I went on to top the league in steals for the eleventh time, breaking the major league record belonging to Pittsburgh's Max Carey. I also stole at least fifty bases for the eleventh time, extending my own league record. One more fifty-steal season, and I'll tie Brock's major league record. I even stole a base off Nolan Ryan for the first time.

I might have been stealing a lot of bases, but the season was by no means a success for me or the A's. The problems started well before Opening Day. When I won the MVP award the previous year, I thought my life would be changed forever. No more unjust criticisms about my performance, no more false accusations. I had records coming out of my ears. I thought this was the time I was going to get my due, my respect. But when I got to spring training, it felt like someone had stuck a pin in my balloon and popped it.

Judging from my conversation with Tony La Russa the year before, I had been under the impression that my contract would be altered if I went out and had a good year. He was the one who told me, "We'll take care of you." My first year under contract, I was the MVP. If that's not a good year, I don't know what is. I didn't say anything to the A's until the end of the season. Then I went in and discussed things on a preliminary basis. I never demanded any specific figures. All I ever asked was for them to be fair. I was putting my trust in the A's. Hey, I was back home, the organization had been great to me, and I was so joyful that I had finally won the MVP. I had hoped this would be resolved before spring training. But talks stalled after New Year's Day when Carney Lansford blew out his knee in a snowmobiling accident. The A's said their priority was to find a new third baseman. I agreed to put everything on hold for a while, but nothing ever happened. Until spring training.

I had a friendly chat with Sandy Alderson, and the next thing I knew, I was the worst thing that ever happened to baseball. It hurt so much. I felt hatred from everywhere, only because I asked. We have the right to ask in our society. If you can't ask, you don't have rights. I asked, then I got punished for asking. All this happened after I was told, face to face, that "We'll take care of you. Continue doing what you're doing, the team needs you, then we'll take care of you." I took them to the World Series with that understanding. But there wasn't a reply. If an employee was told his boss would do something for him, and something wasn't done, the employee would wonder why. That's what happened to me.

We continued talking in spring training, but I never did make any specific demands. I just asked them to be fair. Sandy did offer to throw out the final two years of my contract in exchange for letting me have my case heard in an arbitration hearing. But he'd do that only if he could wipe out two of the most important parts of my contract—my guaranteed salary and my no-trade clause. I didn't think that was an equal trade-off.

Throughout our talks, both Sandy and I did a pretty good job updating the press on the events. Sandy's honest, and I'm honest. I wasn't afraid to talk about it. When writers approach most guys about their contracts, they don't comment. But I don't have a problem being honest to the press. The down side was, much of the other news in spring training was overlooked. I was disappointed because it seemed as if my contract was bigger than spring training itself and what the A's were trying to accomplish. There was less and less talk about what would be one of the biggest news stories of the year—the all-time steals record. It would seem as if being only three bases from Lou Brock's record was better reading material than any business stories. Obviously, the press didn't agree.

Some fans at those spring training games read everything about my contract and didn't appreciate what was going on. I got booed everywhere I went: Mesa, Scottsdale, Yuma, Chandler, even at our home park in Phoenix. I even heard boos from the A's booster club, of all people. At those little parks, you hear everything. I could understand a lot of it. Imagine the guy who comes out to the park, a guy who works an eight-to-five job. He earns thirty, forty, maybe fifty thousand dollars. He knows exactly how much money I make, and he knows I'm bitching about the contract. He wants to know what's my problem. What am I so ticked off about? Why am I always crying? Well, I'd like to ask that fan this question: "What if you went back to work and found out one of your peers just got a raise and his salary is now twice yours?" If you were doing your best every day and felt you produced more than the other guy, you'd be upset, too. You'd go in there and say, "Where's my raise?"

People ask, "Why does Rickey complain so much? Why is Rickey stuck up? What's with him anyway?" Here's the answer: I'm driven to be number one. I don't think I'm greedy. If number one means stolen bases, hits, and runs, it also means dollars. Number one in all categories. That's not being greedy. That's being deserving. That's being number one. That's America.

You want to be the best at whatever you do: money, business, investments. If you want to be just average, that's fine. I don't want to be average. I didn't make it to the major leagues by being average. When I set out to achieve something, I realize I might fail. But at least I give myself a chance. I don't think that's got anything to do with greed. If you ask for a lot of money when you're not successful, then you're greedy. But if you're the best, you deserve the best. That's why you're called the best. Look at entertainers. Look at MC Hammer. He made fifty million dollars in one year. He's the best. Nobody complains about that. Nobody calls him greedy.

It's funny. At the same time I was talking about my contract in spring training, Ryne Sandberg of the Cubs was asking for a contract extension of his own. He was asking for more money than I was making. And what happened? The Cubs told him no. And three days later, I stopped seeing it in the papers. Sandberg was never booed during spring training, but I was. Everyone called Sandberg a great guy. A lot of the same people said Rickey Henderson is a bad guy. What's the difference between us? I would hope it doesn't have anything to do with him being white and me being black.

I don't mind being booed, but boo for the right reason. If I'm playing poorly, go ahead and boo. That's part of the game. If I were a fan and I saw someone playing poorly, I'd boo. In fact, I have booed, at basketball games. When Al Attles was the coach of the Warriors, I used to sit right behind the team bench. This was in the early eighties when Joe Barry Carroll was the center. Those were some bad teams, and

I'd scream so much at those guys. "Boo-ooo-ooo. You should've made that hoop. Boo-ooo-ooo." I'd really get caught up in those games, and my adrenaline would run wild. Al would turn around and ask me, "Hey, Rickey, I know what I'm doing. Could you please get off us a little bit?" I meant no harm, I was just into the game like everybody else. I was a fan, and a fan can sometimes get very emotional. But there's a difference. I still respected those guys, as bad as they were. I booed them, but I didn't insult them. Some fans get out of hand, throwing things, cussing players, and ridiculing their families. That's uncalled for. That's disrespecting the players as well as yourself.

Everybody thought those spring training boos would carry into the season. Everybody thought that when I was given my MVP trophy on Opening Day, everyone would boo. As it turned out, everybody was wrong about the boos. I didn't hear one boo. Before the Bay Bridge Series—when we played the Giants in our final games of spring training—Sandy and I had talked one more time. We didn't resolve the contract, but at least the season was near and I was eager to start things. He did say we'd get together again during the season. By then I had thought the negative talk had ended, and I was ready to put everything behind me. The crowds in the Bay Area reassured me of my feelings the minute I stepped onto the field. People cheered as if it were still 1990. We played two games in San Francisco and one in Oakland, and the reaction I heard from the home crowd made me think this bad dream was over. All right, let's play ball.

Before the opener, the league president, Bobby Brown, presented me with the MVP trophy at home plate. The place was sold out. And the place was rocking. I stood at the plate, lifting the trophy above my head. And forty-five thousand people were going crazy. It was one of the warmest moments of my career. It was as if all the problems in spring training had never taken place. It proved that the game itself is far more important than anything else that might happen behind closed doors. It showed me that the fans' main concern is what happens on the field, not off it. There was still the hurt I felt from the A's not reaching a conclusion over the contract. But at least I knew the fans were behind me again. And for me, with the season starting, that was the most important thing.

There was one slight problem. Because of all the distractions in spring training, because the contract problem wasn't resolved before I reported to camp, I left camp in worse shape than I had started it. And it showed. In the third game of the season, I suffered the calf injury. That messed up everything. I was just getting over one problem, and now this. The bad dream had returned to haunt me. Naturally, people thought I was faking the injury because of the contract situation. People thought it was related. That made me sick. I know I've got a strong body, but I'm no machine. The press, and sometimes even my managers and trainers, believe it's impossible for me to get hurt. They think, "Rickey can't be injured. That's not possible. Anybody else is believable, but Rickey? No way." People think I'm invincible, and I could never figure out why. I'm susceptible to pain just like anyone else. In fact, the way I play the game, I'm much more susceptible than most everybody else.

My latest injury never seemed to get any better. It only seemed to get worse. First I hurt my calf, then I hurt my ankle favoring my calf, then I sprained my groin favoring my ankle, then I pulled a rib muscle favoring my groin. Everything on the left side of my body was killing me. It was either bruised, beaten, or battered. I went through treatment every day, but it wouldn't go away. I couldn't do anything but play in pain. I even had to drive home crooked because I couldn't sit my normal way.

It seemed as if '91 was becoming like '87 all over again. Sometimes I wish I could throw those two seasons away. Every other year was a fabulous year for me. With the injury and all the crap I was hearing from all sides, I found it difficult to get motivated after that. As the season went on, my motivation came and went, came and went. Not only was I hurt, but Sandy never came back to me for our talk. It was all killing me. The entire time, I tried to fight that, tried to resist being put down, tried to rise to the occasion. But I was like a boxer. I got up, then got knocked down, got up, got knocked down. And every time I got knocked down, it became harder to get back up. Some days I was just completely worn out, drained from the experience. It hurt me, and I saw it hurting my team. A lot of times I couldn't focus on what I should have been doing. There was something wrong. Other players who fell into slumps would find out what was wrong and fix themselves. I could never find out because so much was going on inside my head. I wasn't getting enough hits, hitting .240 and .250, and wasn't getting on base enough. It just wasn't me.

13

"GOT A MINUTE, RICKEY?"

When I'm healthy, I'm usually at the top of my game. And I don't think there's a soul in the press who writes a bad word or talks crazy about me. But when I'm hurt, everybody jumps on the let's rip-Rickey bandwagon.

That includes Kit Stier, who wrote the worst story ever written about me late in the '91 season. Stier is the A's beat writer for the *Oakland Tribune*, and he wrote a column that I'll never forget. He called me a quitter, somebody who doesn't use all his talents. I've come to accept that kind of criticism from people who don't understand what it takes to be a successful base stealer in the major leagues. That's nothing new to me. But Stier made one reference to my momma that was totally uncalled for. I had gone to her for advice, and she gave me some. All children do that, go to their parents for advice. She suggested I talk less to the press until I got my game back together. It was a good idea, but Stier got hold of it and took it way out of bounds. Hey, it wasn't his business. It was nobody's business but mine. I don't know what made him write all that, and I approached him when we got to Toronto for a three-game series with the Blue Jays.

I told him, "What you wrote has nothing to do with baseball, nothing to do with you. What goes on in my family is my business and my business only." I couldn't care less what he wrote if he wrote about baseball. But he dragged my momma into it, and I told him, "You're lucky I'm the kind of person I am. You're lucky I don't kick your ass right now."

Contrary to Stier's article, I had never given up. I hate sitting on the bench. I've said that thousands of times, but it doesn't seem to sink in. At the time, we were ten games out of first place, and the A's were about to miss the playoffs for the first time in four years, but I didn't see anybody giving up. There were times when La Russa wanted to give me a rest, and I told him no. When I don't play, I get bored. The bench is boring, and I can't stay on the bench. I'm not one of those guys who's happy sitting on the bench and getting playing time here and there, who can sit on the bench every day for eight innings, then pick up a bat and hit once in the ninth. I can't do that. If I ever get to that point, I think I'll quit. But here's a reporter telling me I've already quit. Because I'm hurt? Because I'm physically unable to play? That's a bunch of crap.

I did try to cut down on my time with the press at the end of '91, and that's definitely something out of the ordinary for me. But I was going bad and needed to spend more time focusing on my game, so I took a time-out. I had nothing against reporters. I was just trying to cool out. I was hurt and irritated, and I didn't want to let it show to the press. I was afraid I'd say something I'd regret later. I was afraid I wouldn't give reporters respect, and that would be wrong for me as a person. I don't consider myself a hardass. I consider myself easygoing and relaxed. People who know me personally will say I'm one of the most easygoing persons around, and they're envious. But sometimes I find myself feeling frustrated, and it's pretty evident that it's hard for me to keep too much inside. But if I explode at a reporter, I'll look like an ass and embarrass both him and myself. There's no reason for that. So when I don't talk, it's not because I disrespect the reporters, it's because I respect them. And that's the truth.

One problem with the press that involves me and guys like Jose Canseco and Reggie Jackson is being too honest. Sometimes we just can't win. We don't want to tell lies, so we'll tell our inner feelings. But our inner feelings are usually controversial. That's why there are so many boring quotes in newspapers. Not everyone reveals his inner feelings. When I'm talking, the press will come to me because they know I'll have something good for them. The press might not want to talk to some middle reliever who'll bore them to death. Talking to me, they know their stories will be better, their editors will be happier, and their readers will be more interested. I sell papers, and so does Jose. We're a reporter's meal ticket. When we get going, there are always big crowds around us. Even in '91 when I wasn't talking, there would be a big crowd around me just in case I did talk. Maybe another player was boring them, and they needed something exciting. So they came to me.

There have been plenty of times when a writer rips me to pieces in the paper. Like I've said, unless it includes my family, I can live with it. But I can't respect the writer who hides out after he rips me. The best writers are the ones who can show their faces the next day and stand up for what they wrote. Or sometimes if the writer does come around the next day, he'll stand way the hell over on the other side of the clubhouse. It's like, "You know what you wrote, and I know what you wrote, so show some balls. Get the hell over here, and let's talk about it." Then I can tell the writer what I feel, whether I disagree with the article or not. The guy who doesn't come around the next day I'll never respect, and I'll think twice about a conversation the next time. The guy who does come around and acknowledge what he wrote, I will respect. I don't care if he rips me, just be visible. At least I'd know we're on the same wavelength.

The press covers the game today entirely differently than it did fifteen years ago. Reporters hardly talk about the game anymore. They don't talk about the way the game is played between the lines. Sure, they mention it now and then. But it's changed. Television has something to do with it. People know everything about the game before they get their newspaper, so the newspaper tries to give you things not shown on television. Something extra. Something more controversial. In a way, because of this, following baseball is like reading the *National Enquirer.*

Back in the old days, when Babe Ruth went out and ate ten hot dogs and drank a hundred beers, the reporters wouldn't write about it. They'd only write about what the Babe did on the field. He could have fallen down in Central Park drunk as a skunk, but nobody would write a single word. That's why I think ballplayers hung around reporters more back then. Ballplayers enjoyed them more, and they spent more time together and enjoyed one another. We're all part of the human race, and we're all trying to survive in this world together. But nowadays, it's not like that. Nowadays, there are certain things you don't do with a reporter. You don't go out and have a meal with a reporter. You don't go to a party together. You don't do anything to have a good time. You have to be skeptical. Maybe it goes back to when players started making a lot more money than the reporters. It was probably around the sixties. The money changed, and so did the closeness between the players and the press. Maybe it was a jealousy thing from the press, or maybe it was an ego thing from the players. Whatever it is, it's unfortunate.

I have a big goal in baseball that nobody really knows about. It doesn't have to do with playing the game; I already know what I can do in that regard. It has to do with the reporters. I want to be a good guy with the reporters. I've asked my momma, my family, my friends, "How do I go about talking to reporters and have them think of me like Don Mattingly or Mark McGwire, one of those good guys in the game?" How do you get to be a good guy, anyway? I'd like to know.

Maybe I'll never be a good guy simply because of the way I am. Sometimes I look so determined that I scare a whole party of reporters away. Why? They don't know me. They think I look kind of crazy over there in the corner. They think I'm pissed off about something. They think I look like I'm going to kill somebody. La Russa once told me he had never seen a guy who comes to the ball park with such a serious look of determination as mine. That's just me. The press often feels they better not talk to me, so they might write something without talking to me. The next day, the papers might be wrong, and I'd think to myself, Isn't that crazy? I'd like to know what can be done to have players and the press have a better understanding of each other. I don't have to be buddy-buddy with every writer, but at least have some respect for each other and each other's jobs. I don't want to tell the press how to write their stories, and I don't want them to tell me how to play the game. Keeping a positive relationship with reporters can often be tough when the season's going bad for you and your team.

As the '91 season went along, I continued to struggle, and so did my team. We dropped out of first place in mid-June and never returned, though we stayed close until late August, when we lost our momentum during an ugly road trip through Seattle and Minnesota. We were swept in four games by the Mariners and dropped three of four to the Twins, with our only win being an 8-7 decision in which I homered and stole three bases. We ended the trip six games out of first place. That not only hurt our momentum, it helped Minnesota's. The Twins won all their big games down the stretch, and we kept slipping. Second place, third place, and, finally, fourth place. It was the first time the A's had finished that low since '85, the year I left for the Yankees.

We had a lot of problems in '91. Injuries played a big part. From Carney Lansford's off-season accident to the fourteen guys we had on the disabled list, we never seemed to find the right timing or combination that we had in '89 or '90. Whenever the pitching was good, the hitting wasn't. And when the hitting was good, the pitching wasn't. To show what kind of season it was, I hit the first grand slam of my big-league career on the Fourth of July. It came in my 6,228th at bat, off Texas's Gerald Alexander. Big deal, right? Huge deal. That gave us a 4-2 lead in the seventh inning. But the Rangers came back and tied us, then beat us in extra innings. It was a season that just wasn't meant to be.

Because I'm not one to put my inner feelings on display, people seemed to wonder why all the team's problems didn't bother me. Hey, they bothered me. I was injured, but I wasn't going to show everybody how much I was hurt. I wasn't hitting, but I wasn't going to show everybody how much I was pissed off. That's not me. I'm not the kind of person who walks in the clubhouse and annihilates the postgame spread. Nobody will ever see me tearing up things and throwing stuff like Lansford and Billy Martin. I don't care how bad I play or feel, that's not how I vent my frustrations. When things go bad for me, and this is the truth, I'm more relaxed. I'm laughing, I'm messing with people, I'm yacking it up with the fans. When I'm going well, I'm suddenly serious and looking like I'm unhappy. One time in New York, I remember I was in something like a 2-for-48 slump—2-for-48! But the way I was carrying on every day, laughing and joking, people were wondering if this man was hitting .900. That's the way I am, the opposite of a lot of guys. I'm not going to let it worry me. See, when you're going bad and getting all tight and serious, it's nearly impossible to snap out of a slump. You think too much, and you listen to advice too much. But when you relax and be cool and smile, you take the pressure off. It might rub people the wrong way, but that's my philosophy. In the '89 playoffs against Toronto, I didn't smile much at all. Then again, I hit .400 and stole eight bases and won the series MVP.

It's simple to see why I smiled an awful lot in '91. Things weren't going right, and I tried to bounce back like I always have. It just never worked. That is, until the final weeks of the season. I was sitting back on my bed one day trying to figure out what I was doing wrong when something ticked. I was thinking about the injury, then backtracked to the days in New York and tried to remember what I had done to overcome previous leg injuries. I thought and thought, then it hit me. The bandaging! Yeah, that was it.

When I swing, I push my left foot forward with the toes pointing inward, almost in a bowlegged fashion. But with the injury, I couldn't do that. I had no control or strength in my front foot, so it moved forward on its own, with the toes pointing outward. The foot wouldn't give, it wouldn't turn in, and that threw the rest of my body out of whack. It prevented me from getting a good, short, strong stroke. Instead, my swing was loose. After remembering how my ankle was bandaged in New York, I marched into the trainer's room the next day and told our assistant trainer, Larry Davis, to tape my ankle, and I told him exactly how it should be done, exactly the way it was done in New York. Rather than the typical bandaging job, I had Larry criss-cross the bandages, with a tuck here, a tuck there. From that day, I hit everything on the nose.

In my final forty-seven at bats, I had nineteen hits, including five home runs, for a .404 average. It was all so simple. I was still hurt, but the bandage supported the foot and allowed me to use my strength. The whole time before the discovery, there had been nothing wrong with the mechanics of my swing. There was just no snap, and I couldn't figure out why. I was doing the right things and seeing the ball fine, but I'd hit the ball and nothing would happen. It just came down to properly taping my ankle. It was a tremendous difference, a miracle cure. One of our infielders, Ernie Riles, kept telling La Russa that if we had had another month, we could have won the division championship because I was hitting everything. I only wish I had realized this trick earlier.

In the last two weeks, I raised my average from .253 to .268, and my fifty-eight steals moved my career total to within six of the magical one thousand mark. I scored 100 runs for the tenth time in twelve years. Despite my relatively low average, I had an on base percentage of .400, sixth-best in the league. I also homered eighteen times, the fourth-highest total of my career. Five of those homers led off games, pushing another of my ongoing records to fifty. But there seemed to be a lot more negative numbers than positive numbers.

Personally, I didn't like my year at all. It was the first time I was disappointed with my numbers since I returned to Oakland. People said I had an off year, and they had a right to say that. But what were they comparing it to? My MVP year? Sure, then it was an off year. But take every guy who won an MVP and compare that year to some of his others. There are an awful lot of off years in there, aren't there? Not every year can be an MVP year. The only way I couldn't have an off year would have been to win the MVP back to back. I didn't, so it was an off year. I'll still match those two and a half years with the A's against anybody else during the same time. I guarantee you, not a man in baseball did what I did.

Then there's Mike Gallego. Good ol' Mike Gallego. Nobody will ever forget what I said about Mike Gallego during spring training of '91. During my contract talks, I tried to draw a comparison with the press. I tried to say that my style of play warrants a certain type of contract, and that I deserve one type of contract and Mike Gallego deserves another type of contract. I always thought it was a good comparison. How was I to know Gallego was going to have the best year of his career and I was going to have one of my worst? I was hurt, I was dying, and here was Gallego enjoying the best year of his life. If he didn't have his best year, I wouldn't have heard another word about it. But his contract was winding down, and he put up his best numbers. It was amazing. Damn, it was freaky. He ended up close to where I was in a lot of categories.

It turned out to be a great story for the press. How could the press have had it any better? They were saying, "Thank you, Rickey. Sure, you said this way back in the spring, but we're going to dig it up and keep using it." It's funny how the press never forgets what you say. A week ago, a month ago, a year ago, they'll always remind you of something you said if it pertains to the present. Throughout the season, newspapers ran Rickey–Gallego graphs, and ESPN played it up regularly. Oh, man, what are the odds of me saying something like that in spring training and what happened actually happening? I thought it was a great quote; I still do. I said it to prove a point, not to hurt anybody. Hey, I respect Gallego. I remember when I first came back to the A's. One of the best things I liked about the A's was the way they respected you as you, whether you're Jose Canseco or Mike Gallego. I guess it was bad timing on my part.

I went the entire year without once hearing from management about my contract. If I had it all to do over again, I would have tried to resolve it one way or another before spring training. Or maybe I should have done what Sandy suggested and left spring training. Yes, he asked me about leaving spring training, but I didn't want to leave. I wanted to work. As it turned out, there was little work for me in spring training, little work and little peace of mind. It hurt me, and it hurt the club. My chat with Sandy before the Bay Bridge Series was the last word I heard about the contract. He said we'd get together in the season and decide what to do, but it never happened. I was waiting for him. But with three weeks to go in the season, Reggie Jackson told me Sandy had been waiting for me. I didn't think we had that agreement. But, hey, that's the way the year went for me.

I took a lot of heat throughout the season. But I trusted Tony and Sandy. It seemed back in '90 that Tony was meaning more and more to me. He was becoming more like Billy than any other manager I'd ever had. When I look back at the end of '89, I see Billy, my pride and joy, getting into a crash and leaving me. The good Lord had taken away Billy, but he was giving me someone else, Tony La Russa. Billy never let the press dog me about my injuries; he always told them exactly what was wrong with me. A manager's bread and butter are his players. Billy knew that, and Tony knows that. They wouldn't be great managers without protecting their players. Billy used to go to the extreme. Even though the baseball commissioner has a rule allowing writers access in the clubhouse, Billy would often throw them out. Anything that he thought would help the team.

Tony is also good at realizing how the press can dog you. We were great together in '89 and '90. We were buddies. Then all of this other crap happened. At one point, I reminded Tony about his comment that the A's would take care of me. He said he had talked to management and gone to bat for me. But nothing had been accomplished. That was his explanation, though I think he felt inside that I didn't believe him. I did believe him, but I didn't see anything happening. I told him I'd been giving him my heart and soul. But I was starting to have my doubts. I was starting to look at Tony differently. I felt him moving away from me.

One time, Tony told me the press didn't believe I was hurt, so he asked me, "Are you hurt?" I said, "I'm hurt, Tony. I never lie." I asked him, "Tony, are you just like everybody else? Do you feel I'm not hurt, just like everybody else?" He said, "Hold on, back up. I'm not just like everybody else. You tell me you're hurt to my face, I'm protecting you. Until you get well, I won't play you no matter what anybody says." That's all I needed to hear. I continued giving him my respect. I don't want to lose my relationship with that man. Hey, he was only the second man I felt that way about.

Once the season was over, I figured my troubles were over. I could put '91 behind me. Not so. Two years to the month after Oakland was devastated by the '89 earthquake, the city was delivered another major blow when a fire raged through the North Oakland hills, killing 25 people and destroying 3,400 homes. I was in Phoenix on October 20, appearing at a card show, and all I could do was watch on TV as those neighborhoods kept burning down, one after another. One of those neighborhoods was mine.

Shortly after breaking into the majors, I purchased my first home, a single-level condominium on Starview Drive. That place was special to me. I bought it when I first moved out of the family house, and I was keeping it to give to my oldest child. I remember what my stepdad used to tell me. He'd tell me, "Get something you'll keep forever, then pass it down." This is what I was going to pass down, the condominium. I could have sold it many times for a huge profit, but I always intended to pass it down to Angela, my oldest child.

Thankfully, nobody was living there at the time of the fire. During the season, I've let other players stay there. When I was in New York, Don Baylor stayed there when he played with the A's. Reggie Harris, one of our young pitchers, had planned to rent it when he came up from the minors. The only thing I told people was to take care of all my stuff. Whenever I went there, I went to kick back and chill out. I'd go there after a night game if we were playing a day game the next day. It was a great little hideout. Hey, the only reason I didn't go more is because Pamela wouldn't stand for it.

The place had a lot of my personal belongings. Not just furniture and clothes and money and a TV, but a lot of my baseball memorabilia was stored there: bases, balls, cards, trophies. The base I stole to break the all-time Yankees record was in that place. I had two of my cars there, and one was as Testarossa. Yes, I had bought a Testarossa for setting the career steals record. I always wanted one, so I bought one myself when the A's said they wouldn't. It's what I worked so hard for. The other car in the fire was a 1984 Mercedes-Benz that was specially made for me. I had flown to West Germany with my friend Louis Burrell, MC Hammer's brother, just to pick out the car. I'm told only two of this particular model were made, and the other was purchased by Reggie Jackson. After I bought mine, Reggie noticed how nice it was and ordered his own. Because people had never seen a car like that, they always thought it was brand new. It was a wide-body with a 5.4-liter engine, a real beauty. It was my favorite car. Before I went to Phoenix, I had parked the Benz at my condo and taken out the Porsche that I had received from the A's. I almost wish I had left the Porsche in there. I wouldn't have minded losing any car except for that Benz. The other cars were replaceable; the Benz wasn't.

I probably had more stuff in that house than my permanent residence, but it was all burned away. Everything. I returned to the Bay Area the night of the fire, but nobody was allowed in the area. The next day, I got a policeman to drive me through my old neighborhood. It was eerie. The houses and buildings had been flattened. Only the brick chimneys remained. I had lost everything, about $800,000 in damages. And I was one of the lucky ones. Some people lost much more. I wasn't as bad off as Reggie Jackson. Reggie's house looked as if somebody had dropped a bomb on it. He had nothing left. Pow! And this was the third time for Reggie. That same house had burned down twice, and his car dealership with all his cars had burned down years earlier.

I was truly hurt by all of this. Sure, my insurance would cover most of it, and I could rebuild my house; my daughter was going to get that place no matter what happened, just not with as much stuff. But that wasn't the point. I was hurt because lives had been lost and Oakland had taken another pounding. We keep having these setbacks and tragedies. It might take five years for the city to get back on its feet. We've just got to pick up the pieces, pick up one another and live on, prepare ourselves for the future.

14

TO CATCH A THIEF

I don't claim to be the fastest runner in baseball. I don't think I've ever been the fastest.

When I got to the majors, I used to watch Willie Wilson run. Man, he went from home to third and first to third faster than any human I'd ever seen. Now that was a sprint. But stealing bases takes more than just a great pair of legs. It takes heart and soul and guts. Yes, it helps to have better than average speed. But speed is sometimes overrated. Wilson, in his prime, was the fastest in the game, but not when it came to base stealing. Nobody compared with Bo Jackson when he came into the league, but he's not the same since his hip injury. There have been other fast runners, such as Barry Bonds and Willie McGee. But guys like that are afraid to get thrown out. Except for Vince Coleman, I haven't seen anyone come into the league stealing a lot of bases.

Base stealing is an art, just like hitting home runs is an art for the best power hitters. It's something you've got to want to do, and you can't be afraid to fail. If a guy gets thrown out once, the next time he might think he'll get thrown out again, so he'll hesitate. There's nothing worse than getting thrown out, then walking slowly back to the dugout all alone as the infielder throw the ball around in celebration. You're thinking to yourself, "Damn, I ran and they beat me." It hurts, but you've got to have the nerve to march back out there and try it again.

Base stealing is too often taken for granted. I don't think the running game is adequately taught in the minor leagues. I see kids coming up who not only don't know how to steal bases, they don't know how to run bases. Some kids don't have a clue. Younger guys come up to me all the time and ask how it's done; they say they haven't learned a thing in the minor leagues. Organizations probably mention it along the way, but they don't teach it like they should. There aren't enough Tom Trebelhorns who will spend hours and hours teaching a young base stealer. I learned from Tom, and I also learned from watching and talking to other base stealers. I studied everybody from Davey Lopes, who taught me how to read pitchers, to Mike Rodriguez, who taught me about the headfirst slide while we were teammates in the minors.

Although I picked up a lot of things from a lot of people, perhaps the most important thing came from Lou Brock. Lou gave me inspiration. I ran a lot in the minor leagues, and I stole a hundred bases in my first full season in the majors. But I never knew how good I could be until talking with Lou Brock that time in Boston, when he declared I'd be the one to break his career record. In time I developed my own distinct style of stealing bases, but I couldn't have been so successful if not for all the help I've received along the way.

When I came into the league, Lou was a few months from retiring. Campy Campaneris, Bobby Bonds, and Joe Morgan were winding down their careers. Stolen bases were dying down, and I like to think I was one of the guys who brought it back to life. Not only that, I was determined to push the art of stealing to another level.

I've heard managers, always opposing managers, complain that base stealing is counterproductive. That's how Earl Weaver felt. I disagree, of course. People have mathematically broken down the success and failure of stolen bases, saying every steal equates to three-tenths of a run and every time a runner is caught he loses six-tenths of a run. That means a runner must steal more than twice as many bases as he's caught to register a positive run production. The theory might make sense mathematically, but I don't buy any of it. As I told Vince Coleman and Gary Pettis and some of the younger guys, there are all kinds of benefits to stealing a base. There's more to it than just advancing ninety feet. There's the psychological side. A base stealer can distract the pitcher, break his momentum. He can also force the infield to shift, which opens holes for his hitters. Most of all, stolen bases lead to runs.

When Coleman first came up to the majors, he didn't score enough runs for the bases he stole. In his second year, he stole 107 bases but scored only 94 runs. I asked him how he could steal that many bases while scoring that few runs. If someone steals that much, he's got to score more. The whole idea of stealing bases is to score runs. I'm not just running to run, although some people say, "Rickey runs when it ain't necessary." That's not true. I steal bases to get into better scoring position. I steal bases to score runs for my team. I steal bases to win games. That's what got me into the habit of stealing third base. I used to be told not to steal third because I'd already be in scoring position at second base. Yes and no. With one out, being on second base is not true scoring position. To me, with one out, scoring position is third base. That way, all the batter has to do is touch the ball with his bat. Just about every time, I'm scoring. That's not true at second base. There are many more ways to score from third than from second, so I'm not going to wait for the batter to get me to third. I'm going to get to third on my own.

Nearly 80 percent of my stolen bases have come with no more than a two-run difference, and nearly 90 percent have come with no more than a three-run difference. That's why Tony La Russa scares me a little bit. His theory is, if we're down five runs, we could still run. I don't really agree. I feel if it's late in the game and we're losing by five or winning by five, I don't run anymore. That's embarrassing the other club, that's showing them up. But if it's a five-run deficit in the second inning, I'll run. We've still got a good chance, and I'm not going to be conservative. If a runner's daring, he'll have a better chance to overcome those odds. Once in '82, Billy had me stealing a base trailing by twelve runs in the ninth inning. That's a bit extreme, but that was Billy. Another time against Detroit, I stole a base in the sixth inning of a six-run game. Billy had me stealing only because he and Sparky Anderson were feuding at the time. That's when people started thinking I enjoy stealing bases in lopsided games, but I actually hate doing that.

I get asked a lot about what I go through to steal a base. People come up to me and want to know how it's done. It might appear easy. Just run fast, right? Not exactly. There are several things to consider beforehand. It's almost like a sophisticated science, with the base stealer breaking down the act into four systematic parts—leading off, getting a jump, running, and sliding. If one part goes wrong, the whole project is ruined and you're a dead duck.

Even before any of that, a base stealer must know how to read a pitcher. When I first came up, I got picked off an awful lot. I learned to be smart about detecting a pitcher's moves. I never look at computers, printouts, or scouting reports. I prefer to rely on my memory. I keep a mental book on which pitchers I drive crazy and where their weak spots are. A pitcher's move to first base will change from game to game, but that's not the important move. His move to the plate is what I look for, because that's when I run. His move to the plate generally stays the same—unless, of course, he balks. There are certain moves to watch for in a pitcher. Some pitchers have unusual shoulder movements, some sit back on their back heels, some use the slide step.

One theory of mine is to split the pitcher down the middle and watch his chest. That way, if one side moves, the other side has to follow. It's the same in basketball. The defender doesn't watch the head or the feet because that could fake you out. The defender watches the midsection because there's nothing that midsection can do to fake you out.

Lopes could read a pitcher better than anybody, and I picked up some of his concepts while he played with the A's from '82 to '84. He said runners slow down in their thirties and can't rely solely on their legs. He said one day I wouldn't have the same blazing speed. I thought about that for a long time, and now I understand. Lopes was a successful base stealer all the way to his retirement, setting a record of forty-seven steals by a thirty-nine-year-old and twenty-five steals by a forty-year-old. As for me, I've become a smarter runner to offset any speed I might have lost. Reading a pitcher and picking the right moment are more important than having great speed.

For obvious reasons, a left-hander is tougher for me to read than a right-hander. Surprisingly, Brock has said right-handers were tougher on him, but pitchers were different then. When he was in the game in the sixties and seventies, left-handers tended to break the plane of the pitching rubber, meaning they wouldn't throw to the plate if they slid their front foot toward first base. Nowadays they don't break the plane as much. They slide their leg toward first base but still throw to the plate. That forces the runner to stay close to his base. If a pitcher doesn't break the plane of the rubber, he can go to the plate or first base in the same motion. I learned a lot about this from watching a couple of Baltimore left-handers, Mike Flanagan and Scott McGregor. Flanagan and McGregor always had a slight pause that threw me off. As they kicked up their right leg, they could see what I was doing. If I didn't move, they'd go home. If I did move, they'd come to first. I always thought they were balking, but umpires disagreed. Now a lot of left-handers pitch that way, making it absolute murder on guys like me.

Jimmy Key of Toronto is another left-hander I have trouble with. If a runner has any kind of lead at all, Key will pick him off. Any time, any place. But the thing with Key is, he's more readable than Flanagan or McGregor because Key curls his front knee. He doesn't come up straight with his leg like those other guys. When a guy curls his knee, you can see the knee break the plane and you know he's going to the plate.

One year things were so screwed up that it didn't seem to matter if a pitcher was a lefty or righty. In '88, when umpires were told by the commissioner to start calling more balks, it proved to be good news and bad news for base stealers: Good news because umpires finally called all those balks I thought they should have been calling all along, but bad news because it hurt the runners. Before that balk rule, I could easily time the pitcher because he'd go to the plate in one motion. When they started calling balks, pitchers got confused and always seemed to delay before throwing the ball. They'd stand out there as long as they could, making sure they didn't balk. Because runners couldn't tell when pitchers were going to throw the ball, they were mixed up and didn't know when to run. I stole ninety-three bases that year, but I should have had a hundred, if not for the balks.

The new rule took away a lot of my steals. I'd have a base stolen, and the umpires would call a balk and simply give me second base. It wasn't a steal, but a balk. Hey, if the runner fools the pitcher into balking, he ought to be awarded a stolen base. When you have a base stolen and the ump calls balk, the pitcher is thinking to himself, "Great, Rickey ain't stealing off me." All those balks actually screwed up my game in '88, so I'm glad the commissioner put a halt to it after one season.

Earlier in my career, I ran solely on natural instinct. If the pitcher made any type of movement, I'd be gone. Sometimes the pitcher would throw to first base, but I'd be off the bag by so much that I'd have the base stolen. Nowadays pitchers are very different. They come after you, and you've got to know how to read them. Otherwise, you're dead. On the other hand, some of the younger guys are so anxious to throw quickly to the plate to give the catcher a better chance to throw the ball that they're really not concentrating on what they should be doing. They grew up watching me on TV, and they'd get a big kick out of it if I were ever thrown out. I try to make sure I don't oblige them.

A runner had better know how to read a pitcher's moves before trying to steal a base. Otherwise, he'll get picked off on a regular basis. Once the runner knows how to read a pitcher, it's time to work on the act itself. The first step is taking a lead. My main objective when taking a lead is to be relaxed. That's why I constantly wiggle my fingers, to relax. That's also why I take such a short lead. Where some base stealers like to take four or five steps off first base, I usually take a modest three and a half, sometimes even fewer. Maury Wills took big leads. He'd have both feet past the infield curve around first base. With my three and a half steps, depending on the infield, I have one foot on one side of the curve and one on the other, unless it's a place like Detroit, where the arcs are a little farther out. To me, that's a safe lead. That way, I don't have to worry about the pitcher. I don't like him wondering what I'm doing over there. A smaller lead relaxes not only me, but the pitcher. And I like the pitcher to relax. It makes him stop paying attention to me. Once I relax the pitcher, I've got a dynamite chance. I don't want the pitcher to throw to first, I want him throwing to the plate. Runners who get bigger leads can't relax and pick the pitcher's move because they have to anticipate him coming to first base. My lead is just far enough off the base so I wouldn't have to dive back if the pitcher threw over there. I hate diving back.

If the pitcher continually throws over to the base, the runner can get worn out and find it tough to get a good jump. If the runner is more relaxed, he gets a better jump and is able to more easily read the pitcher's move to the plate. Remember, the key for me is reading the pitcher going home, not to first. So if I can fully read a pitcher going to the plate, he can never beat me. Brock tried to learn the pitcher's move to first base. I always wondered why. You don't steal on moves to first base, you steal on moves to the plate. If I know the pitcher's move to the plate and I see something different or unusual, I know he's coming to first base. I know I have to get back.

Most first basemen will talk with me and ask me when I'm going, try to distract me. But it doesn't work. When they get me talking, I'll actually concentrate more. When I'm talking, I'm relaxed. That's me. On first base, at the plate, in the outfield, if I'm yakking away, I'm more relaxed and more at ease. Sometimes the dialogue gets pretty hilarious. Sometimes I'll flat-out tell the first baseman I ain't running. I'll tell him to tip off his pitcher so he won't have to worry about me. I'll be serious, too. It's funny how nobody ever believes me. The pitcher ends up throwing over to first base a half dozen times, but I'm not going anywhere. The first baseman says, "I tried to tell him, Rickey, but he wouldn't listen." Pretty soon I get tired of that. I'll say, "Hey, man, you get over there and tell your friend if he comes over here one more time, I'll just go to second base anyway. One more time, and I'm gone on the next pitch. Tell him that." I talk like that to Cecil Fielder, Don Mattingly, all of them. I feel no pressure on the bases.

People wonder if I run on my own or get a sign from the dugout. For the most part, I run on my own. It's gotten to the point where the only sign I get from the dugout is a red light and only if Tony La Russa decides he doesn't want me running. Maybe Jose Canseco's coming up and Tony wants me to stay put. Usually Tony gives me a red light only when I'm on second base because he knows I'm a mad man when it comes to stealing third; he knows I want third base every time I'm at second. Otherwise, I go when I feel I can succeed. The one thing I truly despise about getting a green light is being forced to run. When I get the go sign, I've got to go. I hate that. When I first started, they did that to me all the time. I told them I couldn't do it that way. I've got to run when I know it's all clear. When I get a sign, I get tense, especially when the opportunity might not be right. It's a forced steal, and you feel uncomfortable. Sometimes you don't get a good jump, and you get thrown out. Now you've hurt your team. A good base stealer should go on his own. Nobody knows better than the base stealer when to go and when not to go.

Once a runner has his lead, the next step is the jump. Some people might think that only the headfirst slide sets me apart from other base stealers like Brock and Wills. That might appear to be the most noticeable difference. But the way we get our jumps from the base is just as significant. They took off with a crossover step, meaning that their first step was their left foot crossing over their right foot. I employ the push step, meaning my first step is with my right foot. As a result, my second step, with my left foot, is almost twice as long as the first. Although Brock and Wills were successful with their method, I think my way is quicker and more explosive because my body is already opened up and balanced. I don't think the crossover technique gets the runner to full throttle as fast.

Stealing second base usually takes me eleven steps. Brock had longer legs, sprinter's legs, and needed only ten steps. I have an explosive first two steps, and getting into a full sprint takes three or four steps. In three or four, I'm at top speed. I feel my first four steps are faster than anybody's in the game. I've been timed from first to second in 2.9 seconds. Even if it takes me 3.1 or 3.2, I'm going to be safe at least 80 percent of the time. A good pitcher–catcher combination can take 3.2 or 3.5 seconds to get the ball from the pitcher to the catcher to second base, so you can see who has the advantage.

The bottom line is the pitcher and how quickly he gets the ball to the plate. Statistically, it's the catcher's fault when someone steals a base. But that's a misnomer. The catcher is at the pitcher's mercy. The catcher has to depend on the pitcher getting him the ball. If the pitcher has a slow move to home, I'll steal the base. I don't care how powerful the catcher's arm is, I'm safe every time. The location of the pitch is also important. If the pitch is up, the catcher will be in a better position to throw. If the pitch is low or in the dirt, he's at a disadvantage.

The most exciting part of my stolen bases, according to what fans tell me, is my slide. If I left the game today, I know I will have left at least one mark on baseball—my headfirst slide. Before I got to the majors, the headfirst slide was rarely done. People were afraid of it. Cobb, Wills, Brock, those guys didn't do it. They didn't go headfirst stealing bases or stretching singles into doubles. Look at the old clips. Pete Rose and some others might have done it every once in a while on a close play, but they never did it as much as players do it now, and that's partly because of the success I've enjoyed. Now almost everybody does it. It's caught on, even for the slow guys. It's a trend I feel I helped develop. It's included in the repertoire of nearly every player in the game.

Some guys still won't try it. Canseco won't. He likes the hook slide. He likes to hook around the bag and grab it on the way. He'd be more successful if he went straight in. When you hook, it gives more time for the infielder to tag you. The bag isn't going to move, so why slide your body away from it? The only time to hook slide is when the fielder is reaching for the ball on the other side of the bag and he's got to come back and get you. Then you hook slide to avoid the bad throw. But a straight steal? You don't do that, not if the quickest distance between two bases is a straight line.

There are several advantages to the headfirst slide. I get to the bag faster. I can see the bag better. And I protect my bread and butter, my legs. Furthermore, contrary to what a lot of people think, it's a safe way to slide. I learned to make it safe. I don't get too many scratches on my arms even though I don't usually wear long sleeves. I'll last an entire season without having a single scar on my arms. People ask how that's possible. Here's the key: Just think of the way an airplane lands. When a plane goes straight down, what happens? It crashes. It's violent. That's why an airplane descends gradually, to land smoothly. Same with a runner. A runner shouldn't jump up and land violently. He should land smoothly. That's why I run so low to the ground just before I dive. As I run for the bag, I run in three stages—down, up, down. When I get my jump, I take off low. Not until my fourth step do I begin to rise; that's when I'm in my sprint. A few steps later, I'm going back down. By the time I slide, I'm so low to the ground that the impact isn't violent at all. There's barely a downward angle, which is why I skid on the dirt so quickly and so far. Some guys who go headfirst begin their dives from high in the air. They come down hard. They come down on the bag at about a forty-five-degree angle, and the infielder can apply the tag more easily. And chances are that their bodies will feel that slide. If a runner dives close to the ground, he shouldn't get hurt. Imagine this: If I dropped a glass from three feet in the air, it would break. But if I dropped a glass an inch from the ground, it wouldn't break. If a base stealer slides headfirst, he must be able to protect his body.

Another advantage is that the runner will get the right call more often. Umpires have a better view of a headfirst slide than a feet-first slide. The guy who goes feet first kicks up his legs and a cloud of dust every time he goes down, and the umpire can't always see enough to make the right call. He has a better grasp when he doesn't have to deal with flying legs and dust. If he just sees hands and face, he'll have a better view. When I first started sliding headfirst, umpires would try to watch where I was tagged. I got called out a lot of times when I was safe. Finally, I went to the umpires and said, "Listen here, pay attention to my hands." When I'm hitting the deck, my hands slide so fast through the dirt that if the infielder hits me on my back or shoulder, it's possible for the umpire to think my hands aren't on the base. So I told the umpires to pay attention to my hands. I started getting better calls after that.

Critics will argue that the headfirst slide does not allow the runner to pop up quickly and advance to the next base if the catcher throws the ball into the outfield. I disagree. I think my slide actually puts the runner in a better position to advance. Where other guys pop up with their legs, I just as easily pop up with my arms. I reach the bag and just push upward. It's simple. I don't waste any time with my slide, and I'm able to see the outfield just as well because everything's in front of me. So if the ball bounces past the infielder, I'm gone. Despite what the critics say, the hands are always quicker than the feet.

Most of what I've discussed so far relates to stealing second base. Many of the same concepts are used when stealing third base. For me, stealing third is easier than stealing second. It's a shorter throw for the catcher, but I get a much bigger lead and need far fewer steps, seven steps instead of eleven. And maybe 2.6 or 2.7 seconds instead of 3.0 or 3.1. I've stolen third base 235 times. Nobody has ever gone after third base like I have. Most guys won't even try taking third.

The year Brock stole 118, he stole third just six times. I prefer stealing third. Sometimes a pitcher will relax when I'm leading off second and ready to take third. To get me, he'd have to turn his body completely around. I watch the pitcher's elbows and shoulders. Some pitchers hold their elbows together; others push them out from their body. The ones who keep their elbows in cannot throw to second without tipping off the runner. Once the pitcher throws back to second, I know his move. I don't care if the pitcher is right-handed or left-handed, he'll never be able to throw to second as quickly as he throws to first. Once I've read his turn, I've beaten him.

Some runners look around for the shortstops and second basemen. Some guys even peer back at the center fielder, thinking he's going to come in from the outfield and catch you off the base. That's ridiculous. Why worry about those guys? Those guys don't have the ball. They can't get you out. Because I've had so much success stealing third, a lot of second basemen—Harold Reynolds does this—will play as close to the bag as the first baseman plays to first. The only thing that does is open up the right side for the hitter. I'm taking away the defense's strategy, creating an alignment that gives my hitters a better chance to hit. Seeing an infielder play close to the bag doesn't bother me. I won't get back until the pitcher turns and throws, so my concentration is only on the pitcher. I don't care if the second baseman and the shortstop meet at the bag and kiss each other. They could be that close, and the pitcher could turn and fake, but I'll barely move. He'll either throw it or he won't. If he does, I'm back. If he doesn't let's get on with the game.

Stealing home is a different story altogether. I've stolen home four times, the last coming way back in '82 against the Angels. Two of my steals of home were against the Angels, and I clearly remember my first. Brian Downing broke his ankle on the play and virtually ended his career as a catcher. Downing leaped to catch a high pitch by Frank Tanana, and I slid as he came down. We collided, and his left ankle turned. He didn't catch much after that, but he successfully continued his career as an outfielder and designated hitter.

One of my old teammates, Mike Heath, got in the way of my chance for a fifth steal of home plate. Billy Martin gave me the steal sign with two outs, and Heath didn't see the sign and almost killed me with his bat. The pitcher had a delivery as slow as molasses, and Billy thought I could score off him. But Heath was concentrating so hard on hitting the ball, he missed the sign. So here I am, sprinting like crazy down the line. And there's Mike Heath, cranking back his bat and taking a wild swing. Obviously, I went down quickly. I hit the ground like a rock. I ducked for my life. Heath made contact—not with me, luckily— and hit the ball to the outfield. Oh, brother, I nearly died. He later said he never saw me coming. I had that base stolen easily. But he hit the ball, and I got nothing. Thanks a lot, Mike.

Rod Carew stole home seventeen times, which is a testimony to Rod's instincts and quickness, but pitchers at that time worked more from the windup than they do now. Now they keep runners closer to third base by working from the stretch. Rod wasn't considered the biggest threat around, so every time he stole home it was a surprise. It was easier then. Wayne Gross, another of my old teammates, stole home three times in his career, and Wayne Gross was the slowest guy in the world. His overall career total was twenty-four. Of course, Wayne had some help. He'd scoot home on the back end of a double steal or with the pitcher in the windup. It helps to have the surprise factor. With me on third, nothing's a surprise. Billy told me to steal anytime I saw the pitcher in the windup, but it didn't happen. I'd love for pitchers to work from the windup when I'm on third. I'd steal home so easily, it would be pathetic.

Although I've said I steal off pitchers and not catchers, there's one catcher I feared more than any other. Bob Boone. He was the toughest and smartest catcher I've ever faced. It seemed that his sole mission in life was to throw me out. He didn't care about the hitter. Boone was so focused on getting me out, he'd almost go as far as calling four pitchouts just for a better chance to nail me. Boone knew I could win the game if I stayed on base, so he'd want me off the bases. He'd say, "The hell with the hitter. Rickey's the money guy. Let's get Rickey now, we'll get the hitter later." Boone figured it was better to stop me even if it meant putting the next guy on base with four pitches. He'd call fastballs on curveball counts, he'd have the pitcher throw outside, high, any place where Boone could get into position to pump to second base.

In my early years when Boone caught, I used to tell Dwayne Murphy, our second hitter, to swing at the pitch, any pitch, no matter how bad it was. Boone had a technique. When he heard the first baseman yell, "There he goes," Boone jumped out in front of the plate to catch the ball. He wouldn't wait. Even if it was a strike, he'd catch the ball before the pitch got to the plate. It's a technique that prevented hitters from swinging, even though the ump would often call a strike. I'd get great jumps and he'd still throw me out. I'd wonder how this guy kept doing it. So I started looking back at the plate while I ran, and I'd see this guy throwing the ball from the front of the plate. Outrageous. I told Murph he'd hit Boone in the back of his head if he swung his bat—just holding the bat out there would keep this guy behind the plate. Once Murph got the picture, I started having more success against Boone.

Incidentally, I never thought a pickoff should be classified in the same category as a caught stealing. I didn't get caught stealing a lot in my early days; I'd get picked off. But my stats read "caught stealing," not "picked off." There should be two categories. That would give a better representation for the pitcher and catcher. Pickoffs are a pitcher's stat, throw-outs a catcher's stat. According to the rule book, if a runner is leaning off the base and picked off without even attempting a steal, he goes down as a "caught stealing." Making two categories would benefit both the pitcher and catcher. As it is, the catcher blames the pitcher if the runner gets a great jump off the base. And the pitcher blames the catcher if the pitcher gets him the ball in time and the catcher still can't throw the guy out. The year I stole 130 bases, I was officially caught stealing 42 times. But I don't remember getting thrown out by catchers very much at all. Unless, of course, Boone was back there.

One of my favorite all-time catchers to steal against was Rick Dempsey. Every time we played the Orioles, I used to get Dempsey so mad. Especially in '85; I stole seventeen bases against the Orioles in '85. I remember one day Dennis Martinez was on the mound, and I had detected something in his move and stole a couple of bases off him. Dempsey began telling Martinez to hold me close to the bag. I had stolen thirteen or fourteen straight off Dempsey, and he was getting frustrated. One time when I came to the plate, he told me he'd get me if I got on base. I told him, if I get on, I'm going. Bam, base hit. Dempsey deliberately stepped in front of the plate, took off his mask, and yelled at Martinez to keep me close at first. When Martinez got into his stretch, Dempsey was ready for me. He was back there with his butt up and his right foot back, all ready to throw me out. Now I was looking straight into Martinez's eyes, waiting for his move, waiting to pick him. Suddenly he leaned toward the plate. That was it. Once he leaned like that, he could not come to first base. There was no turning back. I picked him again. I was gone. Dempsey was so mad because he knew I had it stolen because I got such a great jump. Dempsey got the ball and stood up to throw. Martinez was leaning off the mound to give Dempsey room. But Dempsey didn't throw to second. He wound up and threw the ball directly at Martinez's ankles. He cussed out Martinez and said, "I told you to keep him close." I was laughing so hard, I could barely remain standing.

The catcher I've stolen off the most was Jim Sundberg: fifty-five steals, and he was a six-time Gold Glove winner. The reason was, Sundberg had a big windup before he threw. He could never get me. He was at a big disadvantage for couple of his seasons because he played in Kansas City on artificial turf. John Wathan played his entire career in Kansas City, which is one reason I stole thirty-one times— eighth on my catcher's hit list—with him behind the plate.

I'll dominate any pitcher or catcher on the turf. It's easier to steal bases on turf. Look at Vince Coleman, who went from the Cardinals to the Mets, from plastic turf to dirt.

It will be difficult for Vince to continue stealing at a fast pace if he remains with the Mets and continues to run on dirt. He got a later start than I did, breaking into the majors at the age of twenty-three, whereas I broke in at twenty. He's four hundred steals behind me and just three years younger. Vince is the only player besides myself who has stolen a hundred bases in more than one season, but he might be at a disadvantage because he doesn't take a lot of walks and his lifetime average is under .270.

I remember one time we were on national TV together. Man, he dogged me on national TV. He kidded about stealing two hundred bases in a season, and I didn't get a chance to reply. Because he had played on a turf field, I thought he'd have a shot at my record of 130. But two hundred is another seventy bases. That's a lot of bases, a lot of pounding. Just look at my record year. One hundred and thirty steals, but forty-two times I didn't make it. And that doesn't even include all the other times I hit the dirt. If Vince is talking about stealing two hundred bases, he'd have to pound the ground almost three hundred times. That's twice a day. That's too much.

I later told Vince he could steal two hundred bases, but only if he got on base a lot, only if he stayed healthy, and only if he ran on turf. I told him if he ever plays on a team with real grass, forget about it. He came back and told me the reason I had so many steals was because I ran on dirt. C'mon, Vince. Look at my stats on turf and dirt. We play each team in our division the same number of games, and I have fifty-one steals on the fake grass at Royals Stadium and thirty-three on the real grass at Comiskey Park. When Vince left St. Louis for New York, I knew I'd prove my point. He pulled a hamstring and stole thirty-seven bases in his first year with the Mets. Oh, now he knows how dirt holds back the runner, how it doesn't stay still. A runner gets much better traction on the artificial turf because he can push and pull, push and pull. Does Carl Lewis get better traction on an indoor surface or on a real outdoor surface? Now Vince knows.

15

MAN OF STEAL

don't think my stolen base record will ever be broken, not by Vince Coleman, not by anyone. It's untouchable. If I'm healthy and play for twenty years—the amount of time put in by most guys with career records—then, oh, man, I can guarantee nobody will ever touch my record. They might as well put an asterisk next to my name. I'll be up there with all the other big spenders.

Joe DiMaggio's streak, nobody's getting that. Hank Aaron's home runs, nobody's getting that. Pete Rose's hits, nobody's getting that. Cy Young's victories, nobody's getting that. Nolan Ryan's strikeouts, nobody's getting that. Rickey Henderson's steals, nobody's getting that. Put an asterisk next to all of our names.

Lou Brock set the career record in '79, but he needed 19 years to get his 938 steals. Ty Cobb is fourth on the list with 892 steals, but he played 24 years. I passed Cobb in my twelfth season. I got Brock in my thirteenth.

There's still a lot of time in my career to steal bases. I look at Brock, who had his 118-steal season when he was 35. I look at Davey Lopes, who stole forty-seven bases when he was thirty-nine and twenty-five bases when he was forty. And then I look at the way I keep in shape, the way I train hard in the off-season. I look at the way my running game hasn't slipped like the running games of so many guys who stop stealing bases after a certain point in their careers.

When I'm done playing, I hope to have at least 1500 steals. Even if someone steals seventy bases a year for twenty years, he wouldn't match that record. The only way it could be reached is for baseball to become even more of a running game. I don't see that happening. I don't think teams can run any more than they have been. If there's any more running, the power game would have to take a backseat. And that won't happen.

If I really wanted to, I could steal a hundred bases every year. I truly believe that if the circumstances were right, I could steal 130 bases again. But that's if I were strictly a base stealer and nothing else. I'm not a one-dimensional player. I do too many things on the field to concentrate solely on stealing bases. I want more from the game than just stolen bases. The bottom line is winning. And winning comes when you score more runs than your opponent. That's why I steal bases, to get in position to score runs and win games. It doesn't hurt that every run I score brings me closer to Ty Cobb's 2,245 runs. People say that record's out of reach, but they also said Brock's record was out of reach.

When I look at the all-time steals list, I wonder how different it would look if baseball weren't segregated in the first half century. Because there were very few records or newspaper accounts for the Negro Leagues, we're without a statistical perspective of their achievements. I've heard that the style of play in the Negro Leagues was much different than in the major leagues. When Babe Ruth and those big guys were hitting all those home runs, the action in the Negro Leagues was faster paced, like today's game. They had power, speed, catchers who had good arms, catchers who had good speed, an overall game. They had guys like Cool Papa Bell, an outfielder who played in the twenties, thirties, and forties, mostly for the Homestead Grays. I've seen pictures of Cool Papa Bell; he slid feet first. They said he once scored from first base on a sacrifice bunt, just kept running around the bases. Another guy, Oscar Charleston, was to the Negro Leagues what Cobb was to the major leagues. He was fast and mean and never turned away from a fight. But Charleston and Bell are nowhere in the record books because they played before Jackie Robinson broke the color line.

The Negro Leagues are sort of like a lost chapter in baseball history. Fortunately, they haven't been completely forgotten. People have been recognized and inducted into the Hall of Fame. Charleston and Bell were inducted in the seventies, and I hope many more players from the Negro Leagues get to Cooperstown.

With black players excluded from the major leagues in the first half century, the steals records were being set only by white players. With the exception of Brock and myself, everybody on the list of top ten base stealers played before Jackie Robinson's debut. They all date back to near the turn of the century, and most—guys like Cobb, Max Carey, and Honus Wagner—are in the Hall of Fame. But their stolen bases were achieved differently compared with how we get them today. In those days, runners were given credit for a steal for advancing two bases on a single or one base on a flyout, an infield out, or a fielder's choice. Billy Hamilton played from 1888 to 1901 and ranks third on the all-time list with 937 steals, just one steal behind Brock. But many of Hamilton's steals were earned the old-fashioned way. Imagine how many steals I'd have gotten if they still had that rule in effect. While we're on the subject, they may as well bring back the rule from Babe Ruth's time where guys got credit for home runs by bouncing the ball over the outfield fence—I'd have gotten a few of those, too.

Baseball has come a long way since Jackie Robinson, but not far enough. We still have problems at the management level, and teams are trying to hide the fact. If a reporter asks me if baseball is prejudiced, I won't answer. If I did answer, I would tell the truth. And all hell would break loose. So do you think I'm going to talk about racism to a group of reporters? Hell, no. If I mention that someone is racist or something is not fair because of racism, it would be blown way out of proportion. It would become too crazy.

I saw it happen in 1990 to Jose Canseco. He mentioned something one day about racism in baseball, that teams are more willing to pay top dollar to white players than black or Hispanic players. That story was in the news for days and days. Come on! What is this game coming to? If you say it, people will dog you behind your back because you've said it. But all you have to do is open your eyes and see it for yourself. Where were the black general managers when the '92 season started? Why were there only two black managers? There were fourteen openings from Opening Day '91 to Opening Day '92; why was just one black hired?

Once again, it's the same old thing. They say blacks need to get experience in the minors before getting a managing job in the majors. Why isn't that true for whites? Three managers were hired for '92 without any previous managing experience in the minors. Where's Don Baylor? Why have teams been so hesitant to give him a chance? If it's minor league experience they're after, how about Chris Chambliss? He's been successful in the minors. Why haven't teams given Chris a chance? Blacks still aren't perceived as leaders—being able to go from playing to managing like whites—and that's a shame. It's got to change, but first it's got to change in other areas.

I believe that if there were more black writers and more black management, people would get a different perception of black athletes. Right now, we've got many more white writers than black writers and many more whites than blacks in the front office. Does management want us to talk about this? Hell, no. Because if we talk about it, we can't get out of it. And they consider that bad public relations. So you can't say anything. But do you think people are really blind and don't see what's going on? Come on!

I don't think most black people are blind. I don't think most white people are blind. But why does racism still exist in our generation? Players are afraid to say baseball's not equal. Well, hell, yes, baseball's not equal. And unless there are changes, it never will be equal.

Blacks must be represented to make this work. Baseball is America's game, but it's not white America's game. It's for everybody. And that includes non-Americans. Now the major leagues are on the verge of becoming an international game, thanks to the Japanese and their interest in buying American franchises.

I love Japan and the Japanese culture. I go over there frequently because I do some promotional work for the Mizuno sporting goods company. I follow Japanese baseball closely. One of my career goals is to knock the stolen base record out of sight, but I don't want to stop with just the major league record. I want the world record. There's a Japanese player who has stolen 1,065 bases. His name is Yutaka Fukumoto, and he was a left-handed outfielder for the Hankyu Braves for twenty years before retiring in 1988. Fukumoto also owns the Japanese season record with 106 steals in '72. The Japanese like to brag that Sadaharu Oh owns the all-time world homer run record, not Hank Aaron. They're also talking about Fukumoto owning the world steals record, not Rickey Henderson. I'd like to bring the world record back to our major leagues.

During my winter visits to Japan, I've taught some of their players about baserunning. My style impressed Fukumoto, but he had his own style. People in the Dodgers' organization had gone over there and taught their techniques to the Japanese players, and Fukumoto had picked up the crossover step. He slid feet first. He couldn't quite grasp my push-step takeoff and headfirst slide. He said my style is difficult to learn, but maybe someday they'll apply it to their game.

I've worked with Mizuno and the Japanese people to help design what I consider the ultimate shoe for a base stealer. I first worked on the shoe when I was in Japan before the '82 season. There was an extremely light shoe on the market that was produced by another company, and I told Mizuno I wanted mine a hair lighter. They had me hooked up to every electronic contraption imaginable. One test had me running in place inside a huge box with a silver screen displaying the movements of every muscle in my body. Once we engineered the perfect mold for my foot, I had them place track-style spikes underneath. The prongs point inward, giving me more traction and more speed. They wear this line of shoes in Japan, but it's not available in the U.S. The only other major leaguer wearing this type of shoe is Ruben Sierra, and that's only because he conned me into letting him borrow a pair one day. Now he's got his own pair.

Throughout the first thirteen years of my career, I've been able to utilize my speed in every facet of my game. But one area where I back off is the bunting game. Most players who bunt for hits are left-handed batters like Brett Butler and Alex Cole. Usually, when those guys beat out a bunt, they beat it out by a millisecond. Because I'm a right-handed hitter, I take one more step to first base than left-handers, and that one step could be costly. Left-handers can also drag a bunt by running toward first base while the pitch is coming. Of course, if a right-hander were to try that, he'd be dead. Some guys need to bunt. Butler, he makes good contact. But take away his bunts, and he's not the same player. He gets at least twenty hits a year bunting. He needs those bunts. Make me a left-hander, sure, I'll bunt more. By dragging that ball properly, there's no way a pitcher would get me.

If I were a guy who couldn't hit well or didn't make much contact, it would be a different story. I'd bunt more. But I get too pissed off and frustrated when I bunt and get thrown out. It's a situation where I don't give myself a chance. Even when I was younger, I didn't like bunting. Maybe it's because I've had some bad experiences. I've gotten hit in both eyes trying to bunt. In the days when I bunted more, I'd square to bunt, get the head of the bat out, then drop it down. For some reason, the ball always seemed to come back and pound me. One time, the ball kicked up and hit me smack in my left eye. Ouch!

Carew began teaching me his style, and I thought I had it pegged. Then one day I tried to lay down a bunt, and bam! I got it in the right eye. That was bad news. That one almost took my eye out. One year I came to spring training and Billy told me I'd have to start bunting more. Here we go again. But Billy's way of bunting was different. Instead of squaring the body and fronting the pitcher, he told me to just hold my bat over the plate with one hand, sliding the bat under my right shoulder. He said the ball would never pop into my eye that way. Well, he was wrong. Sure enough, I'm trying it one day and I knock myself in the eye once again. Give me a break. I decided then that if I had to bunt again, I'd prefer to quit this game. I'm not bunting anymore, unless I absolutely have to. That's why the third basemen play me way back near the outfield grass. They say, "Go ahead, be my guest. Bunt." No thank you.

Despite my speed, I don't get nearly as many infield hits as I'd like. Because of the nature of my crouched stance and potent swing, I'm generally in an odd position after hitting the ball. I twist my bat around my body, and I'm all tied up. By the time I untie myself and start running, I've lost a lot of time. Don Mattingly used to try and help me get a better jump out of the box, but it didn't help much. With my style, I can't swing and be fully ready to run. I've hit some weak ground balls that I wanted to beat out for infield hits, but I've been thrown out. If I were able to just flat out run after I swing, I'd have a lot more infield hits.

For all I do on the field, whether it's knocking a home run, robbing a guy of a hit with a diving catch, throwing a runner out at home, or scoring from first on a single into the corner, the thing I'm known for most of all is stealing bases. Yet base stealing just might be the most misunderstood act in the game. Nobody appreciates it except your teammates and your manager. Opposing players and managers hate it. The last way they want to be beaten is by the running game. That's why

so many of the best base stealers have been despised by their opponents, from the very beginning of the game.

Everybody hated Ty Cobb. If people think I'm bad, they should
think about Cobb. He was a deadly ballplayer. He cussed a lot, cheated,
sharpened his spikes to slide into people, got thrown out of a lot of
games. They say even his own teammates hated him. He was bad. But
he was successful, a winner, a legend. All the way through time, it was
the same thing. Cobb, Jackie Robinson, Maury Wills, Lou Brock, myself—all great base stealers have to possess a certain amount of arro-
gance to be successful, a me-against-the-world attitude. Some people do
not respect base stealers and, consequently we've all paid a heavy price.
We've all been knocked down at the plate. Brock had his shoulder
broken by Sandy Koufax, and Koufax hardly threw at anybody. But
Brock stole bases. And opposing pitchers didn't like or respect that.

Let's get one thing straight. My legs are my weapons. They're my
entire game. I use my legs to steal bases, to score runs, to chase down
balls in the outfield. I'm only five foot nine and a half, so I rely heavily
on my legs to push off when I swing a bat. I'm only as good as my legs
are strong, so sometimes I have to make sacrifices to keep my legs from
wearing out. Because I put so much effort into the running game, I try
to rest my legs whenever possible. I don't sprint on and off the field like
other guys. I never have. It's not for a lack of hustle, it's for the
protection of my legs.

Nobody puts his body on the line like a base stealer. Nobody
pounds his body to the ground more. It comes with the territory. Even
if I don't steal a base in a game, I might hit the deck a half dozen times.
Like Brock said, "People should give base stealers more credit and
understand that they often come into games a little sore. Sometimes
they need to recuperate." It pisses me off when people say I'm not
hustling today as I did yesterday, that I look different from day to day.
Well, I might have stolen four bases the day before. Do you think my
body doesn't feel those four bases a little bit? Willie Wilson might have
stolen more than six hundred bases, but he said he feels each and every
last one of them.

When I was on the Yankees, Mattingly, a guy I love like my
brother, was always described as the greatest this, the greatest that.
Blah, blah, blah. He asked the reporters one day, "Do you think if I went
out there and played and slid every day like Rickey, I'd be able to do

what I do every day?" The answer's no. All he did was pick up a glove and stand on first base. He'd get mad when people said I wasn't hustling. He'd say, "What's wrong with y'all? This guy is hustling without question."

In those days, if I'd go on long streaks averaging two steals a game, Dave Winfield had to come up and ask me to slow down. He'd say, "Today, Rickey, you don't have to run. You rest, we'll take care of you, we'll get runs. We'll need to have you ready for an important series next week." If the game wasn't tight, I did slow down a little. I learned to preserve myself for a whole season. That's what a base stealer must do. Otherwise, in the last couple of months, I'd have nothing left. I learned to save myself.

That's why I'm still playing this game. That's why I'm still having so much fun. That's why I'm still running crazy around the bases.

Looking back on my career, I've stolen bases on good teams as well as bad teams. Every team is different, and I've learned to adapt to different teams. The year I stole 130 bases, I stole because the team had nothing else; I was the guy who had to make things go. I've also been on power teams where stealing bases wasn't as important, and that's when I was able to learn to become a better all-around hitter.

The game has changed dramatically during my career. When I broke into the majors, the game was deep on pitching. Pitchers seemed to dominate the hitters more back then, and teams could depend on their pitching to carry them through. Later on, the power game became the focus. Then the speed game. Now it seems there are power hitters and base stealers, whereas pitchers are harder to come by.

Nobody knows what the future holds, but you can bet the game will continue changing to a certain degree. And you can bet there will be guys who keep the tradition of the great base stealers, guys who follow in the footsteps of Billy Hamilton, Ty Cobb, Cool Papa Bell, Oscar Charleston, Jackie Robinson, Maury Wills, and Lou Brock. All those guys had to be confident, maybe even cocky, to be so successful. But all those guys ignited their teams, made their teammates play at a higher level. It's a thrill to be mentioned in the same breath as those guys, and it's a greater thrill to have passed each of them on the all-time list. They're the ones who paved the way for the next generation of base stealers, including me. That's why one day I'd like to pass the torch. I'd like to teach the next generation about the art of base stealing, whether it be as a coach or simply a guide who shows up every spring training to instruct the young players.

With the career record already under my name, there won't be many more times when I'll steal a base, then lift it out of the ground and hold it high to the crowd. Maybe I'll do that when I steal my 1,066th base, passing Yutaka Fukumoto for the world record. I do know I won't be going through any more game-stopping ceremonies like the one following my 939th steal. Maybe they'll do something like that during my last go-round, my final season. That would be a nice way to go out, a nice way to retire.

Then, watch out. I'll be looking to break more records—in the old-timers' games.

INDEX